A Teenage Girl in Auschwitz

Basha Freilich and the Will to Live

DOUGLAS WELLMAN

North Carolina

Published in the United States by WriteLife Publishing
(An imprint of Boutique of Quality Books Publishing Company)
www.writelife.com

978-1-60808-289-6 (p)
978-1-60808-290-2 (e)

Library of Congress Control Number: 2023939311

Book design by Robin Krauss, www.bookformatters.com
Cover design by Rebecca Lown, www.rebeccalowndesigns.com

First editor: Caleb Guard
Seond editor: Andrea Vande Vorde

This book is dedicated to the millions of people who suffered at the hands of the Nazis during the Holocaust, and to their families who survive them. It is not only a memorial to the lost and broken, but a reminder that evil continues to exist in the world and we should never believe "That cannot happen here."

And to my wife, Deborah, with my love. As always, her continuing support and reassurance encourage me through the rough spots of life.

Acknowledgements

My friend, Patti Hecksel, is the initiator of this project, for which I am deeply grateful. After reading one of my previous books, *Surviving Hiroshima: A Young Woman's Story*, Patti immediately recalled Bess's story, which was told to her by Bess's grand-daughter, Renée, years ago. Patti's introduction to Bess's family was the step that set me on the road to taking Bess's story to the world.

Bess's daughter, Evelyn Kaplan, has been absolutely essential in putting this work together. She provided pictures, documentation, and personal stories that gave life to the work, taking it beyond simply historical documentation. This was an understandably emotional process for her, but she never faltered.

Bess's granddaughter, Renée Harper, sourced and provided documents from Nazi archives, creating a broader historical context for the author to more fully understand Bess's life, and the lives of those who suffered alongside her in the camps. Her numerous contributions are greatly appreciated.

The opportunity to quote the exact words of the participants in an event is frequently denied to historians. Bess was adamant that her story be told to the world, and did so to all who would listen. Two of her recorded testimonies are foundational to this book and the author wishes to extend his personal, heartfelt thanks to those who provided them:

Josey G. Fisher, Director, Holocaust Oral History Archive at Gratz College, graciously provided the transcript of the interview she conducted with Bess in June, 1981, as well as the transcript of the interview Helen Grossman conducted with Dora Freilich in October, 1984.

Georgiana Gomez, of the University of Southern California Shoah Foundation, kindly provided a recording of the interview Marc Seligman conducted with Bess in October, 1996.

The author is grateful to them for providing the means by which he could use Bess's own powerful statements to help tell her story.

The outstanding work of editor Caleb Guard is greatly appreciated by the author. Although this is the story of one young woman, Basha's story is a component of a story which encompassed the entire world. Telling the world story without overshadowing the personal story was not an easy task. The author is grateful to Caleb for providing the assistance to tell both stories with clarity.

Editor Andrea Vande Vorde painstakingly scrutinized the text of this work, adjusting the author's well-intentioned, but sometimes misguided, adventures with the English language. Her careful, professional work is greatly appreciated.

Rebecca Lown created the striking cover for this book, which boldly visualizes the story and turbulent times in which it is set. Her beautiful work is always appreciated.

Book designer Robin Krauss has once again turned a stack of my manuscript pages into a beautiful and readable text, which is gratifying and greatly appreciated by the author.

The author wishes to express his sincere gratitude to publisher Terri Leidich for understanding the value of this work, not just as an individual's personal story, but as a component of a painful, historical tragedy that should never be forgotten. Basha's story will now live on through the dedication of Terri and Writelife Publishing.

Foreword

The archives of history record episode after episode of humankind's cruelty to its own. They show that humanity apparently has a virtually limitless capacity for inhumanity. Wars are generally fought for territory and power, with lives lost in that quest. However, sometimes loss of life is the goal, not collateral damage. People of societies, races, and religions may be victimized simply because they are different from others. Those differences breed hatred, which may culminate in a program of mass genocide.

It is improbable that the average citizen—and even most historians—could come close to correctly estimating the number and scope of history's genocidal atrocities without committing themselves to a significant period of study. In countries with moderately good educational systems, many may be at least superficially aware of acts of genocide which have occurred over the past few centuries; however, the facts of these events are often elusive. Josef Stalin in Russia, and Mao Zedong in China, for example, launched programs of genocide against their own people, which took the lives of millions. However, as closed societies, exactly what happened and the exact number of lives destroyed is, to some degree, a matter of speculation. In this regard, the Jewish Holocaust, perpetrated by the Nazis in the mid-twentieth century, is unique for the abundant documentation left undestroyed by the Nazis, the statements of captured Nazi concentration camp guards, and the eyewitness accounts of liberating Allied troops, all supported by photographs and motion picture footage. Most importantly, many surviving victims told their personal stories to the newsreel cameras, reporters, and later, in books and articles. Some left oral histories recorded at educational institutions and historical foundations. Unlike the atrocities of previous centuries, many victims precisely documented their stories in their own words. It is the testimonies of Basha "Bess" Anush Freilich, a victim of the Jewish Holocaust who was imprisoned in the Auschwitz concentration camp at fourteen years old, that form the basis of this book. As you will learn, Basha had a very special reason for telling her story, and her determination to do so may very likely have contributed significantly to her survival.

Although this book focuses on Basha and chronicles her personal struggles, frequently quoting her directly, it is by extension a chronicle of the lives of millions of other innocent Jews whom the Nazis caught in their murderous grip, as well as political opponents, Gypsies, homosexuals, minor and major criminals, and leaders of faith communities, whose actions, words, or sometimes simply their very existence, put them at odds with Nazi totalitarianism. They were smaller in number, but their individual suffering was equal. The author has combined their stories with Basha's testimonies to tell a story that focuses on one, but represents millions.

Dates and Spellings

The Nazis intended not only to eradicate the Jewish people, but also as much of the documentation of their existence as possible. They symbolically destroyed works of Jewish art, literature, and music whenever possible; whitewashed Jewish contributions to medicine, law, and society; and discarded family ancestries the Jews had carefully maintained for generations. This last matter creates a particular problem for historians. Much material which would have been invaluable for research simply no longer exists, consumed in the flames—figuratively and literally—of Nazi hate.

The author has done much to ensure that this work is accurate, but gaps remain. The problems begin with Basha. In two of her oral histories, she states that she was born in 1928; however, camp records from Auschwitz list her birth year as 1926, and that birth year appears on her United States immigration paperwork and the various forms of identification which followed. When children arrived at Auschwitz, older prisoners frequently advised them to add a year or two to their birthdate to avoid immediately being sent for execution, as happened to many of the younger prisoners. If a child stated that he or she was older than their actual age, and they appeared strong enough to work, they stood a better chance of being assigned to living quarters—a barrack, rather than dying quarters—the crematorium. It is quite possible that this is what Basha did, and that it was easier to keep that birth year than attempt to change it in the already complex immigration process. It will likely remain unknown whether or not that is correct.

Basha's siblings present the same problem. In her testimonies she identifies them by their birth order, but only two by age. Based on various bits of information available, the author has reached an approximation of their ages which should be close, if not absolutely accurate.

Names provide another challenge. Sometimes the Nazis transliterated them in the camps. For those who later made their way to the United States, imigration officers, hopefully with the consent of the émigré, Americanized the names by choosing ones that sounded like the original and spelling it to conform with English language norms. For first names this was not a particular problem, however, changed last names present an issue for tracing families. Basha's family uses Anush as her maiden name, but Anuz and Enish also appear in family histories. Since the Nazis apparently destroyed all Polish records, it is not clear for certain which is correct, if any.

Historical Perspective

Ideally, Basha's story would be told without any extraneous matter. However, decades after the events, many readers may not be familiar with the historical context of the times, which makes understanding this tragedy more difficult. The author has provided historical notes to place Basha's experiences in the context of the events that swirled around her. These notes are placed at the end of the chapters, rather than within, to avoid disruption of her personal story. Those familiar with the times may choose to skip over these notes, while other readers may find them helpful. The usual research citations appear in endnotes at the conclusion of each chapter.

Direct Quotes

Basha was intelligent, well-educated, and multilingual. The English language oral histories she created clearly and emotionally present her struggles. The author has frequently chosen to use direct quotes from the testimonies because they provide much more than information; he feels they provide a window into her heart. Since she is responding spontaneously, without preparation, to questions posed by her interviewers in a language that was relatively new to her, there are occasional grammatical errors in the quotes. Other than slight editing for clarity, the author has presented her words as she spoke them to retain as much of the emotion that was clearly heard and seen in the interview recordings.

Author Background

The author is not Jewish, nor does he speak Hebrew, Yiddish, Polish, or German. He has been extremely careful to accurately present material used from research documents in those languages. Any cultural or translation errors are unintentional.

Intent

As will be revealed, Basha had specific reasons for wanting the story of her and her family told, even though the process of reliving those events to tell it was painful. The author is honored to participate in the achievement of her goal, with the sincere hope that no one in the future will ever have to share a similar experience.

Douglas Wellman
St. George, Utah
September, 2023

Prologue

"It's very sad for me to talk of this bitter period of my life. It's carved in my heart and in my soul and I tried to push it away in my under conscious, but I feel in order for me to function normally that's what I have to do. There are many nights when all this comes back to me, and sometimes I feel like I'm going to explode from sorrow and from pain, but the world must know and it must be told. We must stay on the guard that the Holocaust, God forbid, shouldn't repeat itself; that what I went through should never happen again. That this should be the last Holocaust on earth, and that my children, my grandchildren, and their children's children should never experience what their mother and grandmother and great-grandfather went through. I pray to God that they should never know from such sadness, humility, pain, starvation, suffering, and desolation. It's for them that I'm revealing the story of my tragic childhood."

Basha "Bess" Anush Freilich
December 23, 1928–September 18, 2006
Interviewed by Josey G. Fisher
Director, Holocaust Oral History Archive
Gratz College, Melrose Park, Pennsylvania
Interview conducted June 5, 1981

CHAPTER 1

The Train

Poland
January 30, 1943

I t was cold, bitterly cold. The Nazi Gestapo, troops, and
local police had stormed the Jewish ghetto of Pruzhany,
rousting the residents from their homes and forcing them
into a milling, anxious crowd. A formerly pleasant, unremarkable
neighborhood, the Nazis had set aside this section of the city,
forced Pruzhany's Jews into it, and surrounded it with barbed wire
and guards. The once happy district was now a squalid community
of hunger and fear, where residents walked the streets at their
own risk. The Nazis created over one thousand such ghettos in the
countries they had conquered, a fact that, at that moment, meant
little to fourteen-year-old Basha Anush, her five siblings, parents,
and elderly grandfather. They were cold, hungry, scared, and
staring down the barrels of weapons pointed at them by shouting,
cursing troops. What was happening to other Jews was not their
primary concern. This was happening to them.

The arrival of the large, armed force was not a surprise, but still
a shock. Rumor traffic in the ghetto had been alive with stories of
the Jewish population of Poland being relocated to work camps.
Or worse. When the ghetto elders gathered to speculate on their
fate, it was generally agreed that the likelihood of still more misery
being inflicted upon them was a question of *when*, not *if*.

Over a period of days, police and German occupation forces

loudly and forcefully demanded that the residents hurry from their homes. Basha's mother told her to wear as many layers of clothing as possible, partially to fend off the vicious Polish winter, and partially because they could take few belongings with them. As the frightened throng was herded to the assembly point, they shivered—from both cold and fear.

As the assembly location came into view, the citizens of the ghetto got their first clue as to what was going on. A line of horse-drawn sleds was waiting for them. Weeks before, they had been gathered at the same place and stood for hours in the cold, without even an opportunity to relieve themselves.

As would be expected, Basha remembered the experience vividly.

"It was a month before they evacuated us. They told all the Jews to come to a certain place and a certain street there—a big street. Everyone [had] *to come to stand in fives, the whole families, everyone together, and then we didn't know what was happening. We thought then they were going to kill us or shoot us.*

"It was a very, very cold day. I remember we stood out there in the street with little children, babies. We were all hungry. We were standing the whole day. We were freezing, the weather was just terrible that day, and they let us stay the whole day. Then the Germans came and counted us. They counted the whole population. After they counted us came the order for us to go home, back to our houses.[1]

"And God, it was so much joy. Everyone was so happy; everyone was running to his corner—to his house. I'll never forget my brother, Berel, when he walked into the house. He fell on the cold floor and kissed it. He kissed the whole floor for an hour, he kissed it. He was so happy that we came home. I won't forget it until my last breath. And my father took a few pieces of wood that he

had and he lit up the oven and it started to get warm. And my mother saved for a rainy day three carrots. And she put it in the oven and every kid got a slice of the carrot. And we were so happy. [I'll] never forget it, we were so happy that we came home. And all of us were together again. But it didn't last too long. It didn't last too long. This was, we find out, they gathered us together to see how many sleds they would need for the whole city to take us to the trains to the station." [2]

Initially, approximately eighteen thousand Jews stayed in the Pruzhany ghetto, including Jews the Nazis removed by force from smaller-area towns and brought to the Pruzhany ghetto to create a centralized Jewish population. The Jewish people, along with several other groups, had been declared enemies of the German state. First, the Nazis removed them from the general population in German-conquered lands, isolating them to make them easier to control. Eventually, they would be eliminated entirely. Sickness, starvation, and the terrible cold weather took about six thousand lives prior to the evacuation of the Pruzhany ghetto. It required some planning in order to expedite the transport of the large remaining population to ensure the least opportunity for rebellion. The Nazis procured sleds locally and from the surrounding towns, but it was virtually impossible to move that many people quickly. The entire operation took about a week. Not everyone was willing to wait peacefully for their fate. On a dark night, several of the town's young people attempted to escape by cutting the wires that surrounded the ghetto, but the Nazi guards were vigilant.

"We heard so much shooting during the night, and we didn't know who it was or what it was," Basha remembered. "In the morning, we saw the best kids in our town just lying in the grass and all of them dead. They shot them all." [3]

At the embarkation point, the armed, shouting troops maintained a reasonable amount of order as they loaded their Jewish captives onto the sleds. To her relief, Basha's entire family was on the same sled. Each sled had two Nazi guards keeping an eye on their victims, but Basha's brothers also kept an eye on the Nazis. As the trip progressed and they passed a forest; they believed they could jump from the sled and escape. They whispered the plan to their mother, but she begged them not to do it.

"No, my kids, I don't want to see your blood spilled in front of my eyes." [4]

Could they have escaped? Basha would never know.

Outside of the ghetto, the Gentile residents of Pruzhany watched the operation with varied reactions, from indifference to joy. Anti-Semitism may have been the rule, rather than the exception. To make their situation even more disheartening, the path of the sleds was lined with many citizens cheering, jeering, and calling out anti-Semitic epithets. These people had formerly been their neighbors. While the Jewish community of Pruzhany had remained close-knit and somewhat isolated from the Gentile population, they still had some interaction with them. During the Russian occupation, Basha's father secretly ran a kosher butcher business from their home against the orders of the Russians, but he sold meat to Gentiles as well as Jews. Basha would clandestinely make the deliveries to them. She hid the meat from the watchful Russians by carrying it under her dress. Unfortunately, sometimes blood would seep through the wrapping paper and stain her dress. She was ashamed to go to school in soiled clothes, but her father told her to make these deliveries, and she dutifully did. She would never say no to her father.

"When a parent said something," she remembered, "it was holy." [5]

One of her father's Gentile customers was the Markovich family. They were wealthy and lived in a very large house on acres of property. Mrs. Markovich was always very kind to Basha. Basha made her deliveries on Friday, which was typically Mrs. Markovich's baking day. Having sufficient flour and sugar to bake was a sign of wealth at that time, and having fresh-baked goods was a rarity among the poor. After school, Basha would have to stand in line at the store for hours just to get a piece of bread. The wait for sugar could be three days, so when Mrs. Markovich gave Basha a piece of cake, and sometimes a few pieces to take home to her siblings, it was a great treat. On cold winter days, Mrs. Markovich always checked to made sure Basha was bundled up as warmly as possible before she let her go back into the cold for the walk home.

As the caravan of sleds made its way through the city of Pruzhany, Basha looked out into the jeering crowd, and there stood Mrs. Markovich and the rest of her family, "laughing, clapping, and carrying on with everyone else." Basha was crushed. "I, as a child, knew something is very, very wrong with this world. And I felt no desire, already, to live." [6]

After about two hours of freezing on the sleds, the caravan arrived at the railroad station in Linova, Poland. There her family was roughly ordered onto the station platform with hundreds of other anxious Pruzhany citizens. To control the chaotic scene, Nazi *Schutzstaffel* troops—the dreaded *SS* with the Death's Head medallion on their uniforms—screamed, cursed, and swung batons, beating their victims on their heads for no reason other than a malevolent hatred of Jews. If someone was brave or foolish enough not to comply with orders immediately, the guards released their savage attack-trained German Shepherd dogs on the defenseless victim.

Basha was stunned. It was too much for a teenage girl to comprehend.

As the cursing and screaming continued, German troops and local police forced the terrified citizens of Pruzhany to board the train. Basha, her family, and their neighbors did not ride in passenger coaches but in *güterwagons*, thirty-two-foot freight cars designed to carry horses or cattle. The Nazis packed as many people as they could into each car, to the point that movement was virtually impossible. If one was standing when they went in, they likely remained standing. If they had managed to sit, they would unlikely be able to get up. Even breathing was difficult in the cramped, stifling car.

In the mass bedlam, the Nazis forced Basha, her mother, and five siblings into a car as guards stood alongside the door beating them with clubs as they entered. The family had remained together to that point, despite the confusion, but now Basha's father was missing.

"We were afraid to be separated from him and we didn't know for how long, but at the last minute, somehow, a miracle happened and he snuck in. As the Germans looked away, he joined us on the wagon, and we were very happy. But we were beaten over the head with big clubs, all of us, [and] they put so many people in the wagon, you could hardly stand up. We couldn't stand up. There were hundreds of people in this wagon." [7]

The Nazis had complete control of the Polish railway system, having seized it immediately after conquering Poland and incorporating it into their own system, the *Deutsche Reichsbahn*. This gave them complete control of when, where, and how they shipped their human cargo. Caring nothing about their victims, the quality and creature comforts of the train cars were irrelevant to them. The Nazis used passenger coaches when available, primarily for expediency, not passenger comfort. When they were not available, which was most of the time, animals were displaced from the *güterwagons* to make room for humans, as was the case with Basha and her family. These boxcars generally had only one small, uncovered window for ventilation. In the harsh Polish winter, those near the window were subjected to freezing temperatures, while those in the middle of the car would nearly suffocate from the heat of overcrowding. Basha soon regretted her decision to wear several layers of clothing. She became ill and fainted. Guards did not give the prisoners food, water, or access to toilet facilities. The three-day journey became unbearable. Some had mental breakdowns and some died. Desperate from thirst, many drank their own urine.

As they rode in the boxcar, Basha's mother, in an apparent attempt to cheer her up, told her to look outside.

"My child, come, stand on my shoulders and look out the little window and see what a beautiful world it is there. It's worth living in this world. It's a nice one."

Basha rejected the idea, afraid that she would injure her mother, but her mother insisted, stood up, and lifted her up high enough to see through the little window. As they passed through a town, Polish girls walked to the movie theater with German soldiers.

"Why are we different from them? Why are we different?" she asked her mother.

A Polish woman was walking with her child and Basha shouted to her, begged her to throw her a snowball that they could eat for liquid. The woman looked at her, grabbed her child, and ran away. [8]

Others in the boxcar looked at the little window and had another idea. A man in Basha's car managed to squeeze through the small opening and jumped from the train. There was a burst of gunfire. Unknown to the prisoners, there were two Nazis with machine guns lying on the roof of the car to eliminate escapes. Shots rang out periodically along the trip. Basha took another peek out the window and saw bodies from previous trains frozen in the snow. It was the same story on every transport: men jumped to escape, and failed.

As the train rolled through the Polish countryside, there was a sudden stir of excitement. The older men, and those with a little more understanding of the situation, realized the train had passed the Majdanek camp. If the Nazis intended to kill them immediately, Majdanek would have been a logical destination. They knew it had extermination facilities. Perhaps things were not as bad as they seemed, the older men speculated. Perhaps they would not be killed after all. It was a meager hope, but they would tightly grasp whatever hope they could get.

After three hellish days and nights, the train finally came to a stop. It was the middle of the night, but when the *SS* guards forced open the boxcar door, rows of high-powered lights virtually blinded the occupants, turning night into day. The *SS* troops shouted, cursed, and jerked the occupants out of the cars and onto the ground. In the chaos, Basha noticed an officer who seemed to have some authority as he pointed at various prisoners and shouted orders to the troops. Basha would remember him and later learn his identity. He was Dr. Josef Mengele, a name that has ever since been associated with barbaric medical experiments and murder.

Jammed nearly immobile for days in the cramped cattle car, the prisoners could barely walk. Basha struggled to force her knees and feet to take a step. Her younger brother, six-year-old Shlomo, had caught a cold before they were loaded onto the trains. He had been sick and feverish for the entire trip, and was weak from the lack of food and water. When a soldier pulled him from the car, he fell near the tracks, unable to stand. Nevertheless, he picked up a cup he found on the ground, packed it full of the dirty snow, and offered it to their mother, who had just been pulled from the train.

"Here, Mommy, put it in your mouth. It's going to melt; it's going to be like a good drink."

An *SS* guard walked up to him, drew his pistol, and shot him in the face, killing him instantly. [9]

Welcome to Auschwitz.

Historical Perspective
on Chapter 1

Pruzhany

The city of Pruzhany, as noted in the text, has a long history. As political powers and governments changed throughout this region, so did the spellings, and even names, of cities. Pruzhany during Basha's youth was spelled Pruzany, a relatively small change. Other cities mentioned in this work are identified by the name and spelling correct during World War II. When the modern name is significantly different, the current spelling is also included.

Güterwagons

Moving as many prisoners as possible as quickly as possible was the objective of using rail transport. Nevertheless, the Nazi penchant for organization cropped up in this task as it did in most others. The *SS* wrote a manual on exactly how their human cargo should be shipped in the *güterwagons*. Each freight car was to be loaded with fifty Jews (or homosexuals, Gypsies, or other unfortunates) with fifty boxcars per train, for a total of 2,500 persons per trip. This apparently struck them as a nice, orderly way to conduct this business. However, despite the carefully detailed process, the *SS* frequently forced one hundred or more victims into each car, leaving virtually no room for the occupants to move. As the trip wore on, some additional vertical space was created as occupants died, but the corpses lying on the floor continued to make movement difficult. This simple act of moving people from one place to another is another example of the callous disregard the Nazis displayed for those they considered subhuman.

Notes

1. Bess Freilich interview by Josey G. Fisher, June 5, 1981, Holocaust Oral History Archive of Gratz College, Melrose Park, PA, 2-1-18.

2. Bess Freilich interview by Marc Seligman, October 20, 1996, University of Sothern California Shoah Foundation, 7.

3. Bess Freilich interview by Josey G. Fisher, 2-1-19.

4. Bess Freilich interview by Marc Seligman, 10.

5. Ibid, 3.

6. Ibid, 10.

7. Bess Freilich interview by Josey G. Fisher, 2-1-19.

8. Bess Freilich interview by Marc Seligman, 11.

9. Ibid.

First, the Russians Came

Pruzhany, Poland
1928–1939

S tepping from the train into the chaos of Auschwitz, Basha was abruptly thrust into an environment that could not have been more different from the one she left only days before. The plot of land, roughly one thousand by four hundred yards, with its twenty-two drab buildings, shared only one commonality with her previous peaceful Pruzhany neighborhood: it was populated by Jews. However, in this case, that was not good—not good at all.

Pruzhany, now part of Belarus, is located on the road from Brest to Moscow. The closest large city is Brest, about eighty-seven miles to the northwest. Pruzhany is a small city with a large history, especially for the Jewish people. The Jews began to slowly settle in Pruzhany in the middle of the fifteenth century. In 1453, Jewish elders constructed the first synagogue and formed a *hevra kadisha*[10] ("sacred society") of Jewish men and women to ensure that Jewish burial traditions were observed, and to keep accurate family records of the Jewish community.

As was common in much of the world during this period, many Pruzhany residents earned their living through agriculture. The land is productive, with many lakes and a variety of plants and animals, but winter can arrive in September and stay until April. Temperatures may reach 80°F in the summer, but winters are dependably frigid. As political forces changed, frequently through military action, governments were overthrown and laws changed. Pruzhany became part of Russia and then Poland, but for the most part, Jewish religion and culture thrived until the middle of the twentieth century. By 1927, the year before Basha's birth, almost 60 percent of the population of Pruzhany was Jewish.[11] For Basha and her siblings, Pruzhany was an excellent place to grow up. At least, it started out that way.

According to her testimonies, Basha Anush was born on December 23, 1928, although wartime Nazi documents list the year as 1926. Basha may have been counselled to tell her captors she was older than she was to escape the possibility of an immediate trip to the gas chamber. This may account for the discrepancy in her records. There is no way to determine that with any certainty today. However, it is a certainty that she was the first child of Isaac Anush and his wife Chava (née Garber), lifelong residents of Pruzhany. Six brothers quickly followed: Berel, Hillel, Bezalel, Asher, and Shlomo, as well as one sister, Reshele. Basha did not give the birthdates of her siblings, but from elements of her testimonies we can determine that Berel was likely born in late 1929 or early 1930, Hillel in 1930 or 1931, Bezalel in 1932 or 1933, and Asher in 1935. There is strong evidence that Shlomo was born in 1937, and Basha stated that Reshele was born in 1939. All of them were children when the war broke out.

In a world before televisions, computers, and cell phones, the family was very close knit, engaging in activities together, rather than individually. Isaac and Chava had plenty of love to lavish on their children, and the children responded in kind to their parents and one another. The Anushes were not wealthy, and Isaac had his work cut out for him keeping food on the table for his growing family. Fortunately, he was an energetic and determined man with a strong work ethic. He would look for and pursue opportunities to make money, sometimes successfully and other times not. For a while he went to neighboring villages and purchased horses, which he would then bring back to Pruzhany to sell at a profit, and his kosher butcher business was marginally profitable until the Russians declared it illegal. The family's house was on a large piece of property and had two big sheds in the back where Isaac kept his calves. As his family grew, so did his sense of responsibility, and he worked hard to provide for his wife and children. Fortunately, the family was devoted to one another, rather than material things.

". . . you didn't have to have a lot to make children happy in those days. It seems nowadays children have so much and sometimes they're not happy, but we were happy with very little. If we had a dress made once in three [or] *four years as a child, I was happy. I was happy when I came home and I saw a smile on my mother's face and I knew that she can make Shabbos—that she has food to put on the table—because she was smiling, and that made me happy, that made my day when I came home from school and I saw her, and I saw that the house is peaceful and everything was fine. That made me very happy."* [12]

To improve their situation, financial aid frequently came from family in the United States. All of Isaac's brothers moved to America before World War II, as well as Chava's sister, Celia. Chava and Celia adored each other, and their separation broke their hearts. Although far from wealthy, Celia did whatever she could do to help her sister and her family. Basha's daughter, Evelyn Kaplan, remembered the stories her mother told her.

"[Basha's] [A]unt Celia would send packages all the time full of clothing, chocolates, toilet paper, and things that were hard to come by in Pruzhany. There was such excitement in the house when the package arrived from Aunt Celia! Such joy . . . delicacies never seen before!" [13]

Basha remembered:

"Aunt Celia, who went to America, she worked very hard and every month sent us $17, $19, $20. Whenever she could spare, she sent [it] *to us and that helped a lot."* [14]

Chava's father, Shlomo, an accountant, also moved to the United States in search of a better life, but that better life was elusive. Unable to find work in his field, he took a job carrying ice to buildings in Manhattan, from the bottom floors to the top. From his hard, physical labor he was able to spare enough money to send some to Chava—his youngest daughter—and her family. He had a special love for his granddaughter Basha, since she was named after his wife who had died in the flu pandemic that followed World War I. He eventually decided to return to Pruzhany, not because of the backbreaking labor, but because in America he was required to work on Shabbos. Devoutly religious, he took his savings and returned to his homeland.

"He lived with us and we loved him, we adored him. He was a very intelligent man. Very intelligent. See there [in the United States] *he couldn't live out his Jewishness the way he was used to. That's what brought him back."* [15]

Back home, surrounded by family, and with savings that stretched much further in Poland than they did in New York City, Shlomo was free to pursue the activity which he cared about the most: studying the Torah. Every day he could be found in the local synagogue with a group of elders, studying and discussing the Jewish scriptures. Like most children with a generous grandfather, particularly when they know they are the apple of his eye, Basha quickly learned the best way to extract a little money from him.

"So, whenever I needed a couple of pennies I ran to the synagogue and begged him. When he was by himself, he gave me only 10

cents. When his cronies were with him, I got double, he gave me 20 cents. So, I always looked to where he was sitting, studying the Torah with all his acquaintances, you know, people that he loved, spent time with. So, I tried to come to the synagogue when they were all there, so he gave me more money. He was a very sweet person. Everyone loved him, whoever knew him." [16]

Basha's daughter, Evelyn, heard the stories, but one in particular stands out in her mind.

"She knew she couldn't ask her parents for something frivolous; every cent was used to feed the family, but her grandfather never said no. I recall one story she told me. She desperately wanted a yo-yo. He asked her how much it cost and he gave her the money. It was such a grand day for her!" [17]

The community was aware that Basha's grandfather had financial resources. Some of the Gentiles came to him periodically, requesting that he loan them money. He did it primarily to keep peace for his family in the community. "[H]e wanted to live with them, you know, like human beings. He wanted peace with the neighbors. And they asked and he gave. He never got it back, of course," Basha remembered.

Basha was sent out on Fridays to collect the loan payments. She got a few vegetables, scallions, and radishes as interest for the loans, but rarely money. After the war when Basha returned to Pruzhany, she met one of the women who had borrowed money from her grandfather. The woman admitted that when the Anush family was driven from their home, her son-in-law had been the first to break into it and steal their furniture. "That was the thanks that we got from giving them the money. At that time, it was a lot of money. They were the first ones to enter our house after the Germans evacuated us, and they robbed all the furniture and cleaned the house out." Grandfather's gesture had not been entirely in vain. The family lived in peace with their Gentile neighbors.

"Yes, we played, and they were [our] neighbors. We were neighbors and we lived in harmony. This was until the war broke out, and then it was a different period altogether."[18] All the children greatly appreciated Grandfather's loving attention and treats, but he had a very special gift for Basha. He planned to pay for a good, Jewish education for her. The Polish public schools were good, but Grandfather insisted she have not only an excellent education, but one that was steeped in Jewish religion and tradition. There was a private Jewish school in the area, but it was quite expensive. The student body was comprised of children from wealthy parents, and the steep tuition hindered families in the Anushs's income bracket. Grandfather had the financial means, and he was more than willing—in fact, insistent—on investing them in his granddaughter. A good education was not the only reason that Basha was excited about her attendance in a Jewish school. The family, particularly Basha's mother, was very religious. Chava was a member of local Zionist organizations, and hoped the family might one day emigrate to Israel. They spoke Hebrew at home, and tried to do business primarily at Jewish shops where the proprietors also spoke Hebrew.[19]

"Religion was very important; very, very important. My grandfather was in the synagogue . . . and my mother was very religious, too. She went to shul on the holidays, and my father put on a tefillin *every morning. When it came to Shabbos you could feel it in the house; you could touch Shabbos in the house. In the summer, the kids were cleaned and washed, and [we] put on the best that we had—the little that we had. And the candles in the house—the Shabbos candles—so beautiful, the candles*

were. We would play in front of the house all clean. And so were the holidays, too. It was very nice until things got much worse when the Germans came." [20]

Basha's time in the private Jewish school was productive. She began to learn languages, and over the course of her life she learned several. She was also educated in the arts, and was proud to show Grandfather her work. "I'll never forget the day that I put some painting on the wall, and he was standing and looking at the painting. He remarked, 'I wish God would give me the years to see Basha become a decent person and grow up.'" He must have had a premonition. Basha recalled, "And the next day we lost him. Like he had a feeling. I've never spoken about this, you know. Life wasn't the same for us." [21]

In addition to the bereavement at the loss of their beloved grandfather, there were practical, financial implications for the family. Basha remembered painfully:

"I still went to that school, and a lot of times I had to stay home. It sent you home if you couldn't pay. And that was very harsh on me. I felt very, very bad, and when the person that took care of the payments, when he came in, my stomach turned. I felt so humiliated, because in the middle of the class I had to walk out and go home until my father paid, and it wasn't easy for [him]." [22]

Isaac Anush did his best, and the family struggled on.

Dora: Basha's Soon-to-Be Friend

In another area of Pruzhany, Dora Golubowicz grew up with quite a different perspective on Jewish life in the small town. Dora's father owned a bakery and they were wealthy. She and Basha had not yet met at that point, but they would soon be thrown together by the war, and their lives—in good times and bad—would intertwine thereafter.

Dora said her family was conservative but not orthodox. In fact, she said the synagogue the family attended was considerably more orthodox than her father, but they maintained strong Jewish faith. They did not always go to their synagogue on Shabbos, and her father frequently had to work at the bakery on weekends. When he did, he tried to stay in the back and let his Gentile employees handle the public transactions.

Dora's neighborhood was almost exclusively Jewish, but she met Gentile children at school, and they went to each other's homes to play. Dora did not recall encountering any anti-Semitism in her childhood. She attended a public school that included classes on religion, but the Jews and the Gentiles had separate classes, and there was no attempt to influence or discredit anyone's religious faith. She said the public school teachers treated her "absolutely good," and the quality of instruction was such that by the time they finished seventh grade they had the equivalent education of a high school graduate in the United States. The family also had teachers who came to their home to teach Hebrew and Yiddish.

The family had sufficient wealth to employ a maid, a Gentile woman who spoke Yiddish as her family did. They could afford amusements and vacations. She remembers a youth filled with fun. "We had a marvelous life." [23]

All of that would change at the end of the 1930s. Wealth would no longer matter—if you were Jewish.

Germany
1932–1939

Basha knew little about world politics during the 1930s, and that was rightly so. Ideally, children should be free from adult worries and allowed to peacefully enjoy the blessings of youth.

However, she was aware there were things going on in neighboring Germany that sent ripples of concern through her community. Her mother whispered of them with friends who gathered in their house, and old men huddled on street corners, frowning as they read newspapers aloud. Their concern centered on a brash, outspoken German politician named Adolf Hitler. He said he was going to restore Germany to its former glory and solve all its problems. Many of the problems, he proclaimed, were the fault of the Jews.

In the aftermath of World War I, Germany was in an economic and political freefall. The population had been crippled by inflation and unemployment, and rival political factions fought in the streets. Paul von Hindenburg, a highly acclaimed WWI field marshal, began his second term of office as president in January 1932, but at the age of eighty-four, he was beginning to lose his grip on his physical and mental abilities. Worse, he was losing his grip on Germany. Several political parties fought for dominance, but the two most powerful groups—the far-left communists and the far-right National Socialist German Workers' Party, known as the Nazi Party—gained support among the population. Hindenburg needed a strong ally. He was a conservative, so aligning with the communists was unthinkable. The alternative was the Nazis, led by Hitler—a former WWI German Army lance corporal. Hitler had a gift for oratory that many said was almost hypnotic. Even his numerous detractors would listen. Many Germans considered him and his brown-uniformed followers little more than street thugs, but Hindenburg did not have a lot of choices in the matter. He appointed Hitler chancellor on January 30, 1933. Hitler remained in his place, at least publicly, until Hindenburg's death on August 2, 1934. At that point, Hitler combined the offices of chancellor and president, giving himself total control over Germany with the new title of *führer*: leader.

Hitler immediately turned his attention to his political opponents. He eliminated them. Many found themselves incarcerated in prisons that would later be known worldwide as *Konzentrationslagers*—concentration camps—usually abbreviated KL, followed by the camp's name. Other dissidents disappeared or died. The Nazi Party banned newspapers and magazines with opposing political opinions, and eventually took control of radio stations and motion-picture production. Hitler and the Nazis controlled everything in Germany. This state-controlled media subjected Basha, her friends, neighbors, and everyone else in the world to story after story that extolled the wonderful improvements the Nazi rule created. Others, like Basha's mother Chava, spoke with Jews who had fled the country. They told a very different story. Despite the chilling militarized political muscle of the Nazis, even those who opposed Hitler had to admit certain things were improving. From February of 1933 to spring of 1937, unemployment fell from six million to less than one million,[24] and German national pride, which had suffered a beating after the humiliating Treaty of Versailles that ended World War I, was returning.

Hitler's vision for Germany extended beyond its borders. In his 1925 autobiography, *Mein Kampf,* he clearly stated his goal for Germany was additional *Lebensraum*—living space. Since he could not create more land, his only alternative was to take land from someone else. The likelihood of multiple nations willingly ceding their countries to Germany was improbable. That meant he would have to seize land by force. Lands east of Germany were soft targets for invasion, but strong military action was not immediately necessary. Austrians spoke German, and many were pro-Nazi and welcomed the *Anschluss*—annexation—of the country. Similarly, Czechoslovakia had a large Germanic population in the Western area of the country known as the Sudetenland, which had been created after World War I. The Czechs agreed to allow the Sudetenland to be self-governing, but Hitler was not satisfied with that. He demanded that the Sudetenland become part of Germany, and Great Britain and France—signers of the Treaty of Versailles—meekly gave the territory to him.

To virtually everyone in Poland, including Basha's family, it was clear their German neighbor on the west had become dangerous, particularly for the Jews. Travelers who had passed through Germany, and German citizens who had fled the country, told stories of abuse. There was no denying Hitler's obvious conquests, and it was apparent that, his ego fueled by success, he was determined to seize more land. To broaden the scope of his attack, Hitler sought Russia as an ally. Led by Joseph Stalin—a man of the same character, or lack of it, as Hitler—the next target became Poland. They agreed to split the country in half, eradicating Polish culture and subjugating the population to little more than servitude.

Hitler began an anti-Poland publicity campaign in early 1939, but he needed a reason for all-out war. The Poles did not give him one, so he had to create one by staging a false flag attack on a German radio station in Gleiwitz, Germany, on the Polish border. Then, with carefully rehearsed theatrical outrage, he announced a "defensive attack" against Poland on September 1, 1939. Unlike the previous conflicts, this one would be no walkover. The Poles fought back. An existing mutual defense pact forced Great Britain and France, who had tried so hard to stay out of war, to aid Poland. They declared war on Germany.

As Basha, her family, and the rest of the world watched powerlessly, World War II began.

Pruzhany
September 1, 1939

Although Basha did not specifically mention it in her test-imonies, it is likely the last thing she expected on the morning of September first was the news that her country had been invaded. That is not the kind of thing nine-year-old children anticipate. On the other hand, she was not entirely ignorant of the political situation, particularly the plight of the German Jews. The Zionist organizations to which Basha's mother belonged, heard and spread the news of the Jewish persecution going on in Germany. It was a topic of concerned conversation for the community. Basha and the other children would eavesdrop as Chava shared the stories with their neighbors, picking up as much information as they could. What they heard was hard to believe. Basha remembered: ". . . [T]hey told such horror stories, but we didn't want to believe, we couldn't believe that something like this could ever happen in the twentieth century. We thought it was just rumors. Nobody—in our wildest imaginations—we couldn't believe such things. [25]

The adults could, and did, believe. It was clear that a wave of anti-Semitism had engulfed Germany, as well as some of their Gentile Pruzhany neighbors. The ethnic peril was not likely to go away; in fact, they assumed it would get worse. The best remedy for their situation, one they were all excited to pursue, was to emigrate to Palestine. Chava's Zionist friends provided ample information and education about moving to the largely Jewish area of the Middle East. The Anush children, and a substantial number of their friends, were steeped in Jewish tradition and understood the implications of moving to the birthplace of their faith. The older teenagers, eighteen and nineteen years old, went to the *hakhshara,* an agricultural training camp that prepared Jewish children to assume a productive role in their Palestinian community when they arrived. Basha was too young to join the *hakhshara*, but in the end, a vast gulf of bureaucracy separated her desire to move to Palestine and the ability to actually do so. Emigration required a special government certificate, and a quota limited the number of certificates issued. Basha said her father struggled and prayed to receive the certificates, but he could not cut through the red tape. As happens in many situations, the rich and powerful pushed for preferential treatment and received it. In 1938 and 1939, the Jewish leaders moved to the top of the list. Had it not been for the quota, Basha believed half their community would have left for Palestine.[26]

Blitzkrieg

When Hitler pulled the trigger on his war machine, the citizens of Poland were stunned by the speed at which the German Wehrmacht troops overran their country. He launched a new type of warfare—*blitzkrieg*—lightning war. The modern mechanized force he had secretly built stormed over the Polish border, clashing with Polish forces, which still depended on horses for transportation. When the Russians attacked from the east on September 17, it was clear the Polish situation was hopeless. Polish military forces had an abundance of bravery, but that would not be enough. By October 6, German and Russian forces controlled all of Poland. The Poles never formally surrendered.

In accordance with their previous pacts, the Germans and Russians split Poland into two zones, with the Russians gaining slightly more territory. Pruzhany was in the Russian sector of Eastern Poland, so Basha and her family suddenly found themselves under the watchful eye of Russian troops. Many Poles, particularly Jews, considered this a stroke of luck. They knew how the Nazis treated Jews, and they felt safer under the Russians. This was true to some degree, but they would soon discover brutality was going to be the rule from now on, no matter who was in control.

It did not take long for Basha and her family to feel the impact of Russian dominance. The Russians were as anti-Semitic as the Germans, although, at that point, somewhat less brutal. They wasted no time in enforcing their anti-Jewish prejudices, and immediately clamped down on the observance of Jewish religious rites. That included a prohibition on kosher meat, which had a devastating impact on Isaac Anush's butcher business and his ability to earn a living. The Russians were strict about enforcing the regulations. At one point, they had an undercover agent watching the Anushes' house, suspecting that he was continuing to ply his trade. They were suspicious of everything. An undercover agent even entered their house and challenged Chava, saying, "It is the middle of the week, it is not Shabbos. How come you wash the floors?" The implication was that Isaac had been butchering the calves in his kitchen, and the agent wanted evidence. Occasionally he found some. Basha remembered:

"He was forbidden and, my father I remember, he was in jail so many times. We used to bring him soup to eat. I was allowed to bring him, as a little girl, soup to him. And he was more in jail than he was out of jail, because they didn't like him to do it, [kosher butcher] *but somehow, he had to make a living."* [27]

Isaac continued at his trade the best he could, secretly butchering and selling kosher meat to the Jewish community and (supposedly) friendly Gentiles, like Mrs. Markovich. With the serious economic strain on the family, Basha's eleven-year-old brother, Berel, stepped up to help support the family. Chava had acquired some tobacco, which she rolled into cigarettes during the day. When Berel came home from school, he took the cigarettes out onto the streets and sold them, primarily to Russian soldiers. Despite the policy of Jewish persecution, Basha said the Russian soldiers, for the most part, left them alone. Kosher meat was prohibited, but cigarettes were okay. The small amount of extra money helped keep food on the table.

No Jew, man, woman, or child entirely escaped the heavy hand of Russian oppression. Living quietly was not enough; being a Jew was the problem. Basha's life was disrupted like everyone else's. The Hebrew schools had closed. Jewish education was allowed to continue but was limited to history and literature. Yiddish was allowed to be spoken, but Hebrew was strictly forbidden in speech or print. It was a criminal offense to possess books printed in Hebrew. Russian troops and local police arrested violators of this rule. Basha had a large library of Hebrew books but disposed of them immediately. "I burned my books. I was very much afraid to keep them in the house because it was against the law. The penalty for teaching Hebrew was worse. Some of the teachers that they let them remain in our town, that they didn't send to Siberia, they knew Jewish and they started to teach Jewish in the Jewish schools." Others were not so lucky.

"They were sent to Siberia, yes, quite a few of them." [28]

Eliminating Hebrew education created time for the Russians to promote their own agenda. Local Polish communists assigned to be youth leaders enrolled young people in the *Komsomol,* the communist indoctrination program, designed to prepare young people for membership in the Communist Party. Basha and her siblings were too young for the *Komsomol,* but enrolled in the Pioneers, a militaristic communist youth organization.[29] These programs bore some similarity to the *Hitlerjugend* (Hitler Youth) and the *Bund Deutscher Mädel* (League of German Girls), focusing on political indoctrination and physical fitness. Instead of studying Hebrew, the Anush children and their friends learned to march.

While Basha's father was attempting to work around Russian oppression to earn a living, the father of her soon-to-be best friend, Dora Golubowicz, faced a variation on the same problem. The Russians brought their system of communism with them, which meant that anyone with a business automatically became a "class enemy." Being a class enemy was dangerous. Russian political commissars deported many of them to Siberia.

> *"I was thirteen at the time, and they gave you passports. In other words, everybody had to carry a passport. It's your name, your birth, a certificate and, if your father had a business, then you had a number. The number was bad; it meant you exploited people. If people worked for you, then you exploited them, because in Russia, you know, everything belonged to the government. You worked for the government . . . if people were happy working for you, it didn't matter. You got this eleven [number on the passport denoting one who exploits people]."* [30]

The Russians wasted little time confiscating businesses and property.

> *"My father was very upset when they took* [his bakery]. *They let him stay for a while in the bakery because they needed the bread . . . so he was working in the bakery* [as a baker], *which he never did before, because he inherited* [the bakery] *from his father and he was the boss. Now he had to go in the back and work with everybody together."* [31]

Unlike the bakers, Dora's father was not allowed to take a salary. The family was supposed to live off their savings. That was part of the price to be paid for being an exploiter.

The communist regime did not spare children. Dora became a member of the *Komsomol*, and community life revolved around Russian communist indoctrination. A local Jewish man, who was a communist sympathizer, organized a social group for boys and girls, both Jewish and Gentile. The group would meet at night and have dances and parties, as well as political discussions. The social aspect of the group immediately interested the children, including Dora, and they were excited at the prospect of fun evenings. Shortly before the launch of the organization, the man pulled Dora aside. "'You are not going to belong,' and I said, 'Why? I never did anything wrong.' 'You are not going to belong because your father is an [exploiter].'" The dreaded "number eleven" socially blacklisted Dora and her family. Despite the obvious trend toward oppression, few Jewish families tried to leave Pruzhany.

"They didn't understand," Dora recalled.

They would understand soon.

The New Normal

The communist system introduced a new factor into Basha's life, one that would impact her for years to come: hunger. Many shops and stores had closed, and Basha's family, along with the other residents of Pruzhany, could no longer easily obtain food. Under their communist system, the Russians periodically brought in food and distributed it to the community, but the citizens had no choice of what, or how much, they would receive. Whatever the Russians brought in was all that was publicly available. Basha would sometimes stand in line for hours to get food for her family, and bartering became a new way of life. Families exchanged foodstuff, or traded clothing and possessions for food, but no matter how meager or bland the allotment may be, the Russian distribution was the only certain way to obtain food. If Basha had to stand in line to get it, she stood in line.

Basha watched as the residents of her once peaceful community began to show signs of stress. Some citizens, both Gentile and Jewish, chose to make their lives marginally easier by collaborating with the Russians. There was also a significant portion of the Jewish population who were communists, or communist sympathizers. There are estimates putting this number at 30 percent of the Jewish population, although some historians believe the number was much lower. Whichever the case, this caused stress in the community, and the Jews' resentment toward the Gentiles increased. Ultimately, it did not matter. The Jews and Gentiles both suffered under the Russians, who ran Eastern Poland as they wished. They treated Poland and its population as their possessions.

The planned enslavement of the Jews had begun, and Basha was in the middle of it.

Historical Perspective
on Chapter 2

Tefillin

Tefillin are small black leather boxes containing scripture from the Torah. One is worn on the head and the other on an upper arm, attached by straps. They are worn during weekday morning prayers, but may be worn anytime during the day.

The Gleiwitz Incident – The Beginning of WWII

In early 1939, the German propaganda machine manufactured a variety of insults and injuries to Germany which the Poles had supposedly inflicted, but Hitler needed a bigger event to justify war. Reinhard Heydrich, director of the German International Criminal Police Commission, and Gestapo chief Heinrich Mueller, devised a plan for a "false flag" attack on Germany. On August 31, under the command of *SS* officer Alfred Naujocks, an *SS* detachment attacked a German radio station on the Polish border at Gleiwitz. The German troops killed radio station personnel and broadcast a brief anti-German announcement. To make the attack look like it had originated in Poland, an *SS* detachment killed prisoners from the Dachau concentration camp by lethal injection, mutilated the bodies with gunshot wounds, and dressed them in Polish military uniforms. They transported the bodies to Gleiwitz in the convoy with the attack troops. Following the successful attack on the radio station, the *SS* scattered the bodies of the prisoners at the scene, along with Polish weapons, to support their contention that the event was a deliberate attack on Germany from Poland.

Hitler immediately broadcast the news of the outrage of the "Polish attack" and stated that he had no choice but to launch a defensive war against Poland. On September 1, 1939, the Germans invaded Poland from the west, and on September 17, the Russians attacked from the east. The Polish Army fought bravely for six weeks, but did not have the resources to fight a two-front war, and British and French troops did not arrive in time to defend the nation.

The Militarization of Germany

In defiance of the Treaty of Versailles, Hitler built a mechanized military force second to none. His new Panzer tanks and mechanized infantry units stormed over the German-Polish border with unanticipated, never-before-seen speed. In the skies, his Luftwaffe air force ruled. Stuka dive bombers destroyed ground targets and their shrieking sirens terrifying the population. The Poles countered with antiquated aircraft, and much of their artillery and equipment was pulled by horses. They fought a defensive fight, but when the Russians attacked from the east on September 17, it was clear that Poland would fall. Some Polish troops fled to neutral Romania to reorganize, and some Polish pilots made their way to England, where they formed a Polish unit in the Royal Air Force.

The Division of Poland

In accordance with the Molotov-Ribbentrop Pact, Poland was divided between Germany and Russia, with the Russians getting slightly more territory. The western section, occupied by Germany, had a more ethnically homogeneous Polish population than the eastern section, occupied by Russia, that had a multitude of ethnically Ukrainian and Belarusian residents. Some of those residents welcomed the Russians, including some Jews, who felt that the Russians had saved them from falling into the hands of the Germans. Polish Jews fled the country if they had the opportunity, but many fled only from the western section to the eastern section, choosing what they believed was the lesser of two evils. Hitler immediately enacted his *Lebensraum* policy, forcing Poles from their property so German colonists could take their land. The conquerors deemed a few Poles worthy of "Germanization" and allowed to remain, but many others were shipped off to the KL camps. Basha and her family remained in the eastern section of Poland, controlled by the Russians.

The Salvation of Pruzhany

It did not take long for the Russians to forcefully impose their will on the citizens of Eastern Poland. According to Pruzhany resident and chronicler Zalman Urievich, invading Russian troops immediately destroyed the cities of Shereshev, Kartuzy, Bereza and Selcz. Fortunately for the residents of Pruzhany, a man named Geurshon Urinsky had an idea to save their city. He formed a committee that set out little tables with lemonade, little breads and cigars on the road into town. They greeted the Russians with a smile. The surprised Russian troops ate what the citizens provided, smoked the cigars, thanked them, and then moved on without destroying Pruzhany.[32] Other cities were not so lucky.

The Russian People's Commissariat for Internal Affairs, known as the NKVD, [33] took charge of the populations of Russian conquered territories, including eastern Poland. The NKVD ruthlessly eliminated anti-communists, killing 20,000 to 30,000 captured Polish Army officers,[34] and sent many Polish troops to enslavement in Siberia. Russian authorities removed Poles from government positions and rounded up police, judges, priests, rabbis, and many teachers, deporting approximately 320,000 innocent civilians to Gulags in Russia. Most victims never returned to Poland.[35] The NKVD arrested suspected Zionists, many of whom were never seen again. The NKVD made an occasional exception for young Jews who were stanch communists, and some of them were allowed to take positions in the government, but non-Communist Jews faced persecution.

Notes

10. Chevra Kaddisha, "Glossary: C," Jewish Virtual Library, accessed September 4, 2021, https://www.jewishvirtuallibrary.org/glossary-c.

11. Joan and Bobby Engel, "Pruzhany History," accessed September 5, 2021, http://www.flora-and-sam.com/pages/PruzhanyHistory.htm.

12. Bess Freilich interview by Josey G. Fisher, 1-1-4.

13. Evelyn Kaplan, telephone interview with author, July 21, 2021.

14. Bess Freilich interview by Marc Seligman, 1.

15. Ibid, 2.

16. Ibid.

17. Evelyn Kaplan, telephone interview with author, July 21, 2021.

18. Bess Freilich interview by Josey G. Fisher, 1-1-4.

19. Bess Freilich interview by Marc Seligman, 4.

20. Ibid.

21. Ibid, 3.

22. Ibid.

23. Dora Freilich, interview by Helen Grossman, October 24, 1984, Holocaust History Archive of Gratz College, Melrose Park, PA.

24. William L. Shirer, *The Rise and Fall of the Third Reich: A History of Nazi Germany* (New York: Simon & Schuster, 1960) 231.

25. Bess Freilich interview by Josey G. Fisher, 1-1-5.

26. Ibid, 1-1-6.

27. Bess Freilich interview by Marc Seligman, 3.

28. Bess Freilich interview by Josey G. Fisher, 1-1-7.

29. Ibid.

30. Dora Freilich, interview by Helen Grossman, 1-1-6.

31. Ibid.

32. Zalman Urievich, "Pruzhany Jews in Ghettos and Camps," Pruzh.

org, 1958, accessed September 16, 2021, https://www.pruzh.org/yzkor_ pruzhany/guettos_camp.htm.

33. "NKVD," Wikipedia, accessed March 25, 2023, https://en.m. wikipedia.org.

34. "NKVD Prisoner Massacres," accessed March 25, 2023, https:// en.wikipedia.org/wiki/NKVD_ prisoner_massacres.

35. Ibid.

CHAPTER 3

Then the Germans Came

I t should have been clear to even the most casual observer of the international scene that neither Adolf Hitler nor Joseph Stalin were trustworthy men. When men unworthy of trust unite, there is always the question of who will betray the other first. The answer came on Sunday, June 22, 1941 when Hitler stabbed Stalin in the back by breaking their treaties and attacking Russia. Unfortunately for Basha and her family, the road to Russia was through Poland.

Pruzhany
June 22, 1941

Once again, it is likely that neither Basha, nor anyone else in Pruzhany, was expecting an invasion on that Sunday night; however, they did not expect an entirely peaceful night, either. The Russians had announced there would be a military drill, so the citizens prepared for a certain amount of activity and noise. Consequently, when the activity and noise started, it took a while for the citizens—and especially the Russians—to realize this was not a drill; it was the real thing.

As one would expect, it was another unforgettable night for Basha. The children were on vacation from school, and prepared to go to bed. It was a warm night, and the Anush family had the windows of their house open. Chava was standing in front of one, enjoying the pleasant breeze and looking out over the town, when suddenly the sky was lit by explosions.

"That evening, somehow, there were maneuvers. All the lights in the town were to be out, and we expected . . . there was a lot of planes were going to be in the sky, and they were going to practice, and we didn't expect anything at all, but during the middle of the night there was a terrible bombardment." [36]

A Russian soldier was passing their house. As he looked into the sky, he yelled to Chava proudly above the din, "Those are ours!" It took another minute or two before he realized something was wrong. "What's happening? They're real bullets and real bombs! It's our planes that are flying there!"

Basha said: "They didn't know themselves that it was like a *blitzkrieg*, and they were very confused. Our town was right near the border [of German-occupied Poland], and we were the first ones to be taken over by the Germans." [37]

Bombs fell all over the neighborhood, sending people running in fear. Basha and her family fled their home, running to her aunt's house, which was constructed more sturdily than theirs. From there they looked out the windows and saw fires all over their city. Basha could see their house surrounded by flames. Miraculously, the structure was spared. They remained at her aunt's home until the night of terror was over.[38]

Across town, Dora's experience was slightly different. Two years older than Basha, she was being prepared for a place in communist society. The communist system of government imposed on Pruzhany expected something of everyone, including children. The ranking political forces assigned youth leaders to educate children for their expected role in the regime. The youth leaders evaluated the children and enrolled them in training programs which they felt appropriate for the individual's age and abilities. Medical personnel provided basic nursing training to many young girls and directed them down the path to that career, which was particularly needed in time of war. On the night of the invasion, Dora and her group took part in the Russian military exercise. Children from different public schools participated as units, with each school approaching the objective from a different direction. As they marched to their assigned assembly point—a cemetery—groups of aircraft roared over their heads. "Look how we are performing!" a Russian soldier in their group shouted. Moments later, his pride turned to confusion as bombs began to fall on them.

". . . [T]*here started to be explosions, and there is fire and people falling, and that is when Germany broke the treaty with them over Russia. They started advancing. And people started running. The chaos was unbelievable. We didn't know what was happening, but we saw that there were casualties already, lying on the floor. Our parents were running.*" [39]

The next day, German troops marched into Pruzhany. Panzer tanks shook the ground with the din of their clanking steel tracks, adding to the chaos. Terrible confusion and fear overwhelmed Basha.

"*I remember I tried to sleep that day. It was the first day after the night* [of the bombardment]. *It was not because I was sleepy, but I just felt that if I go to sleep that all of these terrible things that were happening were going to disappear. I knew that, God forbid, my family is going to be hit by a bomb. I didn't want to see. I felt if my eyes would be closed, I just won't see it is happening to them. I didn't want to see it. Like I wished it should happen to me first, not to them. The whole day, it was terrible, the whole time. It was upside down. People were running, people were leaving the city, a lot of them.*

"And of course, if you had little children—we had a baby six months old in the house, and one was a year old—there was a house full of children, little children, and how can you leave everything and just run? We couldn't. So, the families that had children remained." [40]

The Russians were just as anxious as the citizens of Pruzhany, perhaps more so, to get out of the way of the German military onslaught. They fled, leaving warehouses of weapons and food, some of which fell into the hands of Pruzhany citizens before the Germans took control. Russian soldiers had been billeted in Dora's house, and their retreat was anything but orderly.

"They tried to get on one truck; they tried to get one thousand people on one truck, hanging . . . from all sides, just to get out. They wanted to go back to Russia, and this is when the whole thing was starting." [41]

At first, some Pruzhany citizens held out hope that things might not be as dark as they expected. One citizen, Shloimke Saphirshtein, ran into a German officer he met during World War I. The officer made a "good news, bad news" comment that summed up the situation. The German said, "Jews shouldn't be afraid of us, the army, but when the Gestapo comes, it'll all be very serious. Look for a chance, save yourself. Runaway." [42]

He was correct to a degree. Many German soldiers went about their jobs without displaying any particular hatred for the Jews, but when the Gestapo arrived it was, indeed, very serious and they inflicted immediate humiliation and persecution. Jews could no longer walk on the sidewalks; they had to walk in the street gutter. They had to wear two yellow star patches on their clothing, one on their chest and one on their back. Germans felt free to plunder Jewish homes without fear of punishment.

Rousting the Russians from Eastern Poland and pursuing

them into Russia bolstered the sense of invincibility felt by many German troops after their long string of victories. With their self-image as members of the Master Race, the Gestapo took the lead executing the principal Nazi plan: the seizure of Polish property, the enslavement of the Poles, and the eradication of the Jewish race. They wasted no time. The Nazis immediately marked Jews of intellect, education, and power, for death. Basha remembered:

"Two days later, already, they started the killing business. They took the whole elite from our town, and they took them outside the city. We didn't know what happened to them. Those were doctors, engineers, and lawyers.

"They took our Rabbi. [He] was a doctor of philosophy, and he was also a major in the Polish Army. Brilliant person, brilliant person. They took him out, and they tied him to a horse and dragged him like this on the ground through the whole town the whole day. Later on, they shot and killed him." [43]

The Germans took the prominent citizens of Pruzhany to a rural area where the Jewish children used to go to summer camp. They never came back. Any questions about how they had been treated prompted a chilling answer: "It was a day later. A dog came . . . and he was holding in his mouth an arm with a coat that a doctor wore [with] a Red Cross [on the sleeve]. He was holding it in his mouth." [44]

To organize the process of Jewish isolation and persecution, the Germans formed ghettos all over Poland, one of which was in Pruzhany. In July, the Gestapo commandant informed the citizens of the impending creation of the ghetto, and that Pruzhany was now part of Eastern Prussia and the Third Reich. Again, the most optimistic of citizens hoped that being officially part of the Third Reich would bring some citizenship rights. They quickly discovered the only right it brought was the right, and obligation, to build the wall that would imprison them.[45]

Nazi authorities set aside a section of the city exclusively for the Jewish population, and surrounded it with barricades, barbed wire, and German guards. They forced the Jews to abandon their homes and move into this secluded area, and non-Jews to move out of it. In perhaps their only bit of luck, the Anush family's house was already inside the designated ghetto area, so they did not have to move, but they were not left entirely alone either. The Nazis searched the surrounding towns for Jews, and those captured were taken to Pruzhany and forced into the already crowded ghetto. They expected the citizens of Pruzhany to take them in, which they did. Entire families ended up living in one room. Basha heard how some of the Jews from other towns were horribly mistreated as they were marched to Pruzhany.

> *"I remember from one town, it was* [name indistinguishable on interview recording] *the name of it, that they made the people crawl from their town on their knees, which was maybe 100 km from our town, and they had to crawl, all the people, the children and women. They were crawling, none of them was allowed to stand up, crawling like this, and they brought them like this to our ghetto. Of course, they brought only maybe 10 percent of the population. Most of them died along the way. These people that remained alive, the population of our ghetto greeted them with open arms. I mean, they shared the piece of bread that they had and gave it to them. They took them into their houses. They tried to make them comfortable under the circumstances, and they remained in our ghetto."* [46]

The Anush family took in two women who had been brought from Bialystok. Young Basha immediately struck up a friendship with them." I got very attached to them." The women reciprocated the friendship, and the relationship became a bit of enjoyment for Basha in the midst of the misery that surrounded her. When it came time to transport the residents of the Pruzhany ghetto to the concentration camps, the Germans took the people from Bialystok first. The two women went on the first transport, and Basha and her family on the second, two days later.

"I was attached to the women. There was so much pain in my heart. They took them away. I knew I'm going to be next, but I remember crying all day and night just because I had so much sorrow that they weren't with us anymore, even though it had only been two days." [47]

To no one's surprise, the Jews in the ghettos received miserable treatment. Oppression was plentiful, and food and basic necessities were scarce. Winter was the worst. In addition to all their other problems, they had very little wood to heat their homes against the brutal Polish winter. Cold and hunger were a way of life. Young children do not understand these things. Basha remembers the day when she and her brothers went to their mother begging for some food, a bite of anything.

Chava stretched out her arm. "Here, my children, bite on my flesh. Maybe this will still your hunger."

Basha had an aunt who was slightly better off financially than the Anush family. "So, she came in one day and brought a piece of bread to my mother. It was very cold that day, and she was covered up. I'll never forget it. And she gave my mother the piece of bread. And she left because she couldn't see the situation that was going on in my house, little children all very hungry and cold."

Chava began to weep.

"Can I ask why you were crying?" Basha asked.

"She brought us a little bread."

Basha was too young to understand her mother's humiliation. Chava cried for a week, and it broke Basha's heart. [48]

Basha's sister, Reshele, was an infant, and Chava was so malnourished that she was unable to produce breastmilk to feed her. Although she was terribly frightened, Basha occasionally slipped out of the ghetto to a German troop facility near her old school, where she could steal food. At first, she took things that would not be noticed, like potato peels. Not the potatoes, just the peels. She brought them home for her mother to cook. However, Reshele became ill, and Basha began sneaking into the German food storage area to take things that were more substantial. One day she had taken a little bit of farina from a German pantry and was spotted by a German soldier as she was making her escape. He yelled at her, and she was certain he was going to kill her. She ran as fast as she could.

"He wanted to kill me, and I felt any minute the shots were piercing my back, but I started running and he shot like out of nowhere. He shot just in the air. He was shooting at me, but somehow, I ran away." [49]

Death by gunshot is something to fear, but so is death by starvation. When the hunger became extreme, Basha again found herself willing to risk the guns. Outside the ghetto, much of the Pruzhany lifestyle had not changed. The Gentiles had many of the items they had before the Russian and German invasions. They had regular bazaars, just as they had before the war. Basha knew food was on the other side of the wire, where Jews were not allowed. Hunger is a strong motivator. When she felt the hunger was going to kill her, she and one of her brothers removed the yellow stars from their clothing, sneaked into the ghetto, and made their way to the bazaar. They would take a few articles of clothing—their mother's dress or shoes—in the hopes of trading them for a few potatoes. At the risk of their lives, they could eat for one more day. [50]

To aid them in controlling the ghetto, the Germans authorized the formation of a *Jundenrat*—Jewish Council. At first the *Jundenrat* was comprised of four members, but it grew to twenty-four. They were elders in the Jewish community and provided a degree of self-regulation over the ghetto, but they were primarily tasked with implementing German orders to the population. Some *Jundenrat* members preferred the traditional Jewish term, *kehilla*—congregation—but whichever term they used, its power to govern was limited to whatever the Germans wanted. And they wanted a lot.

In addition to *Lebensraum,* Hitler had long envisioned the Eastern European countries as a source of disposable slave labor for his war machine. Virtually every day, the *Jundenrat* received a demand for men and women who would be assigned to work details known as *kommandos.* The jobs assigned to women involved knitting gloves and hats for German soldiers to fend off the cold Polish winter. The jobs for men involved physical labor, frequently outdoors, regardless of the season. Any man not capable of performing physical labor was expendable. *Jundenrat* members did their best to fill the labor quotas with the healthy and protect the elderly and frail. Basha knew these men.

"They were Jewish people, but they worked very hard, and they tried very hard for the population. In fact, when things got real bad, they saw that they can't tolerate it; they saw what was going on and a lot of them just couldn't take it. [They] *committed suicide, and those were very brilliant men, very brilliant, all professionals, very highly educated people. A lot of them came from Warsaw. They ran away and came to our town. They were real educated, very fine, nice people. Their hearts couldn't take it. They couldn't take what was happening to their fellow Jews, and they looked for a way out, and one day we found them all*

there. They just got together, all of them in one room, and they committed suicide." [51]

The mass suicide attempt was a shock. The group had gathered at *Jundenrat* member Velvel Shraibman's home on the ghetto border. They blocked the windows and sealed the doors, lit a fire in the fireplace with the chimney blocked, and intended to die by asphyxiation. To ensure their escape from their moral dilemma, they also took doses of poison. The next morning, all of them were either unconscious or dead in the smoky room. Not everyone felt sympathy for the survivors. Some felt these intellectual men had "... no right to give up or become disillusioned, and they must be an example to the others, and not break [the] Jews' morale in [the] ghetto." [52]

Perhaps, but they were not just leaders; they were also human beings who had a crushing emotional burden forced upon them.

The Germans demanded that Pruzhany have a functional *Jundenrat* so there would be no leadership vacuum in the ghetto. Basha said the community chose another *Jundenrat,* consisting primarily of lawyers. The men selected were known to be fine men—honest, and dedicated to serving the people as best they could. Although there was no food to distribute and everyone was starving, the new *Jundenrat* went about the business of organizing the *kommandos* and providing something of a buffer between the average citizen and their oppressors. [53]

With the population subjugated and fearful, the Germans felt free to take anything they wanted from the ghetto residents. Sometimes it was common items such as warm winter coats. Other times, the demands were much greater. One day a German officer came to the *Jundenrat* and told them they would be responsible for collecting five to six kilos of gold from the Pruzhany ghetto. To encourage compliance, the German officer told the *Jundenrat* that if they did not receive that amount of gold, they would kill everyone in the ghetto. The community took this message very seriously. For most people, any gold they had included jewelry such as earrings, bracelets, and wedding rings. No matter how great the emotional attachment to the item may be, the population knew it would do them absolutely no good to keep it if they ended up dead. Chava surrendered her wedding ring. Her father, Shlomo, had taken a significant portion of his earnings in the United States and used it to buy gold. Part of his motivation may have been speculative, Basha said, since he apparently expected the price of gold to rise, but she also believed he was saving it as an inheritance for his grandchildren. He once showed Basha the large number of gold watches, watch chains, and miscellaneous gold jewelry items he had acquired. This he dutifully surrendered to the *Jundenrat* for the sake of the community.[54]

The other community organizations were quite different. Many of the youth lacked confidence in the *Jundenrat*. The *Jundenrat* negotiated the best circumstances possible for the people of Pruzhany, but some young men interpreted this as weakness and, therefore, unsatisfactory. They wanted active resistance. They wanted to stage a rebellion. They formed the Fight Organization, a loose group with initially poorly defined objectives. They wanted to fight back against the Germans, but they did not have a specific plan. They considered things like burning down the ghetto to panic the Germans while the Jews escaped, or staging a mass escape of the youth into the nearby forest. The *Jundenrat* was generally opposed to these ideas, since it would unquestionably bring the wrath of the Nazis onto the Jews that remained.

In mid-1942, the youth began to organize teams of twenty to twenty-five young men who focused on collecting guns. Many of the youth had been given jobs working for the Germans outside of the ghetto. The Russians had left behind warehouses of weapons, so these young men searched for them and smuggled them into the ghetto. It was fairly easy to conceal revolvers, but they had to remove the wooden stocks from rifles to sneak them past the eyes of the *SS*. Once inside the ghetto, local craftsmen made new wooden stocks in the basements of supporters.[55]

One day the Germans ordered the *Jundenrat* to assign some Pruzhany youth to *kommandos* detailed to remove tree stumps in a field outside the ghetto. This work put them in the proximity of the forest, where Soviet partisans waited. The partisans urged the young men to join them, but members of the Fight Organization were cautious. One concern was that while they were working on a *kommando*, the *Jundenrat* was responsible for them. Multiple escapes into the forest while on a *kommando* would quite likely result in the murder of *Jundenrat* members. Nevertheless, Basha was aware of at least one occasion when a group of Jewish youths had been assigned to a forest *kommando* fled when the German guards looked the other way. The group ran en masse into the forest and joined the partisans. However, for the most part, members of the Fight Organization found other opportunities to flee the ghetto and join the partisans. Other Pruzhany partisans acted when they heard of their colleagues in the forest, and looked for opportunities to join them. The resistance group in exile grew.

Like most guerrilla operations, they did not have the manpower or firepower to match their enemy, so they relied on surprise, attacking and escaping before the enemy could retaliate. One day, a car with Nazi soldiers drove into the ghetto where Basha was standing, and their presence frightened her.

"They were so vicious. They were walking and killing people."

The Nazis then drove into the nearby forest, directly into a group of partisans lying in wait. Basha saw the results. "They came back. Nothing happened to them, but the car was full of [bullet] holes." [56]

The small attacks had little tactical value, but they kept the *SS* troops looking over their shoulders, and provided an emotional boost to the community.

Like everyone else in Poland at this time, the partisans had needs. They would occasionally slip into *Jundenrat* meetings looking for bread, boots, or other basics. The ghetto residents had almost nothing for themselves, but they did their best to give something.

On January 27, 1943, two partisans slipped into the ghetto from the forest to meet with members of the *Jundenrat,* hoping to raise some money. In a classic case of bad timing, the chief of the Gestapo had also chosen this time to speak with the *Jundenrat,* and his unexpected appearance resulted in a gunfight. The partisans, armed with rifles, managed to escape, but the Gestapo chief's bullets killed the *Jundenrat* guard and wounded several other members. When the shooting stopped, the Gestapo chief angrily demanded that the *Jundenrat* tell the partisans to surrender by noon the next day, or there would be consequences. He then climbed on his motorcycle and roared off into the night. Now the *Jundenrat* had another dilemma. They had no means of delivering the message to the partisans. [57]

———

One did not have to be a partisan to incur the wrath of the Gestapo and *SS*. Violence and brutality became a way of life for everyone in the ghetto, and a mood of oppression hung on the citizens like a shroud. Chava was despondent, and seeing her cry hurt Basha terribly. Basha said the days were miserable, so she spent time with her friends in a largely futile attempt to cheer each other up. One afternoon, as she sat with the other children, the German soldier that ran the nearby telegraph station kicked the door open with his boot and came raging into the room. He was drunk and began shooting the place up. One person was wounded and then the soldier ran away.[58] No one in the ghetto was safe anywhere, even children in their home.

Basha was too young to be assigned to a regular *kommando*, but she wanted to help her family, so with the aid of a friend of her father's, she got a job working for the Germans outside the ghetto. The German Army had occupied many structures in Pruzhany, using them as offices, barracks, and storage facilities. In one large villa that was being used as a barrack, the entire main floor had been converted to a kitchen and dining hall. Adjacent to the building, a garden had been planted. The garden needed tending, and that was a job appropriate for Basha's age and abilities. The job came with a wonderful surprise. "There was a Russian woman, and she was an angel. She was an angel, this woman,"[59] Basha remembered fondly.

The woman immediately took a liking to Basha and became very protective of her. When the weather was bad, she found reasons to bring Basha out of the garden and into the house. Although the water pump was right next to the kitchen, the woman delegated pumping chores to Basha as another way of getting her into the house when the weather was bad. Once inside, away from the view of the Germans, the woman would give her a piece of bread, or whatever food was available. For Basha, who lived with constant hunger like everyone else in the ghetto, this small act of kindness was truly monumental. The Russian woman also had sympathy for Basha's family.

"She used to give me the peels of potatoes to take back to the ghetto. When I brought it home, my mother was so happy. She used to put water in it and make soup. At the bottom of it [the

package], *she would always find a few potatoes. Small pieces of bread. She gave me small pieces of bread. Sometimes they used to look, the Nazis, when I came from work to the ghetto. Where the ghetto met the outside. So, they looked, and if they would see a piece of bread, they would spill everything out and I would get beaten. But she put it so, she disguised it so they could never find it, and I brought it home. It was like a holiday in the house whenever she gave it to me. She was very, very good."* [60]

Basha's devotion to her mother and family is clear throughout her testimonies. The kindness of the Russian woman not only was a step toward easing their hunger, but an emotional boost for Basha, as she could see the happiness it created in the Anush home.

— • —

Malnutrition makes it hard for the body to fight off illness, and Basha's baby sister, Reshele, became very ill. She was taken to the makeshift ghetto hospital that was set up in a former high school. The diagnosis was scarlet fever. Basha admitted that Reshele's birth caused some resentment in her. She was used to being the only girl in the family and was happy with the special attention that brought. The resentment did not last long. "She was the most gorgeous baby," Basha remembered.

Reshele's health became another major concern for Basha, especially when she was hospitalized.

"I used to come every day to see her, and one day I came and my mother ... I looked at my mother's face, and I knew the baby feels better because my mother was . . . like she looked much better, and I looked at the baby and she looked very good . . ." [61]

Unfortunately, Reshele's battle was not only against disease. Hitler's policy, and therefore German policy, was to not feed "useless mouths" in the non-Germanic populations. Babies, particularly non-Germanic babies, were not productive. They were useless mouths. In the Pruzhany ghetto hospital, word came down from the Nazi overlords ordering doctors to make room for other patients by eliminating babies. Sadly, that included baby Reshele. Death came by injection.

"The day before I came to the hospital, and I saw she was getting much better because my mother stayed with her, and my mother was so happy. She was getting much better. Then they gave her the needle. The next day, and they killed her." [62]

Reshele was buried in an unmarked grave by Basha and her father. Chava could not bear to go. Chava instructed Basha to look carefully at the location of Reshele's grave in the cemetery with the hope that she would return someday. Basha did return after the war, and spent an entire day searching the cemetery for the spot where they laid Reshele to rest. She could not find her. [63]

By the end of 1942, it was clear to the residents of the Pruzhany ghetto that life was unlikely to get better, and was probably going to get a whole lot worse. The ghetto was not entirely isolated from the outside world, so information flowed in. Much of it was in the form of rumors, and most of the rumors were disheartening at best. Some were outright chilling. They knew the ghettos in most of the smaller cities had already been evacuated. They knew the ghettos in Bialystok and Warsaw still existed along with Pruzhany, but that ghetto residents in other cities had been sent to the concentration camps. And worst of all, they knew some of the concentration camps, like Majdanek and Dachau, were death camps.

"We knew that they killed the whole city, and we heard something about Majdanek, that they were bringing Jews there and they killed them, but nobody wanted to believe that human beings could do that to other human beings. Nobody wanted to believe it until the last moment. We all thought it was only a bad dream; we just couldn't believe that they could take people for no reason, just for being Jewish, and kill them in cold blood. I remember listening to the adults, and that's what they were talking about, but everyone said [the one who brought the rumors] *must be crazy, or lost his mind. He was just spreading fantasies that were not true. How can you take a person and kill, just kill him? Nobody wanted to believe it."* [64]

The rumors became fact on January 28, 1943, the day after the Nazis and the partisans shot it out at the *Jundenrat* meeting. The Gestapo chief had apparently come to tell the elders that the Pruzhany ghetto was about to be evacuated, but never delivered the message due to the gunfight. When word of the pending evacuation came out the next day, some felt it was retaliation for the previous night's incident. It was not. It was just the time for Pruzhany to take its turn in Hitler's plan to solve the "Jewish Question."

The day after the announcement, Basha received a message. Someone came and told her he had been instructed to bring her to a place at the wire that surrounded the ghetto. She went, and found the Russian woman waiting excitedly to speak with her. The ghetto had been closed by the Nazis when the evacuation was announced, so Basha would not be able to see her at her job.

The Russian woman told her, "Basha, I'm going to take you out of the ghetto now, and I'm going to hide you in the cellar. Under the dining room. And you'll survive the war." The Russian woman told her she could bribe a guard to sneak her out.

A chance for survival, no doubt, was a tantalizing proposition for Basha, but what about her family?

The Russian woman told her that, unfortunately, she could only rescue Basha.

"I didn't have the heart to leave my family, to leave the other kids, and I was thinking, 'why am I better than them that I should survive and God knows what's going to happen to them?'"

Basha declined the offer. The next day, the sleds arrived.[65]

So far throughout the ordeal, the Anushes retained their faith. It was very important to them, especially under the trying circumstances.

"The only popular word in the ghetto was a *Nes*, [a miracle]: *Nes min hashomayim* [A miracle from heaven]. And *Nes* never came." [66]

Basha's grandfather Anush arrived at their house the day before the evacuation. He had remarried after the loss of his first wife, and had two daughters, but he felt compelled to spend this time with his grandchildren. When the Gestapo arrived around noon, the family was as prepared as they could be under the circumstances. Grandfather Anush, whom Basha described as a tall, nicely built man, wore his best dark suit, the one he wore on holidays. He carried a cane as a fashion item, which was common in that day, not because he needed it to walk. The Nazis did not care about fashion. They saw an old man, and the cane may have made him look feeble. Feeble people could not work, and if they could not work the Nazis had no use for them. Her grandfather walked with Basha into the courtyard of their home, holding her hand, perhaps to engender some sympathy for a loving grandfather and granddaughter. "Sympathy from them you couldn't get," Basha remembered. [67]

Without any discussion, an *SS* man took a revolver and shot him, point blank. Basha was still holding his hand as he fell at her feet. The family was horrified, bursting into tears.

"That's how it started. My grandfather was lying in the courtyard. It was the last time. I have a picture [in her mind] of my home, and my last look at my life, and my grandfather lying covered with blood."

Chava grabbed Basha and said, "Go, my child, try to survive. And if you remain alive, tell daddy to say *Kaddish* for us." [68]

With that, they were marched to the sleds and taken to the train. The first two nightmares were over. The big nightmare was about to begin.

Historical Perspective
on Chapter 3

Operation Barbarossa

Hitler's alliance with Russia appeared to be an unlikely partnership from day one. Hitler and Stalin were diametrically opposed on the political spectrum, and it was no secret that Hitler had low regard for the Russian people. However, what Hitler knew and Stalin did not, was that Hitler had no intention of keeping Russia as an ally. In fact, his plan was the exact opposite. He intended to use Russia and its military forces for as long as they were beneficial to his plan of land conquest, then break their treaties, reverse his political course, and conquer them as well.

The German plan, which had been brewing for quite a while, was named Operation Barbarossa. This was an extension of Hitler's overall plan for seizing *Lebensraum* for Germany. In addition to its vast lands, Russia was rich with oil and agricultural resources that would feed Hitler's military machine, and he planned to reduce the Russian people to virtual slavery to further his purposes. Masked by the ruse of friendship, Hitler felt the trusting Russians would be vulnerable to a surprise attack which would lead to a quick victory.

Initially, Operation Barbarossa was successful. German troops captured roughly five million Russian soldiers and treated none of them like former allies. Over three million Russian prisoners were killed, some executed outright, and others starved to death along with many of the Russian population. The Nazis killed roughly one million Jews during this campaign.[69]

Operation Barbarossa started out very well for Hitler, but he soon learned that the winds of war blow both ways.

Notes

36. Bess Freilich interview by Josey G. Fisher, 1-2-10.

37. Ibid.

38. Bess Freilich interview by Marc Seligman, 5.

39. Dora Freilich, interview by Helen Grossman, 1-2-12.

40. Bess Freilich interview by Josey G. Fisher, 1-2-10.

41. Dora Freilich, interview by Helen Grossman, 1-2-13.

42. Zalman Urievich, "Pruzhany Jews in Ghettos and Camps," Pruzh. org, 1958, accessed September 16, 2021, https://www.pruzh.org/yzkor_ pruzhany/guettos_camp.htm.

43. Bess Freilich interview by Marc Seligman, 5.

44. Ibid.

45. Zalman Urievich, "Pruzhany Jews in Ghettos and Camps," Pruzh. org, 1958, accessed September 16, 2021, https://www.pruzh.org/yzkor_ pruzhany/guettos_camp.htm.

46. Bess Freilich interview by Josey G. Fisher, 1-2-11.

47. Ibid.

48. Bess Freilich interview by Marc Seligman, 6.

49. Bess Freilich interview by Josey G. Fisher, 1-2-12.

50. Ibid, 1-2-15.

51. Bess Freilich interview by Josey G. Fisher, 1-2-13.

52. Zalman Urievich, "Pruzhany Jews in Ghettos and Camps," Pruzh. org, 1958, accessed September 16, 2021, https://www.pruzh.org/yzkor_ pruzhany/guettos_camp.htm.

53. Bess Freilich interview by Josey G. Fisher, 1-2-14.

54. Bess Freilich interview by Marc Seligman, 8.

55. Zalman Urievich, "Pruzhany Jews in Ghettos and Camps," Pruzh. org, 1958, accessed September 16, 2021, https://www.pruzh.org/yzkor_ pruzhany/guettos_camp.htm.

56. Bess Freilich interview by Marc Seligman, 9.

57. Bess Freilich interview by Josey G. Fisher, 1-2-14.

58. Zalman Urievich, "Pruzhany Jews in Ghettos and Camps," Pruzh. org, 1958, accessed September 16, 2021, https://www.pruzh.org/yzkor_ pruzhany/guettos_camp.htm.

59. Bess Freilich interview by Marc Seligman, 9.

60. Ibid.

61. Bess Freilich interview by Josey G. Fisher, 1-2-12.

62. Bess Freilich interview by Marc Seligman, 4.

63. Bess Freilich interview by Josey G. Fisher, 1-2-13.

64. Ibid, 1-2-15.

65. Bess Freilich interview by Marc Seligman, 10.

66. Bess Freilich interview by Josey G. Fisher, 2-1-17.

67. Bess Freilich interview by Marc Seligman, 12.

68. Ibid.

69. "Operation Barbarossa," Wikipedia Foundation, last modified April 10, 2023, https://en.wikipedia.org/wiki/Operation_Barbarossa# References

CHAPTER 4

Day One: Auschwitz

February 3, 1943
Oświęcim, Poland

The sign on the railway platform read, "Auschwitz." Basha had never heard of it, but from this day forward she would never forget it.

The forty-four railway lines that converged near Oświęcim, Poland—which was called "Auschwitz" by the Germans—made it an ideal rail transport hub for shipping cargo. Heinrich Himmler, German Reich Leader (*Reichsführer*) of the Protection Squads (*Schutzstaffel*, or *SS*) and his colleagues took note of this convenience and determined it was an excellent location to ship their special cargo: human beings. More specifically, Jewish human beings. With that in mind, they created *Konzentrationslager Auschwitz*—KL Auschwitz—the first of forty such camps and sub camps in that area. Auschwitz II, named Auschwitz-Birkenau, soon followed as a concentration and extermination camp, complete with gas chambers. Auschwitz III-Monowitz was created as a labor camp to staff the nearby IG Farben plant, part of their chemical empire, which was a vital component in the Nazi war machine. Smaller subcamps, such as Budy, sprang up as needed to achieve various Nazi goals, the foremost being to deal with the "Jewish Question" by destroying the Jewish race.

Basha did not know any of this at the time. What she did know was that her brother lay dead on the ground with a bullet in his head, and Nazi *SS* troops screamed at her as they beat everyone with clubs and rifle butts, releasing their German Shepherd dogs on those who reacted too slowly from uncertainty and fear.

It all happened quickly. Lying on the frozen ground, Shlomo's body was still warm as SS troops forced Basha and her horrified family off the train. There was no time to mourn. Fear overpowered their grief. Basha remembered:

"They were confusing us. First they told us to stand here, and then they told us to stand there, and we were running from one place to the other."

It was total chaos, an overwhelming scene of crying, cursing, screaming, and beating. Basha ran to her mother, gave her a kiss, and was roughly pushed aside by *SS* guards. She then ran to the line where her father and brothers stood. She had enough time to say goodbye, but no time for kisses. Pushed aside again, Basha was anxious to rejoin her mother, who was holding Asher in her arms and leading Bezalel by the hand. As she ran toward them, a girl Basha knew from school grabbed her.

"Come, follow me. The young girls have to stay in this line!"

Basha reluctantly complied. It was obvious that any type of resistance was futile. The enormity of the overall experience was overpowering.[70]

"The stench of the burning flesh was just terrible. The chimneys were burning, and we saw the fire, and the skies were red for as far as you could see. And we asked, 'What is it, the chimneys?' And they said, 'It's a factory.' It was a death factory." [71]

Taking a place in line with the girls her age, Basha scanned the crowd for her mother. She quickly spotted her; she was not far away. Chava was quite tall and stood above most of the crowd. In the glaring lights, Basha could easily see her and her two brothers standing in a long line that led to a row of open trucks. She watched as her mother tried to climb into the back of a truck. An *SS* guard struck her on the head with a club. She fell. Basha did not see her get up. She never saw her mother and brothers again.

Cursing *SS* guards marched Basha and the other young girls in one direction, and her father, Berel, and Hillel in another. For the captives, particularly the younger ones who had less life experience, a reasonable question would be: "What is this place, and why are they doing this to us?"

It would seem impossible that one man, Adolf Hitler, with an insatiable lust for power and a demonic hatred of the Jews, could be responsible for the hell on earth that Basha and her family had just entered. However, he was a charismatic man, and his message resonated with many suffering in post–World War I Germany. He needed someone to blame for the country's troubles, and he chose the Jews. People began to listen to him. Soon, he had sufficient followers to impact the fate of Germany, and that would impact the fate of the Jews. His anti-Semitic rants became public policy, and he developed a loyal and efficient leadership cadre that shared his devotion to conquest and hatred for the Jews. They intended to raise the status of Germany in world politics, and part of that would entail the extermination of the Jews. Basha, bewildered, stood shivering at Auschwitz as the hatred of the *SS* troops visibly boiled all around her. One did not have to understand the motivation for the situation to be a victim of it.

In February of 1943, fourteen-year-old Basha Anush shed her identity as a Polish schoolgirl and became Auschwitz prisoner 33327. It was tattooed on her left arm, so she could not forget it.

Ever.

Induction

SS guards, shouting and menacing their young captives with clubs, forced Basha and the other young girls, to march to a processing location at Auschwitz II–Birkenau, which was located less than a mile west of Auschwitz I. There, humiliation was added to their anxiety as their captors shaved their heads.

"One sister didn't recognize the other, because within minutes we looked so different."

The guards told them to wash, and then issued them concentration camp uniforms.

"They took off our clothing, and they gave us some dirty khaki pants. It was too short for some gals, too long for others. And we looked so terrible. We hated to look at each other without hair." [72]

The thought of surrendering her clothing filled Basha with fear. It was not parting with her belongings that terrified her, but the knowledge that her mother had sewn jewelry and money into the clothing of each of her children. Chava hoped they would have the opportunity to use the valuables to secure better treatment, or perhaps even bribe their way to escape. In theory it was a great idea meant to save her children. In practice it was the opposite. It put Basha's life in danger. She knew her mother had sewn the valuables into the clothing, but she did not know where.

"In this whole chaos, with [the] beating and the yelling, screaming and the dogs, I was all shook up. I just couldn't find the place where [Chava] sewed it in. I was trembling because they [the SS guards] said if [they] find it [instead of Basha surrendering it] they're going to shoot me." [73]

Basha frantically searched her clothing for the hidden stash of valuables. The multiple layers of clothing she wore made the task more difficult, but she finally found where her mother had hidden everything. The discovery brought mixed feelings.

"There were American dollars there. And there was jewelry and gold that [Chava] *sewed in. Between the cotton they used to wear for insulation in the coats in Europe. That's where it was. And I was happy that I found it. And we threw it all—*[we were] *in circles—and we threw it all in, in the middle on the floor. And with every $20 bill* [I] *threw, my heart was bleeding because I knew there were times when we were so hungry that maybe, if my mother would change one $20 bill, maybe we would* [have] *had food for a couple of weeks. But my mother always thought it's going to get worse. And besides, we had so many children. In Europe, you couldn't get married if you didn't have . . . a dowry to give. That's what she was saving money for, and here I was, throwing it.* [But] *I was happy I could find it."*[74]

Guards ordered the frightened young girls, with their shorn heads and ill-fitting uniforms, to march double time from the building to a barrack. *SS* guards, standing on both sides of the doors, beat them as they exited the building and beat them again as they entered the barrack. The barrack contained rows of bunk beds stacked on a wooden floor, where the cracks between the planks filled with dirt and spilled filth. The guards continued to abuse the girls, swearing and beating them as they scrambled to find a bed.

"There were three bunks, and I hid on the first one [lowest bunk] *just to run away from the Germans. It was the easiest one to run into, but as the girls came in running, and they were beating us, everyone was beaten up so badly, a lot of them—the first bunks— were taken already, so a lot of them jumped on top* [beds] *and that's* [when] *the bunk bed broke and all of the girls* [fell] *on top of me, with the wood, with everything. I remember them jumping*

down and screaming, 'Oh, there's a girl there. She's lying. She's bleeding.'

"Everything was on top of me, the wood and the bricks . . . and the Germans ran through the halls and [whoever] *they could* [get to] *they just beat every one of them up. When they left, I remember everybody was confused, everybody lost—they lost their minds— they just became crazy. Some of them undressed. Some of them, they stood on top* [of the bunks] *and they gave speeches. They didn't know what they were talking* [about.] *Nobody made sense because right away the shock, the shock it devastated us."* [75]

The continuous brutality of the *SS* guards immediately began to take an emotional toll on the young girls. Basha was a victim of this hysteria along with everyone else. When the commotion died down, Basha, still bleeding, searched for her mother, even though she had witnessed her being beaten as she attempted to get on a truck.

"I, too, was very confused. And I saw a gal lying there on the ground, and I held her head, and it came to my mind that this is my mother. This gal was a cousin of mine. I knew that we belonged [to the same family]. *She was a cousin of mine. My own flesh. But I thought it was my mother. I couldn't . . . I couldn't tell. I was so . . . I could see that I was losing my mind. And I thought, 'Mommy, mommy, come on, wake up. You'll be okay, mommy. You'll be okay, mommy.' And here was the gal, she was dead already. She was dead. She was dead. Her name was Sema. I knew we belonged to each other, but I couldn't tell. I thought* [she] *was my mother."* [76]

After two or three days of indoctrination and nonstop mistreatment, the *kapos* sent Basha and the rest of the girls to work and assigned them to a *kommando* that moved stones. As usual, there was no right way to accomplish the task. Whatever they did likely brought a rebuke from the *SS* guards and frequently a beating.

> *"We had to go to work to carry stones, big stones. If you took a small one, you got beaten. And a big stone, you couldn't pick up, so you got beaten, too."* [77]

Throughout the days of hard physical labor, the girls tried to make the best of it by talking and getting to know one another. One day, Basha was on a *kommando* of five, talking with a German girl about her age named Hilda. Suddenly, Hilda became very excited and smiled.

> *"She was working with me. We* [were] *trying to pick up a stone, and she started to scream. 'Oh my God, here is Heintz! Heintz is here!' And I said, 'What do you mean?' She said, 'I sat with him in school. We sat together.' She said, 'Oh my God, I must go talk to him.' She left her shovel and went over and she said, 'Heintz, don't you recognize me?'"*

But this was not school anymore. Heintz was an *SS* guard.

> *"And he said, 'Yes, Hilda, I recognize you.' And he took the gun and shot her."* [78]

The brainwashing of German youth had been successful. Heintz did not see Hilda as the schoolgirl, the human being, he had sat next to just a few years before. Heintz, like millions of other German boys and girls, had been indoctrinated by the Nazi youth programs to believe Jews were subhuman and unworthy of life. Hilda was no longer a person to him.

As Basha and the young girls struggled to survive, her father and brothers also struggled, assigned to a labor *kommando*. At this early time in their imprisonment, Isaac had already nearly been worked to death. Fortunately, his sons were there to help him. Despite their best efforts, there was no way to protect him or themselves from the wrath of the Death's Head Units.

At the conclusion of a long, hard day of labor, Isaac and his sons, along with the rest of their *kommando*, stood in the freezing cold and wind as the guards slowly and laboriously counted the prisoners. The guards kept meticulous records, and each prisoner had to be accounted for at all times. When he was finally dismissed from formation, Isaac rushed for the warmth of the barrack. Perhaps because his vision was obscured by the rain, or due to fatigue and his haste to get inside the warm building, Isaac failed to notice a fresh concrete slab that the Germans had laid in front of the building. He walked through it. The results were predictable, immediate, and terrifying.

The *SS* troops stormed into the barrack, and the ranking guard screamed that they would kill everyone unless the man who stepped in the concrete identified himself. Another prisoner, a terrified man from their town, [79] immediately pointed to Isaac. The guards dragged Isaac outside and beat him terribly. They kicked and stomped on him, and even pelted him with rocks. Witnesses later told Basha that her father did not look human when they finished with him, and they did not think he would live. When the beating was finished, Berel and Hillel rushed to him, but that further angered the guards, and they beat the brothers as well. When the abuse finally ended, the brothers carried Isaac into the barrack and nursed him as best they could. In addition to tending to his immediate physical injuries, they had to figure out a way to get him to work. If he stayed in the barrack the next day, he would be considered useless and taken for the "selection." The selection consisted of those selected to go to the crematorium. The following morning, despite their own painful injuries, Berel and Hillel carried their father to the work site, saving his life. [80]

The routine was relentless, day after day. Drawing on her own experience, Basha said that if a prisoner could survive the first few weeks, if they did not die or go crazy, they had a chance at survival. Despite the abuse heaped on them, her father and brothers managed to sustain themselves mentally and physically. They had been prisoners for six weeks when a guard came to the barrack with an attractive offer. He told them there was an opportunity for the younger prisoners to be moved to a different camp where life would be easier for children. He offered them the option to register for transfer. Anxious for a better opportunity for his sons, Isaac encouraged them to register.[81] They did, and climbed aboard the trucks that would take them to the new camp. In reality, this was nothing more than another cruel Nazi trick, but Isaac and Basha would not know that until much later.

The Structure of Terror

Although everything in Auschwitz looked chaotic to Basha, she quickly learned that the *SS*, with its characteristic Germanic sense of order, had devised a system of badges worn by prisoners that allowed the guards to immediately know quite a bit about them. She was given the familiar yellow Star of David to identify her as a Jew, but all prisoners wore an inverted triangle—with the point down—that was color coded to identify which group of unfortunates they belonged to. The principal groups were:

Red Triangle: Political prisoners, especially communists, socialists, and leftists.

Blue Triangle: Foreign forced-labor prisoners from countries occupied by Germany.

Green Triangle: Career criminal or dangerous person.

Purple Triangle: Almost exclusively Jehovah's Witnesses, with a few fringe religions.

Pink Triangle: Homosexual men and sexual offenders.

Black Triangle: The "asocials." Roma (Gypsies, later changed to a brown triangle) mentally ill, alcoholics, drug addicts, pacifists, draft dodgers, vagrants, prostitutes, and lesbians.

More information could be provided by adding other elements to the badge, such as an additional triangle, bars, colors, or letters. If a guard had a specific hatred toward one group of people, the badges made it easy to find victims to abuse.

Prisoner "Self-Administration": the Kapos

Basha quickly learned, and would soon personally experience, that the *SS* guards were not the only ones doling out abuse. Maintaining order and discipline in a concentration camp that could house as many as one hundred thousand inmates was an enormous task. To reduce the number of *SS* troops required, and the associated costs, camps relied on a large number of prisoners whom camp administrators gave the title "prisoner functionary," or *kapo*. *Kapos* could number as many as 10 percent of the prison population. They also used the term "prisoner self-administration," a euphemism that implied prisoners had some voice in their treatment. Nothing could have been further from the truth.

Being a *kapo* brought significant privileges which made con-centration camp life less miserable. *Kapos* had private rooms, extra food, cigarettes, and sometimes even alcohol. The trade-off for these comforts was that they were required to abuse their own people. If they wanted to keep their privileged job, they had to be as brutal as the *SS* guards. Some ensured their position by being even more brutal. For a few, their barbaric treatment of the prisoners earned them a postwar trip to the gallows.

The basic *kapo* positions consisted of:

Lagerältester: Camp Leader

Blockältester: Barracks Leader

Stubenältester: Room Leader.

Vorarbeiter: Foreman of a work *kommando.*

Sonderkommando: Special unit of prisoners assigned to aid in the gas chamber executions.

For Basha and her fellow prisoners, the most feared of the *kapos* wore the green triangle badge of the career criminal. The *SS* preferred to pull *kapos* from this group, thinking, generally correctly, that those who had already shown a predisposition toward brutality and murder in their civilian lives would have no trouble transferring their vicious street skills to the prison population. The reviled green badge *kapos* were a daily component of Basha's life.

———

After all she had been through, one might assume Basha felt that things could not possibly get worse; but suddenly and unexpectedly, Basha was told that she was being moved to a different camp. She was being sent from Auschwitz-Birkenau to Budy.

Budy was a *Strafkompanie.* A punishment camp.

Historical Perspective
on Chapter 4

Hitler and Anti-Semitism

Since the middle of the twentieth century, the name Adolf Hitler has been synonymous with anti-Semitism, persecution, and murder of the Jews. He did not create anti-Semitism; Jewish discrimination and persecution had run rampant in Europe during the Middle Ages, with forced conversions to Christianity or expulsion from certain countries. However, until Hitler there was never a truly viable movement to destroy the entire race.

As far as can be confidently determined by the historical record, Hitler was not raised to be an anti-Semite. There are various theories about what may have turned him toward anti-Semitism, but there does not seem to be one single, clear motivation. He stated he began to have an aversion toward the Jews during his time as a struggling artist in Vienna before World War I. That is certainly possible, although historians have noted that his principal art patron in Vienna was one Samuel Morgenstern, a prominent Jewish man in the city. Hitler either had not become an anti-Semite at that point, or was willing to set aside his bigotry for the sake of making a living.

World War I was clearly a turning point in Hitler's life. Although born in Austria, he was a devoted German nationalist and enlisted in the German Army in 1914. He saw a great deal of combat, much of it serving as a messenger between various frontline and rear command positions. He was twice honored for bravery with the Iron Cross medal, first class and second class, but never rose above the rank of lance corporal during his four years of service. When Germany surrendered in November of 1918, Hitler was in an army hospital recovering from temporary blindness caused by poison gas. It was during this time that the stab-in-the-back myth was born. Many felt, erroneously, that the German Army had not lost the war, but rather, that the German government had stabbed its valiant troops in the back under pressure from powerful people, predominant among them, the Jews.

However it evolved, by the end of World War I Hitler had become a vocal anti-Semite. In November 1919 he wrote a lengthy letter to someone he addressed as Herr Gemlich. Among other accusations, he stated that he believed Jews were incapable of being true Germans because they were an "alien race" and were untrustworthy due to their devotion to money. During this period he also became interested in the philosophy of Austrian politician, Georg Ritter von Schönerer, who believed Jews could never be acceptable as German citizens because their racial and religious bond would always be stronger than their devotion to the German nation.

Hitler had become a well-known political figure in Germany by 1925. He was opposed, and even feared, by many, but was attracting a large following from the political right who feared communism even more. Despite serving a prison sentence for a failed revolt against the German government, which became known as the Beer Hall Putsch, his following grew. That was the year he published his autobiography, *Mein Kampf*, a turgid, rambling polemic of his beliefs. Principal among them was his hatred for the Jews, on whom he blamed most of Germany's problems. He accused them of being both money-hungry capitalists and communist revolutionaries. The obvious political contradiction apparently did not bother him, or many others, as it turned out.

Hitler was an extremely powerful speaker, with many noting a crowd-engaging intensity in his eyes. On the platform he had a presence many described as hypnotic. Others said it was demonic.

Whichever the case, Hitler used his vast persuasive powers to continually, maliciously vilify the Jews. Supported by his powerful political machine, he became Chancellor of Germany. Then, suddenly, unlike the other anti-Semites in the world, Adolf Hitler had the power to turn his murderous words into action.

The Nazi Party and Anti-Semitism

On August 2, 1934, the death of German President Paul von Hindenburg gave Adolf Hitler and his National Socialist German Workers Party—the Nazis—full control of Germany. He christened his new movement the Third Reich—Third Realm—the successor to the Holy Roman Empire (800–1806) and the German Empire (1871–1918.) He and his nascent empire builders wasted no time in eliminating their political enemies. They jailed communists and socialists. Those with anti-Nazi opinions now took frequent, uncomfortable looks over their shoulders. The Nazi regime quickly launched an assault on the media, and shut down newspapers, magazines, books, and radio broadcasts critical of Nazism. The Jews were high on the Nazi list for elimination, but the process would go slightly more slowly as Hitler built the infrastructure for such a massive task.

Key People and Organizations

The list of miscreants in the Nazi hierarchy is long, from Hitler himself to the Gestapo informants on each city block who reported their anti-Nazi neighbors to their Gestapo handlers. Some in this massive group were in positions of influence that had a great, and chilling, impact on Jewish life, and the lives of all Germans. A few of the worst deserve special attention.

(Paul) Joseph Goebbels

As the Reich Minister of Propaganda, Joseph Goebbels

wielded enormous power in the Nazi government. He was different from most other members of the party, which was initially heavily comprised of thugs, rogues, and misfits. Goebbels was a man of intellect who held a doctorate of philosophy in literature. He was a talented writer and a dynamic public speaker. Most of all, he was a virulent anti-Semite.

Goebbels was devoted to Hitler and was highly esteemed by his boss. That was fortunate for him, since Goebbels was apparently hated by pretty much everyone else. Short in stature with a congenitally deformed right foot, he was anything but a prime example of Hitler's vaunted "master race." An obnoxious martinet, he was given the nickname "Poison Dwarf."

Personality aside, his skills were perfect for his role in the Nazi regime. He understood that people make decisions based on information. The people who control information control how the public perceives a situation—or a race of people. Lies become the truth when the truth is hidden. With all mass media in his power, his staff churned out a constant stream of anti-Semitic material designed to present the Jewish people as undesirable, and potentially dangerous, to Germany. He funded films such as *The Eternal Jew* (1940), to vilify the Jewish race and present them as a parasitic people unworthy of human life. The repetition of this degrading image of the Jews slowly seeped into the consciousness of the German people, particularly the indoctrinated young girls and boys of the Hitler Youth, who would grow up to take their place in the Reich, and for some, to run the concentration camps.

Heinrich Himmler

With his round spectacles and unimposing physique, Heinrich Himmler looked much more like a chicken farmer—his previous occupation—than the leader of the *SS*. He was born into a conservative Roman Catholic family and did well in school, but he was physically weak and had chronic stomach problems. He did poorly in athletics. At the outbreak of World War I, he joined the Landshut Cadet Corps, and then enlisted in a battalion of the Bavarian Regiment in 1917. He hoped to become an officer in the German Army, but was still in training when Germany surrendered. His feelings of anti-Semitism began to develop while he was a student at the Technical University of Munich, although he appears to have gotten along with his Jewish classmates. He earned a degree in agronomy, but his career in farming was brief. He was fascinated by politics and military affairs, and became a member of the Nazi paramilitary unit, the *Sturmabteilung* (*SA*). The *SA* wore distinctive brown uniforms and the public generally referred to them as the "Brownshirts." The requirements for joining the *SA* were low, so the ranks were filled with disenchanted former military men, the unemployed, and misfits with nowhere else to go. Their fundamental persuasive tool was violence; they left the talking to others. Himmler participated in the failed Beer Hall Putsch but was not charged with a crime. From the *SA* he joined the newly formed *SS*, and rose to a position of leadership quickly. As membership in the *SS* increased dramatically, Himmler convinced Hitler that the *SS* should be a separate, elite military group. Hitler appointed Himmler *Reichsführer-SS* in 1929. The *SS* force of 290 men quickly multiplied to thousands, tens of thousands, and then hundreds of thousands of fanatics who saw themselves as a racially superior body that would lead Germany to a new place of world dominance. It was the *SS* that would run the concentration camps.

Himmler used his position of power to indulge his ideas of Aryan racial supremacy, targeting the Jews in particular. He had an obsessive devotion to the occult, which included a fervent belief that his *SS* troops were heirs to the ancient Germanic knights, destined to play a pivotal role on the world stage. Although many, including Hitler, thought Himmler's mysticism was odd at best, no one stopped him. He was successful at what he did, and that was sufficient to overlook his eccentricities. As important to Hitler was Himmler's unquestionable loyalty and devotion, which earned him the nickname "True Heinrich." Hitler was Himmler's master, an arrangement that worked well for both.

Myths and fantasies aside, Himmler was a very, very dangerous man. In addition to building the *SS*, he, with the enthusiastic assistance of Reinhard Heydrich, created the *Einsatzgruppen*— the death squads—that followed German troops into occupied areas to kill Jews, intellectuals, Russian commissars, and anyone perceived to be a threat to Germany. The concentration camps were originally built to isolate and silence political prisoners, but Himmler added extermination facilities to systematically murder those who did not fit in with the German vision of Aryan supremacy. The Jews became his principal target.

Reinhard Heydrich

Adolf Hitler described Reinhard Heydrich as "the man with the iron heart." Quite an endorsement, coming from one of the greatest mass murderers in history. Of all the evil characters in the Nazi regime, Heydrich seems to have come by his evil nature naturally, rather than by some event. The list of his atrocities has filled volumes, but a few stand out as being critical in the story of the Holocaust.

Heydrich was born into a family of culture and wealth in Halle an der Saale, Prussia in 1904. His father was a prominent composer and opera singer who founded a music conservatory where Reinhard's mother taught piano. Heydrich was a talented violinist, but rather than choosing a career in the arts, he joined the German Navy in 1922. His reputation as a rogue with women overshadowed whatever naval skills he had. He was dismissed from the Navy in May of 1931 under the charge of "conduct unbecoming an officer and gentlemen," for promising to marry one woman and then marrying another. He immediately joined the Nazi Party, and the *SS* shortly thereafter. Heydrich's wife, Lina, was an ardent Nazi and arranged a meeting on his behalf with Heinrich Himmler. Impressed by Heydrich, Himmler immediately hired him to be part of his new security service, which eventually was named the *Sicherheitsdienst*, or *SD*. Heydrich rose through the ranks, and in 1934 also became the head of the feared Gestapo, the German secret police. Through chicanery and brutality, Heydrich rose in power throughout the 1930s.

Heydrich's career of Jewish persecution included organizing the *Kristallnacht*—the "Night of Broken Glass"—a series of coordinated attacks on Jewish synagogues and businesses throughout Germany on November 9, 1938. After the occupation of Poland, he created the *Zentralstelle IIP Polen*, Central Office, Poland, unit of the Gestapo, whose primary responsibility was the ethnic cleansing of Jews from the country. In 1942 he chaired the Wannsee Conference, which formalized the "Final Solution to the Jewish Question." The "solution" to the question, of course, was the deportation and extermination of the Jews. Heydrich had mercy on no one, but above all else, the Jews took the brunt of his hatred.

Adolf Eichmann

Born Otto Adolf Eichmann in 1906 in Solingen, Germany, Eichmann's family moved to Linz, Austria in 1913. His performance in school was very poor, but during this period he met older youth who were members of right-wing militias, and he became interested in the Nazi movement. He left school without attaining a degree, worked in several sales jobs, and moved to Germany in 1933 when the Nazi Party was banned in Austria. He joined the *SS*, and in 1934 transferred to the *SD*. He was eventually placed in the Jewish Department where, using any tools at his disposal—including violence—he worked on "encouraging" Jews to emigrate from Germany, and established the ghettos to contain them until they left, voluntarily or not. After the German invasion of Russia, Nazi policy changed from relocating the Jews to killing them. Eichmann reported to Reinhard Heidrich and supervised a staff devoted to sending Jews to the concentration camps, where approximately 75 percent of them died. Eichmann personally visited Auschwitz while Basha and Dora were imprisoned there and cheerfully announced the new, faster solution to eliminating the Jewish race with Zyklon-B, stating that he "would jump laughing to his grave for his role in killing four million Jews." His vocal and enthusiastic approach to his murderous job allowed him to reach the rank of *SS-Obersturmbannführher*, lieutenant colonel.

The SS-Totenkopfverbände—Death's Head Units

Like virtually every organization in Nazi Germany, the *SS* was complex. Hitler apparently believed having divisions with overlapping jurisdictions kept them competing with one another, which brought good results as well as offering him a level of security against one organization gaining too much power and challenging his authority.

The word *Schutzstaffel (SS)* translates into English as "protection squadron." In the 1920s, competing political parties, like the Nazis and the communists, frequently articulated their political positions with their fists and clubs. Brawls were common. The predecessor of the *SS*, the *Saal-Schutz* (Hall Security) was originally developed to keep order when Hitler and his colleagues spoke in public during those times of turbulent, and frequently violent, political upheaval. Under Himmler's direction, the small group grew far beyond its protection role, first becoming an elite paramilitary force, and then a major component in Nazi intelligence, counterintelligence, security, and terror operations. The *SS* had three major divisions: the *Allgemeine SS*, the general *SS* used for racial policing; the *Waffen-SS*, the armed *SS* military unit; and in 1933, the *SS-Totenkopfverbände,* the Death's Head Units with the skull-and-crossed-bones insignia on their uniforms. It ran the concentration camps. They were trained in the extreme Prussian military manner until "the juice boiled in their tails," and a talent for sadism was recognized when it came time for promotion. For the *Einsatzgruppen* murder troops and the concentration camp guards, the Death's Head emblem was chillingly appropriate.

Beginning in 1935, the Dachau concentration camp became the training facility for all *SS* Death's Head concentration camp guards. Although this was intended to create a uniform policy for the operation of all the camps, it appears that actual policies remained flexible at the whim of the individual camp commandants. There were written policies prohibiting abuse of detainees when the camps were originally built to house political prisoners, but by the outbreak of World War II, abuses and atrocities became more of the rule than the exception. Much of this was the result of the long, intense propaganda campaign of the Nazi government, presenting Jews as subhuman. A remarkable number of men and women were simply brainwashed out of their sense of humanity.

The Camps

The Nazi concentration camps, which have become synonymous with inhumanity, persecution, and murder, were likely not in the original Nazi plan for the Third Reich. The Nazis built the camps as a matter of necessity, as they eliminated their political opponents from power and influence, and separated them from the general population. They simply needed a place to put them. The first camp was established in 1933, and the number of camps expanded as the need arose. Roughly 80 percent of the first inmates were communists, who were designated "enemies of the state," in a primarily political purge.

The successful isolation of political enemies presented a new opportunity for the hierarchy of the Third Reich to handle elements of society whom they felt were undesirable. Reinhard Heidrich was particularly vocal about broadening the scope of potential victims beyond the political arena, and the term "enemy of the state" became "antisocial malefactor."

Antisocial malefactor charges were somewhat flexible to the degree that the government could generally find an excuse to imprison a particular individual if they were intent on doing so, but there were three general categories of offenses; "professional and habitual criminals," "anti-socials," and "the work shy." Professional and habitual criminals were defined as those who had been imprisoned for six months or more on three separate occasions. Anti-socials included beggars, homeless, Gypsies, prostitutes, homosexuals, gamblers, alcoholics, brawlers, habitual traffic offenders, and psychopaths. Heinrich Himmler defined the work shy as those who, "could be proved to have refused, without adequate reason, employment offered to them on two occasions." [82] Some of the mentally ill were sent to euthanasia facilities, which were part of the Nazi racial purification program. Initially, many citizens applauded this act as an improvement to German society. Undesirables were gone from the streets. Exactly where they had gone was likely unknown to many.

Theodor Eicke, a man with an unblemished record of previous employment failure, [83] was appointed by Himmler as the Commandant of Dachau in 1933. Eicke wrote the Disciplinary and

Penal Code, which specified the punishments that could be meted out to prisoners for disobeying camp rules. The punishments were harsh, but it would be years before the creation of the extermination camps. Putting prisoners to work as slave labor was more productive than killing them outright. If they were worked to death, so be it. There would always be more. Labor camps were predominant until the enactment of the "Final Solution to the Jewish Question" in 1942, which preceded the construction of extermination facilities and camps. As many as 2.3 million men, women, and even children, were forced into the camps between 1933 and 1945. An estimated 1.7 million died there.

The number of concentration camps and sub-camps grew to more than one thousand facilities by the end of the war, but there was a certain amount of standardization in their design. *SS* planners wanted isolated locations to hide their activities, but they preferred these locations to be reasonably close to urban centers so *SS* personnel had access to entertainment. The *SS* built other labor camps adjacent to industrial sites so prisoners could work as slave labor without having to be transported. Camp guards assigned prisoners to build roads and structures, particularly in isolated areas that had little infrastructure.

The camps were designed in three sectors: a headquarters area for administrative functions, a residential section for *SS* personnel, and a prisoner compound surrounded by barbed wire and guard towers. Concentration camp officers lived in luxury. The residential area had gardens and numerous forms of recreation for the camp staff, and the food was good. Guards under emotional stress by the grim nature of their work found diversion in this area. Whether or not the guards were stressed seems to depend on the degree to which they were brainwashed against the Jews and other victims. Some *SS* troops appear to have adapted to their job with relative ease, but for others, the treatment of camp prisoners created serious moral distress. Historian Nikolaus Wachsmann recounts one such example. A young *SS* physician, Dr. Hans Delmotte, suffered a breakdown after witnessing his first selection at the Auschwitz ramp. He appeared paralyzed and had to be escorted to his quarters, where he got drunk and vomited. The next day, still dazed, he demanded to be transferred to the front, as he could not participate in mass slaughter. He was placed under the wing of his experienced colleague, Dr. Josef Mengele, who gradually persuaded him of the "necessity" of mass extermination in Auschwitz.[84] Delmotte calmed down. Apparently, an inconvenient sense of humanity could be overcome.

Dr. Eugen Kogon was a German historian, journalist, socialist, and vocal anti-Nazi. The Gestapo arrested him for his opposing political beliefs in 1936, 1937, and 1938. Since periodic jailing had not "reformed" him, in September 1939 he was sentenced to imprisonment in Buchenwald concentration camp. He would spend six years there and was eventually marked for death. He narrowly escaped when the camp's medical doctor, who had befriended him, smuggled him out of the camp in a crate. Kogon returned to journalism after the war, and wrote of the structure and operation of the concentration camps, and his own personal experience.

Kogon details the system of induction used at all the camps, and the accompanying barbarity. The camps kept meticulous records, and guards immediately sent new prisoners to the camp Political Department where a file was started on them, including their personal history, police record if any, and a photograph. The data was entered on a file card, along with any other pertinent information, including transcripts of Gestapo interrogations. The process was accompanied by the brutality which the prisoners would henceforth experience daily. A favorite *SS* tactic at induction, according to Kogon, was to ask the prisoner why they had been arrested. The prisoners generally did not know, which gave the guards an excuse to lash them with a whip. Lashings and beatings would continue, with or without an excuse. An indoctrination lecture followed, which detailed camp policy and the things the prisoner could not do, which was virtually everything, and the harsh penalties, including death, that would be applied to rule breakers. [85] From there the prisoners were sent to the showers to discard their clothing, and generally, all hope.

The Hitler Youth

Participation in youth programs was compulsory in Nazi Germany. The *Hitlerjugend,* for boys, and *Bund Deutscher Mädel,* for girls, had a major impact on the worldview of German youth as they moved into adulthood. The boys' program centered on physical fitness and was basically a preparatory program for military service. Instructors usually held classes outdoors and designed them to be both instructive and enjoyable. The girls' program also stressed physical fitness, but instructors primarily taught domestic classes, which prepared the girls to be good wives and mothers. The Nazi government was actively preparing for war and encouraged motherhood to ensure a supply of young soldiers.

A critical component of the youth groups was indoctrination in the Nazi political philosophy, which included a significant amount of anti-Semitic propaganda. With no contradictory information, many German youth took this as gospel. By the time they became adults, this training had been so ingrained in them that many believed Jews were subhuman. Many assigned to work in the concentration camps had little or no sympathy for their victims.

Some of the most vicious fighters toward the end of the war were former *Hitlerjugend* in the *Waffen-SS.* Many chose to fight to the death, even when it had become apparent that the Nazi cause was lost. It was not just Allied troops they were after. German citizens who tried to surrender their homes to the approaching Allies, rather than have them destroyed in the fighting, were in danger of being killed by young *Waffen-SS* soldiers who viewed them as traitors. At his trial at Nuremberg, former Hitler youth leader, Baldur von Schirach, confessed that the Nazis corrupted youth on a scale probably never before seen in history.[86]

Schirach was one of the few Nazi leaders who took responsibility for his actions. It was believed he had been killed in the battle for Berlin; in fact, he heard his death announced on BBC radio. However, on June 5, 1945, he heard a radio report stating that other Hitler Youth leaders had been arrested. His conscience won the battle with his will to escape, and he surrendered to Allied authorities. Imprisoned, he wrote to his wife: "I want to speak before a court of law and take the blame on myself. Through me, the young have learned to believe in Hitler. I taught them to have faith in him; now I must free them from this error. Once I have had the opportunity to say this before an international court of law, then let them hang me."[87] He was tried, convicted, and sentenced to twenty years in prison. He was released in 1966.

Notes

70. Bess Freilich interview by Marc Seligman, 14.

71. Ibid.

72. Ibid.

73. Ibid, 15.

74. Ibid.

75. Bess Freilich interview by Josey G. Fisher, 2-2-24.

76. Bess Freilich interview by Marc Seligman, 16.

77. Ibid.

78. Ibid.

79. Bess Freilich, interview by Fisher, 2-2-23. Long after the war, Basha and her husband met the man who pointed out her father to the *SS*, and he confessed to what he had done. He was racked with guilt, and begged for forgiveness. He told Basha he had lived with this shame all his life and continued to have nightmares about his act. He said he was so scared at the time that his mind did not work, and the event continued to eat his heart out. He asked Basha to speak to her father and ask for forgiveness for him. Isaac had been beaten so badly that even after moving to the United States years later, he had to give up his job because of back pain and lack of mobility. Basha and her husband listened to the man, but did not know how to respond.

80. Ibid, 2-1-22.

81. Ibid, 2-1-21.

82. Heinz Höhne, *The Order of the Deaths Head: The Story of Hitler's SS* (London: Penguin Books, Ltd, 1966) 200.

83. Ibid, 202-3

84. Nikolaus Wachsmann, *KL: The History of the Nazi Concentration Camps* (New York: Farrar, Straus and Giroux, 2015) 371.

85. Eugen Kogon, *The Theory and Practice of Hell: The German Concentration Camps and the System Behind Them* (New York: Farrar, Straus and Giroux, 1950) 62-3.

86. Ann Tusa and John Tusa, *The Nuremberg Trial* (New York: Atheneum, 1990) 39.

87. Ibid, 40.

CHAPTER 5

Budy

I t is hard to imagine the fear—likely terror—that filled Basha's heart when she learned she was being sent to a *Strafkompanie*. Her life was already miserable in Birkenau and now she was being sent somewhere even worse for an unknown crime.

"If you did something wrong in Birkenau, they sent you to Budy, but what did we do wrong?" [88]

It was a reasonable question. However, the *SS* seemed to make up the rules as they went along, so there was not necessarily a reasonable answer.

From Unbelievably Bad to Unbelievably Worse

The Budy concentration camp was originally nothing more than an acreage near Bór, which was operated as a farm. Located about five kilometers from Auschwitz, selected male Polish prisoners marched there every day to tend the crops before marching back to their barracks at night. The *SS* quickly determined that the daily marches were unproductive—a waste of valuable slave-labor time. So, in April 1942, prisoners built rudimentary living accommodations and an initial group of forty male prisoners took up residence there. At the end of 1942 and beginning of 1943, the *SS* maximized use of its slave labor and transferred more prisoners to Budy to increase the camp's agricultural output. The Nazis forced families in Bór from their homes and businesses, converting their buildings into support facilities for the *SS* guards and *kapos*. Prisoners then built various agricultural buildings such as stables, pigsties, and warehouses, both inside and outside the wire that surrounded the prisoner compound, and Nazi authorities transferred prisoners from Czechoslovakia, Russia, Greece, and Germany into the camp. Budy operated as a typical labor camp until one event changed everything.[89]

On June 24, 1942, a *kommando* of two hundred Polish women marched to a field near the Solo River to dry hay. During one of the periodic prisoner counts, the guards discovered something that never happened before: a prisoner had escaped. The guards quickly spread out and searched the surroundings, but to no avail. The prisoner was gone. In the domain of the Nazi *SS*, an escape was completely unacceptable. This would not be good for anyone—guards, *kapos*, or prisoners.

The missing prisoner was a young woman from Bedów, Poland: twenty-four-year-old Janina Nowak. [90] Her Auschwitz induction photo shows an attractive young blonde woman bearing a slight smile despite her shabby prison uniform. The remaining women in her *kommando* marched back to Auschwitz-Birkenau where an intimidating *SS* political officer grilled them about the missing prisoner. One by one, the women stated they had not heard nor seen anything and had no idea what happened to Janina. Frustrated, the *SS* could do nothing to punish Janina since they had no idea where she was. Instead, they decided to punish the rest of the *kommando*. They began by shaving the women's heads. (The women were Gentiles. Prior to this, only Jewish women had their heads shaved.) The next day the entire *kommando* was designated as a penal company and sent to Budy. A few days later, the *SS* forced another two hundred women, primarily French, Slovakians, and Jews, into the camp. Budy became the collection spot for troublesome prisoners.

Budy was clearly no place for Basha and her adolescent fellow sufferers; in fact, it was clearly no place for anyone. Still, it could have been worse. Basha very nearly fell into the hands of the dreaded Dr. Josef Mengele.

A Run-In with the Respected Resident Murderer

Basha and the other girls were afraid and confused. They knew they were going to a punishment camp, but they had no idea what offense they had committed to warrant worse treatment than they were already receiving. She could ask a guard, but the reply would likely be a blow from a club.

As with many situations in Auschwitz, just when it appeared that things could not get worse, that is exactly what happened. As they formed columns to march to Budy, a group of officers arrived and studied the girls intently. Basha recognized the leader; he was the one she had observed pointing at prisoners and shouting orders when her train arrived at the Auschwitz station. By this point she had learned his name: Dr. Josef Mengele. Mengele was respected and acclaimed by Nazi leaders for making great contributions to medical science, but in the concentration camps, he was known as the "Angel of Death." [91]

With the theatrical exuberance for which he had become notorious, Mengele strode into the barrack with the look of one who enjoyed his job: to torture and kill prisoners under the guise of "medical experiments." As they did almost daily, Mengele and his underlings prowled Birkenau looking for new subjects— victims—for his experiments. Other than being selected for an immediate trip to the crematorium, being selected by Mengele was about as bad as things could get. However, more often than not, when Mengele was finished with his victims, he would send them to the crematorium anyway.

There was no way to hide. The girls stood in line as the medical team slowly walked past them, looking for specific physical characteristics known only to them. The girls could only hope and pray that they did not match the team's needs. Unfortunately, Basha's hopes and prayers were unsuccessful. One of officers grabbed her and attempted to pull her out of the line of terrified girls. She twisted and turned and managed to break his grasp, running like her life depended on it, which it no doubt did. She managed to outrun her pursuers and found a place in the camp to hide, remaining there for two days until *SS* guards discovered her. Fortunately, it was the regular guards who had captured her and not Mengele's team. They gave her the expected mistreatment, and then shipped her off to Budy with a new group of girls. There is no way of knowing what Mengele would have done to her, but he maimed most of his victims in his experiments, and the majority died. Survivors withstood a lifetime of physical and mental scars. Between the two miserable options, moving to Budy was likely the less horrible for Basha.

Life in Budy

Basha's feelings about Budy could not have been clearer:

"That camp was hell. No matter how much you can talk about it, how much you could write about it, there are no words in the vocabulary. You can't talk about it. You can't describe it. It's impossible. They were killing everybody." [92]

The first group of women sent to Budy earned the transfer for misbehavior. However, that did not remain a requirement. The notorious Auschwitz *SS-Oberaufseherin* (female camp manager), Maria Mandl, was known to send women from Birkenau to Budy for the slightest infraction of rules, frequently after beating them herself.

Cruelty aside, the ability to increase agricultural productivity by adding more slave labor was an attractive proposition to the *SS*. Consequently, when Budy needed more laborers, they moved them there from Birkenau, whether they had misbehaved or not. This was the case with Basha. She was strong enough to work hard, so the SS marched her off to Budy to take advantage of that. Unfortunately, the guards and *kapos* did not make a distinction between those sent there for punishment and those sent there for labor. They punished everyone. That was the answer to Basha's question about what she had done wrong: nothing. She had done absolutely nothing wrong.

Basha had been a prisoner long enough to expect that nothing good or kind would happen to her. Her expectation was confirmed at Budy immediately. Her group arrived in the middle of the night and formed a line near the camp kitchen. *Kapos* handed them pieces of bread, then marched them to the barrack. At the barrack entrance, different German *kapos* took the bread away to eat for themselves.

The next morning, after no food and little sleep, *kapos* formed Basha and the new prisoners into a *kommando* and marched to their new assignment. Although the primary function of Budy was agricultural work, the Germans were building a railroad line nearby and transported the girls there to smooth out the railbed. They were ordered to shovel away the topsoil and dump it into carts. This would be a quick and simple task for earth-moving equipment, but it was a backbreaking job for teenage girls. The shoveling was not the hardest part. When the carts were full, six girls worked together to push them to an area where the soil was dumped. It was difficult enough at the beginning when the pile of dirt was small, but the small pile soon became mountainous and the girls struggled mightily to push the carts to the top.

"We had to push the dirt on top, load up the dirt, push it on top of

the mountain with the heavy dirt, and then [when the cart] *was empty . . . it was going down the mountain so fast, and we were so weak, and so tired, and so cold that we were just dragging on the mud like rags and holding onto this little wagon. And we were just coming down dragging ourselves in the mud, and this was the work.*[93]

"And every time the Nazis saw [a girl dragging], *they killed all the six gals. You are lucky if they didn't notice you, that you were dragging on the ground.* [94] *They used to bring from Auschwitz four hundred girls, and in a matter of two days the camp was empty; they had to bring more. They all died. They all died."*[95]

The degree of physical torture at Budy was equaled by psychological and emotional torture. The prisoners were subjected to a daily barrage of sadism and perversion. The suffering of the girls became entertainment for their captors.

Each day, as they marched the three kilometers from Budy to their worksite, an *SS* guard scanned their ranks looking for girls that appealed to him. When he saw one, he wrote down the number tattooed on her arm. The girls selected would appear in a "show" during the midday meal. It was a show no one wanted to be in.

"Those gals, they didn't want it . . . they wrote the numbers down . . . they didn't want to be on the show that they [performed] *every afternoon. So, the gals, around twelve o'clock* [were ordered] *to disrobe, and they had to start dancing. They* [guards and kapos] *were all sitting with their German Shepherds. It was like a valley, and they were sitting all around like in the hills. And those gals had to dance.*

"I saw a friend of mine; her name was Sylvia. I used to go to her house very often. And they took her, and her mother was there too.

Because they didn't have no small children. The mother was very young . . . and both numbers they wrote down. They told them to disrobe. And my God, like I said, right before my eyes, the mother was begging, begging: 'Kill me first, shoot me first,' after she performed the dance. 'I don't want to see my daughter killed. Do it first to me.' And what do you think? They killed the daughter first. And they let the mother see it, and then [they killed] *the mother. They told them to turn around and go* [as though they were rejoining the group]. *Turn their backs, and they killed the daughter first and then they killed the mother. And we had to drag all those people that were killed at work. They grabbed gals, they grabbed me sometimes, they grabbed other gals. And they put them . . . we were like horses. We had to drag the big carts with the dead people. And what can I tell you? It was in the wintertime, and you couldn't see an inch of white snow. The snow was red with blood, dripping from the carts, because it was every day, every day."* [96]

Passing under the daily gaze of the *SS* guards likely created a level of fear and anxiety that no one would understand if they had not undergone the experience themselves. For some of the girls it became unbearable. They attempted to position themselves in the middle of their group as it marched, but someone always ended up on the end, and that meant their tattooed number was clearly visible. Some girls, fearful they had been selected, broke down and chose suicide. Alongside the road to the worksite, there was a well.

"So many gals, they passed by an open well and they jumped into it." [97]

They knew they were going to die anyway, so they spared themselves the humiliation of the show. The *kapos* retrieved the bodies from the well as the rest of the *kommando* stood by watching, then the girls placed the dead on carts and rolled them to the barrack at the end of the workday. Everyone had to be accounted for, dead or alive.

Those not selected to dance in the show were by no means safe from the perverse entertainment the *SS* created for themselves. They would frequently select prisoners randomly and tie them to the perimeter wire.

> *"They used to disconnect the electrical wires, and there were two wires, and the middle was an empty space. So, they grabbed the ten girls and put ten* dogs [one in front of each girl], *and the dogs ripped them alive, just ate them up alive. This happened every day, every day. Every day I thought the next day I'll be there."* [98]

Dora Golubowicz was at Birkenau by this point, but had not yet connected with Basha since their imprisonment. As far as Dora knew, she and her sister were the only survivors of their family. On the train to Auschwitz, family members demanded that their father jump from the train. Exactly how they thought that would benefit the family is unclear, but he reluctantly jumped through the small window. There was an immediate burst of machine-gun fire, and he was never heard of again. One day, their guards assigned Dora and her sister to a work detail that involved moving heavy, wet dirt. The *kapos* did not provide them with wagons, and ordered them to use their coats to carry the mud. The guards exercised the same cruelty at Birkenau as they did at Budy, frequently for their own amusement.

> *"Their enjoyment was our agony. The more agony, the more they enjoyed it, so they used to think of things to do."*

One day was particularly painful for Dora.

> *"They stood there, and they were young soldiers . . . they would say to each other, 'Let's see. Can you shoot her? Shoot her from here?' And he said, 'I will try,' so he did . . . he got her. Another one on the ground dead."*

The victim was Dora's sister. At the end of the day, Dora carried her body back to the barrack to be counted. [99]

There was a constant, oppressive feeling of doom that hung over the girls. Basha felt it like the rest. However, despite the apparent hopelessness of the situation, some refused to buckle and pushed on with unbroken spirits. In Basha's barrack there was a girl she knew from Pruzhany. Her last name was Hermofski, and she was imprisoned in Budy with her two sisters.

"Such beautiful three sisters," Basha remembered. "They were like the elite of our town." [100]

Basha frequently visited the sisters in their home before the war. The Hermofski family was financially better off than Basha's family, so there were certain treats and delicacies available there, which Basha did not get at home. Being elite or well-off meant nothing in Budy, of course, and the oldest and youngest of the sisters were both killed, leaving the third, the one who was Basha's age, mourning her siblings. Despite this, the remaining Hermofski sister never gave up hope. Her undaunted spirit was encouraging to Basha.

> *"We were talking, and I told her if I hadn't promised my mother to live . . . I can't take it no more. I want to die. She said, 'Basha, don't be foolish. Today's Purim in the world. Maybe God will make us a miracle again.' How did she know it was Purim, I don't know. And I will never know. Somehow she knew, and she gave me courage to go on. Two days later, I was carrying the wagon, and there on the wagon she was. They killed her. She gave me life, but she herself died. 'It's Purim,' she said. 'Remember, God will make a miracle for us.'* [101]

Indoctrinating Hatred

For those previously spared a glimpse into the darkest corners of humankind's depravity, Basha's story sounds like something from a perverse horror novel. It is dumbfounding that anyone, particularly young girls, could participate in—and apparently enjoy—the torture and murder of a fellow human being, but that was the impact of the Nazi indoctrination through the *Bund Deutscher Mädel* (League of German Girls). The *SS* guards did not view the prisoners as young girls just like them. They had been taught that the prisoners were subhuman—because they were Jews.

The basic title for female *SS* guards in concentration camps was *SS-Helferin* (*SS* Helper Women), but as with their military counterparts, they each earned a rank. They rose in the camp hierarchy the same way the men did, through aggression and brutality. Most escaped punishment after the war, but at Auschwitz, Budy, and Ravensbrück, Basha was in daily contact with several who became notorious for their cruelty.

Maria Mandl — "The Beast." Beginning in October 1942, Mandl became a domineering figure over prisoners, *SS-Helferin*, and *kapos* at Auschwitz-Birkenau, where she became the *SS-Lagerführerin,* reporting only to the camp commander. She was known for her immense cruelty. Witnesses stated that if a prisoner merely looked at Mandl, she might pull the girl off her job and the prisoner would never be seen or heard from again. Mandl participated in selections for the gas chambers, and was accused of being an accomplice in as many as five hundred thousand deaths of women and children. Curiously, she was a talented pianist with an appreciation for fine music. She organized the Women's Orchestra of Auschwitz from prisoners, which provided music at incoming prisoner transports, roll calls, and prisoner hangings. After the war she was tried as a war criminal, and hanged on January 24, 1948 at the age of thirty-six. [102]

Irma Grese — "The Hyena of Auschwitz." Against the opposition of her family, Grese eagerly began training to be an *SS-Helferin* when she was only seventeen years old, and officially became a guard at the age of nineteen. She soon became a supervisor over as many as thirty thousand women prisoners at Auschwitz and achieved the rank of *Lagerführerin*. She also worked at the Ravensbrück and Bergen-Belsen camps. Armed with a whip, pistol, and German Shepherd attack dog, she committed acts of torture, sadism, sexual abuse, and arbitrary murder. She was tried and convicted of war crimes. Defiant and unrepentant to the end, she was hanged on December 13, 1945 at the age of twenty-two.[103]

Juana Bormann — "The Weasel" and "The Woman with the Dogs." Bormann's motivation for joining the SS in 1938 had nothing to do with politics. She said at her trial that she joined because "I could earn more money." Rising through the ranks, she served in several camps, including Auschwitz-Birkenau and Budy while Basha was imprisoned there. Regardless of her initial lack of political interest, she appeared to take great delight in her job. She was known among the prisoners for her sadism and cruelty, and seemed to particularly enjoy killing helpless prisoners with her attack-trained German Shepherd. She was tried and convicted of war crimes, and hanged on December 13, 1945, at the age of fifty-two. [104]

For Basha, every day she arose, every step she took, and every word she spoke could potentially put her in the hands of these women who had lost all sense of humanity.

Although Basha did not enter Auschwitz until 1943, Heinrich Himmler approved what would become the Auschwitz complex as a concentration camp site in April 1940, and the first thirty prisoners were transferred from the Sachsenhausen concentration camp on May 20 of that year. They were all career criminals and wore the green triangle on their uniforms. They worked as *SS* functionaries, charged with controlling the prisoners who would soon arrive. They quickly established a system of abuse and torture to keep the inmates in line, as well as for their own amusement. The camps grew and the population of Auschwitz and sub-camps like Budy became predominantly Jewish. The Nazis congregated the Jews in specific camps and shipped in Jews from all over German-occupied Europe. The camp eventually held prisoners from Poland, Hungary, France, the Netherlands, Greece, Slovakia, Belgium, Germany, Austria, Yugoslavia, Italy, and Norway. [105]

The mix of languages and cultures was new to Basha. In Pruzhany she lived in a predominantly Jewish section of town, but had friends among the Polish Gentiles. It was not a culturally diverse environment, so many days in Auschwitz, particularly in her early imprisonment, were learning experiences. Basha's daughter, Evelyn Kaplan, remembers a particularly unusual experience her mother told her about being present when a transport train from Hungary arrived at Auschwitz.

> *"Mom happened to be near the platform of the railroad tracks when the doors of the train slid open and the horror of these poor souls was realized. There was the usual screaming of orders, the cries of terror, and the fear of being separated from family. The barking of vicious dogs with foam drooling from their mouths, added more hysteria to the unfolding scene. Most prominent was the countenance of the new arrivals; the fearfulness in their eyes, the bewilderment as to where they arrived after such a horrific journey, the horrendous thought of being separated from their family, and their desperation to find their loved ones who were on a different cattle car.*

"Mom noticed that this transport seemed much different than the others. There were many Gypsies on this train. Their colorful garb made them stand out from the others. Also known as Roma, Mom heard many stories about them. She was fascinated by their appearance. Mom also took notice that there was no selection for the Gypsies. Those with families were sent to special barracks that were marked 'Z' (zigeunerin: Gypsy). A Gypsy who arrived as a single person was often assigned barracks with [non-Gypsy] Auschwitz prisoners. Mom watched as the Gypsies were marched to their barracks.

"As the cattle car was emptied, there was another sight that captured Mom's attention. A bride in her white gown disembarked from the train. It was a sight Mom would never forget. The juxtaposition of the scene: a beautiful young girl in a lovely dress that is now covered in urine, feces, and vomit arriving in Auschwitz, hell on earth, the armpit of the world. She was stolen away from what was to be the most special day of her life only to end up in a nightmare in a devil's playground. Her face was that of a lost soul, frightened, alone. The image was imbued in Mom's memory forever.

"Later that day, after completing her work assignment and standing for hours during the evening roll call, Mom returned to her barracks. She was surprised to see that a young Gypsy girl had been assigned to her group. After a few days, the young girl took a liking to Mom and tried to communicate with her. To survive in Auschwitz, it was an asset to have a friend. Mom introduced her to some of the other girls in the barracks, and the strict rules and routines they were forced to follow. The Gypsy girl caught on quickly and meshed well with the group.

"In the evenings the inmates would reminisce about home, share recipes, and argue about the different ways of cooking a brisket

or baking a strudel. They enjoyed talking about their past romances . . . anything that would make life in the hell of Auschwitz a little lighter, a little easier. One evening the Gypsy approached Mom and placed Mom's hand in hers. She wanted to read Mom's palm. Thinking it would be fun, Mom agreed. She looked at Mom's hand and gently followed the lines in her skin. She closed her eyes, visualizing everything she was about to say. She told Mom, 'You will survive this hell. You will be walking very far . . . it will be very difficult, but you will do it. Your father is alive. He is here in this camp. You will search and find your father. Sadly, the rest of your family is gone . . . ashes in the sky. You will marry a man . . . a very handsome man . . . who has something to do with shoes . . . lots of shoes. It will take you some time, but the two of you will travel over an ocean . . . a most difficult trip for you; but, again, you will survive that too. You will find family upon your arrival. and you will have three children.' Mom had chills throughout her reading. Mom thought, what kind of fairytale is she concocting when you don't know if you will survive another hour? When one wrong step, one wrong remark, one wrong facial expression can mean instant death. Her words, however, were not forgotten and became a source of hope to Mom." [106]

The Gypsy's prediction was eerily accurate.

———

Their uniquely appalling circumstances unified the girls, despite their different homelands, languages, and cultures. A transport of girls from Greece arrived one night and the guards marched them to Basha's barrack. It was another unfortunately memorable event.

"It came in the evening . . . there were a lot of gals from Greece

there. While they gave us a piece of bread, I always remembered the moon was shining. First, was beating us. We were wearing a little dress with nothing . . . torn-up shoes. There they gave you the dresses with stripes. And outside of the barrack was the little kitchen. They gave us a teeny piece of bread and a little ersatz coffee. And while we took it, we went to the barrack because it was a very short distance. The Nazis [that]were staying there, spilled out the coffee, and took away the bread. Took away the bread from us. Some gals pushed it right away in their mouth; they could've choked. The piece of bread . . . the Nazis gave it to them, but then they got beaten terribly. They took all the bread back that they gave. We came [to the barrack] at night, exhausted . . . dead. Dead people."

Jewish prisoners in the camps coined a slang term for this condition: *Muselmänner*: those depleted of emotion, only a pulsebeat from being a cadaver. But in the midst of this hopelessness, there was still a spark of life.

"There was a gal there with the most beautiful voice. From Salonika [Thessaloniki, Greece]. *She started singing the song, 'Mama mama . . .'* [the rest of the song title is indistinguishable on the interview recording] *and God, we were soaked with tears . . . thinking about our life and our mothers. Couldn't sleep. We couldn't sleep. We were crying terribly. She sang it so . . . it broke our hearts."* [107]

Each day, Basha and the other prisoners awoke and functioned in an oppressive cloud of despondency and heartache. There was nothing to look forward to and always the possibility that things could get worse.

"The kommando *was always 350 people, and that's how they wanted it. And when so many died, they brought from Birkenau more. Every day it was changing because it was a deficit."* [108]

Under the constant physical and emotional battering, Basha sometimes lost her will to live, but she never forgot her promise to her mother. Every day, her primary goal was to stay alive so she could one day tell her story to the world.

Basha's *kommando* worked outside regardless of the weather. In the summer they suffered through the heat, and in the winter, the cold.

"The dirt we had to haul, some pieces with the grass, how do you call it, turf. So we had to carry this and it was very heavy . . . on rainy days and cold days. Your hands were cold, and it was very heavy to carry." [109]

The work at Budy was essential to the Nazi cause. The workers, however, were expendable. Those no longer able to labor, even for a few days, became the "useless mouths" that the Nazi regime was so dedicated to eliminating. One day, that reality confronted Basha.

"I felt that my day had come. I got sick, and I felt something very hollow-like in my chest, and I got very sick, burning up with fever. And one morning I just couldn't go to work. So, I thought to myself that I'm going to rip a piece of blanket, and I felt like if I put something on my chest, it's going to help me, and maybe I'll be able to go through the day. [There] was punishment for ripping a blanket. They beat you twenty-five times over that." [110]

Basha carefully arranged the torn blanket around her upper body, then put on her dress, being careful to ensure the blanket was concealed. She hoped it would help, but the fever was not her only problem. She was so sick she could barely move. She managed to walk outside with the rest of her group and assemble for the march to the work site, but it took all her strength. She found a spot where she could lean against the barrack wall, hoping not to fall, and to rest enough to regain a measure of strength. It was still dark, 4:00 a.m., and she hoped the *kapos* would not notice her. On that morning the *kapos* noticed everyone. They decided to begin the day with a severe and lengthy beating that Basha described as agonizing. Finally, it was time to go to work. The *kommando* marched off, but Basha was not with them.

"I couldn't put my feet forward. I couldn't work. So she [female kapos name unintelligible on interview recording], *the Nazi, went over to me, and with* [her] *cane, the round piece of the cane* [hook], *she stuck the cane* [into Basha's dress] *to drag me, and she noticed the blanket.* [111]

The *kapo* shouted the discovery of the torn blanket to her colleagues, and other *kapos* joined her. They tied Basha's hands behind her back and began to administer the twenty-five-lash beating penalty for ripping her blanket.

"I counted. I was still conscious until sixteen. I got twenty-five-lashes and I lost consciousness." [112]

The rain that poured off the barrack roof drained through the assembly area and, over time, had eroded a ditch in the property. The *kapos* dragged Basha's unconscious body to the ditch and threw her in it.

"When I started to open my eyes, I saw like I was lying in a river of blood. The whole ditch with the water was full of my blood. I looked at the sun and I could tell the time . . . and I knew it was close to twelve o'clock [noon]. *And I knew* [that is when] *comes a little truck with the Red Cross signs."* [113]

Basha had seen the little truck with the Red Cross emblems every day, both at Birkenau and Budy. She knew it would pick her up and transport her to Birkenau. She also knew the truck would not be taking her to a hospital.

The little truck with the red crosses went directly to the crematorium.

Historical Perspective
on Chapter 5

Josef Mengele [114]

Josef Mengele was born to a wealthy family in Günzburg, Germany in 1911. He was intelligent and a good student, earning first a PhD in anthropology, and later a medical degree. He had a particular interest in genetics and racial matters. Mengele joined the *SS* in 1937 and eventually served as a medical officer in the Ukraine. After being wounded, he was transferred to the *SS* Race and Settlement Office in Berlin, and then to Auschwitz. With a large pool of helpless prisoners, Mengele was able to perform brutal and unethical medical experiments under the guise of research. [115] Auschwitz chief *SS* physician Eduard Wirths praised Mengele for "utilizing the scientific material at his disposal to make a valuable contribution in his work on anthropological science." [116] Others in the Nazi hierarchy agreed. History now refers to Mengele's "contributions" as atrocities.

Standing at the Auschwitz train station, Mengele stood out prominently for his "elegant looks, high spirits, and theatrical manner, dividing prisoners 'like a conductor' into separate groups. He sent those who appeared capable of work to the camp, and those who could not work directly to the gas chambers.

His initial assignment as physician at the Auschwitz Gypsy barracks provided Mengele an opportunity to study a niche society that did not conform to the Nazi philosophy of Aryan superiority. He moved on to become the senior medical doctor at Birkenau, where his pool of potential victims grew substantially. In the end, statistically, Mengele's victims were predominately Jewish, a fact that was, no doubt, influenced by their prominent numbers in the camp, as well as his own racial prejudice. Physical abnormalities fascinated Mengele, as did twin children. The victims he chose were usually between the ages of two and sixteen years old. Guards stationed at the Auschwitz rail station scrutinized incoming prisoner transports, alert for anyone that met Mengele's criteria. When they spotted anyone that they felt would be of interest to him, the guards immediately pulled the young prisoners away from their families and escorted them to Mengele's special medical facility.

Mengele's experiments were more often than not horrendous, and without any valid medical justification. In one experiment, he attempted to change the eye color of some of the twins by injecting liquid into their eyes. Others were subjected to surgical experiments without anesthesia to gauge their reaction to pain. Some of the twins survived, many did not.[117] It is possible that Mengele, if he had possessed a shred of decency or morality, might have made more positive contributions to medical science. He had been an assiduous student and a dedicated researcher. Had he applied his intellect and talent in positive pursuits, perhaps it would have yielded more beneficial research data. Perhaps, even his obsession with racial biology and anthropology might have led to something of value to humankind. We will never know. Rather than seeking to understand and possibly improve the human experience through his efforts, he adopted the Nazi policy of targeting races they deemed inferior and using science—or the pretext of science—to eliminate them.

SS doctors conducted medical experiments at several of the concentration camps, but Auschwitz, by far, provided the majority of the victims, and Mengele, by far, stood out from the other doctors for his complete lack of humanity and his willingness to perform virtually any experiment, however repugnant. Couched as medical research, he performed excruciatingly painful invasive procedures that were nothing short of degenerate torture. [118] The entirety of Mengele's work shows a man who descended to a level of evil most would find beyond comprehension.

When the German Army collapsed, Mengele disguised himself as a *Wehrmacht* officer and was taken prisoner by the United States Army in June 1945. He was using his own name, but it had not been put on the list of major war criminals yet. For some reason he had not received the traditional *SS* blood-group tattoo, so his *SS* membership was not known at the time of capture, and he was released a month later. Aware he would eventually be discovered as a war criminal, he emigrated to South America where he had several business interests and, likely, financial support from his wealthy family. Despite efforts by Simon Wiesenthal and the Israeli Mossad, he managed to elude capture for the rest of his life. On February 7, 1979, he suffered a stroke while swimming in Bertioga, Brazil and drowned. His body was later exhumed and his identity confirmed by DNA testing. Colleagues stated he remained an unrepentant Nazi to the end.

SS-Helferin

Female *SS* staff were not full-fledged members of the *SS* and treated as a step below their male counterparts. They tended to come from the lower or lower middle class, and were generally unskilled. Nazi editors skillfully crafted newspaper advertisements which appealed to the patriotism of the young women. Some women joined the ranks of the *SS* because it paid better than whatever they were currently doing, or because they were doing nothing at all. Once inducted, the *SS* trained them for a specialty and they received a rank. Many moved up through the system, some reaching ranks and positions of great authority. As with the men, a willingness to mistreat prisoners was considered a valuable quality for promotion. The basic *Helferin* ranks were:

Lagerführerin: Leader of the Camp.

Oberaufseherin: Senior Overseer

Rapportführerin: Overseer of several barracks. The roll-call taker.

Blockführerin: Responsible for one or more barracks, from two hundred to three hundred prisoners.

Hundeführerin: Guard-Dog Handler

Aufseherin: Guard

Of the estimated 3,600 to 5,000 female concentration camp guards, only sixty were charged with crimes and faced war crimes tribunals. All were convicted, and twenty-one were hanged.[119]

Notes

88. Bess Freilich interview by Marc Seligman, 17.

89. "Wirtschaftshof Budy Strafkompanie," Sub-camps of Auschwitz, accessed September 22, 2021, https://subcamps-auschwitz.org/auschwitz-subcamps/wirtschaftshof-budy-strafkompanie/.

90. Séamus Bellamy, "Janina Nowak," Faces of Auschwitz, April 3, 2018, https://facesofauschwitz.com/gallery/2018-4-3-faces-of-auschwitz-janina-nowak/.

91. "Josef Mengele" Wikipedia Foundation, last modified April 17, 2023, https://en.wikipedia.org/wiki/Josef_Mengele.

92. Bess Freilich interview by Josey G. Fisher, 2-2-25.

93. Ibid, 2-2-26.

94. Bess Freilich interview by Marc Seligman, 17.

95. Bess Freilich interview by Josey G. Fisher, 2-2-26.

96. Bess Freilich interview by Marc Seligman, 18.

97. Ibid, 17.

98. Bess Freilich interview by Josey G. Fisher, 3-1-34.

99. Dora Freilich, interview by Helen Grossman, 2-2-27.

100. Bess Freilich interview by Marc Seligman, 18.

101. Ibid, 18-19.

102. Maria Mandl," Wikimedia Foundation, last modified November 21, 2022. httpss://en.m.wikipedia.org/wiki/Maria-Mandl.

103. "Irma Grese," Jewish Virtual Library, accessed September 27, 2022, http://jewishvirtuallibrary.org/irma-grese.

104. "Juana Bormann," Wikimedia Foundation, last modified November 3, 2022, https://en.wikipedia.org/wiki/Juana_Bormann.

105. "Ethnic Origins and Numbers of Victims of Auschwitz," Auschwitz-Birkenau Memorial Place and Museum, accessed September 27, 2021. http://70.auschwitz.org/index.php?loption=com_content&view=article&id=89itemid=173&lang=en.

106. Evelyn Kaplan, email to author, May 25, 2022,

107. Bess Freilich interview by Marc Seligman, 19.

108. Ibid.

109. Bess Freilich interview by Josey G. Fisher, 2-2-27.

110. Ibid.

111. Bess Freilich interview by Marc Seligman, 20.

112. Ibid.

113. Ibid.

114. "Josef Mengele" Wikipedia Foundation, last modified April 17, 2023, https://en.wikipedia.org/wiki/Josef_Mengele.

115. Wachsmann, 436-40.

116. Ibid.

117. Ibid.

118. Ibid.

119. Ibid.

CHAPTER 6
Not Quite Dead

Lying in the filthy ditch in small, lapping waves of her own blood, barely conscious, Basha watched the movement of the sun, calculating the amount of time she had left to live. When the truck marked with the red crosses arrived promptly at noon as it always did, the drive to the crematorium would be brief. The use of a truck marked with the Red Cross symbol was ironic. Although it sounds almost oxymoronic, war has rules which have been agreed upon by international law. [120] Basha knew that the Red Cross symbol on buildings and vehicles designates that the occupants cannot be harmed. Yet under the protection of the truck marked with the worldwide symbol of mercy, she knew the Nazis would be taking her to her death.

Basha was not ready to be murdered. Despondent and in agony, with absolutely no hope for the future, many would remain in the bloody pool and give up. She might have been among them, except for one thing.

"And this came to my mind, that my mother wouldn't like it for me to die; she wanted the people of the world to know. She wanted the world to know." [121]

Recalling her mother's words, perhaps even hearing her voice in her mind, Basha pushed herself to survive. If she remained in the bloody ditch, she would be dead within hours. Her only option was to find the strength to move.

"I crawled . . . [on] both sides [there] was an awful lot of mud

and there were pieces of wood in the middle. And from that place . . . I could go to the latrine." [122]

Camp management had constructed sidewalks of wooden planks to allow people to walk across the rain-soaked compound without being trapped in the mud, which on occasion became almost like quicksand. Exhausted and in excruciating pain, Basha knew she would have no chance of extricating herself if she got stuck in the mud. Healthy people frequently had a hard time breaking free. She summoned all her strength and pushed herself.

"Somehow, with all that I went through, and with all that surrounded me, there was still a will to live." [123]

Basha knew her number had been put on the selection list for the crematorium. She would immediately be spotted alone in the barrack while the *kommando* was at work, so she had to find a place to hide. She knew the latrine offered refuge, although not a pleasant one.

"When I walked in there, I got myself under the whole pile of dirty clothing, because the girls all had diarrhea . . . dysentery, so some of them organized another dress and the filthy ones they threw there. [124]

"Somehow, some girls would give away a piece of bread for a different dress, because [it was assumed] *you couldn't work. Once they saw you with all this on you,* [diarrhea stains] *then they would kill you. So, the girls were afraid and they dropped those dresses off there in the toilet and there was a whole pile, and I went underneath this pile and I just lay there, and I lay there, and I didn't care what was going to happen. I figure I'll postpone it for a couple of hours. But they wrote my number down already, and the little truck* [with red crosses] *. . . came, and they were looking for me all over because my number was marked, and I*

heard them scream '33-3-27' . . . and I just pretended I wasn't around and just lay there. I couldn't walk. I was bleeding all over. I was living, I was not living. I was conscious, I wasn't conscious. I didn't care what was happening to me." [125]

The search for Basha continued, but the truck left. She knew she was spared the ovens of Birkenau for one more day.

Day faded into evening, and Basha knew her *kommando* had returned from its work detail. She needed to join them and, hopefully, get a piece of bread. When one of the girls from her barrack came into the latrine, Basha revealed herself from under the pile of filthy dresses. The girl helped Basha walk to the barrack, and Basha mingled briefly with the crowd, hoping she would not be spotted by the *kapo*. She did not have enough strength to stand for long and had to find a bunk as quickly as possible.

Basha had occupied a top bunk prior to her beating, but she no longer had the strength to climb up into it. Instead, she found a bottom bunk, crawled into it, and tried to stay warm and rest. Ultimately, the bottom bunk became a problem. In the middle of the night Basha saw the *kapo* waving at her. She wondered if she had been caught, but the *kapo* was apparently unaware that she was listed as missing. Instead, a chore had to be done and Basha was easily within reach. The latrine was off limits at night, and the girls were required to relieve themselves in buckets placed in the barrack. When they became full, a prisoner was selected to carry them to the latrine to dump the waste. The *kapo* selected Basha. Basha said she did not even look human at that point, and did not think she could stand or walk, let alone carry the two heavy buckets. The *kapo* could easily see her condition, so she may have selected her from all the rest of the girls as a special act of cruelty. She struck her with her stick and demanded that she get out of bed. Basha said she would try, and begged the *kapo* not to beat her.

"I couldn't even walk. 'How am I going to carry the buckets?' I asked. She said, 'I'll help you walk.' She put a stick . . . put it in the back of me to give me balance to be able to walk those couple of steps, and she told me to pick up both buckets. Both buckets. And to carry [them] *to empty . . . to the latrine. I'll never forget. I begged her, I begged her, 'Please, I'll do it, I'll be able to do it. I'm still strong. But don't beat me. If you beat me, I won't be able to do it.' Somehow, she held me in the back. I walked outside."* [126]

As Basha staggered toward the latrine with the heavy buckets, they passed an *SS* guard who took interest in the young, female *kapo*. He began to flirt with her, and the *kapo* flirted back, then showed off for him by hitting Basha again. Basha had summoned strength from somewhere to carry the load, but that was reaching its limits.

"I begged her, I begged her, 'Bitte schlagen Sie mir nicht, schlagen sir mir nicht [Please don't beat me, don't beat me] *because I'll never be able to carry those buckets.' And she started to scream at me, I should shut up, and started to hit me again. And then—I'll never forget it until I die—I turned to this guard, and I begged him please—in German—'Bitte schiessen sir mir* [Please shoot me]. *Please do me a favor. Kill me. I can't go on like this. I don't want to live no more.'"*

The guard's response was typically heartless.

"He said, 'Sie alte sau' [You old pig]. *He said, 'I don't want to waste a German bullet on you. You'll die any minute now any-how.'"* [127]

The *kapo* again beat Basha with her stick, forcing her forward. The walkway through the mud was only a single plank wide, which meant she had to put one foot in front of the other rather than walking in a normal fashion. This was a fairly simple task for a healthy person, but it required more balance than Basha's weak muscles could provide, especially while carrying the buckets. Her inner strength could no longer command her worn-out body.

> *"It was impossible for me to do, and I fell down and all those buckets on top of me with their dirt, with everything, and she hit me again, and then I gave up. I gave up and they threw me in the morgue."* [128]

The Pile of Death

It is likely difficult for the average person to imagine a place so permeated by a sense of doom that constant death becomes normal and unremarkable. Basha had watched for months, as girls her age, hundreds by now, succumbed to disease, beatings, and murder. Thoughts of her mother had kept her going, but her body could no longer comply with her will. She finally reached the conclusion that death was preferable to continuing her horrible life. Death would be her escape. Death was so rampant, even for an extermination camp, that it exceeded the murderous capabilities of the killers. In a perverse twist of fate, Basha would have to wait in line to be killed.

Despite her numerous wounds, Basha was still conscious. She remembered being carried to the morgue and being thrown onto a pile of bodies. Most unsettling for her later was the memory that, like herself, not all of them were dead.

> *"They had a morgue in the barrack for the dead people they kept that died during the night, and they kept me there, and there were dying girls lying there and they were pinching me. I'll never forget, I was lying in a pile of dead bodies, some were dying, some were dead already. And I was lying like this on top of them* [as] *I spent the night."*

Basha found herself in the same situation she had been in only

a few hours earlier. Lying brutally beaten, waiting for the truck
with the red crosses to arrive. With characteristic punctuality, the
truck arrived promptly at noon. Having lain motionless through
the night, Basha had regained a small amount of strength. She
was determined not to be carried to the truck. The other living
prisoners were carried, but she walked.

> *"The* [truck] *came and I walked in. I remember like it was now.
> I picked my right foot, my right foot, I picked up like this. I knew
> where I was going, and somehow in my mind the thoughts passed
> by. I knew it then, but I prayed to God it should be easy and it
> should be fast. And that's the only reason I picked up my right
> leg. Like it was a superstition. I walked into that little truck,
> and I remember there were olives laying there all over. Because
> they were probably taking . . . there were transports from Greece
> at that time, and they were probably taking the people to the
> crematorium there, and the Greek people, they lived on olives.
> They probably brought it with them, and there were olives laying*
> [on the truck floor.] *Then I just prayed to God that this journey
> shouldn't end because I knew where the stop will be, that it was
> going to be in the crematorium. Sure enough, it was a small trip.
> It wasn't too long of a trip."* [129]

The truck stopped and the doors were jerked open. Basha
painfully crawled out, but no one followed her. Everyone else
was dead.

Historical Perspective
on Chapter 6

Too Many Dead

The *SS* killed so many prisoners every day, and so many others died of disease and neglect, that the *Sonderkommando* had more work than it could accomplish. There were limits to the number of corpses the crematoria could dispose of per day, and when the limits were exceeded, the piles of corpses grew until the *SS* executioners were forced to slow down their activities. Some prisoners, including Basha, got a last-minute extension of their lives.

The dead presented Auschwitz camp management with some critical problems, the worst of which was the health hazard the stacks of bodies created. An outbreak of disease would affect everyone in the camp, not only the expendable prisoners. Auschwitz medical officers were deeply concerned, and chief physician, *SS-Hauptsturmführer* Dr. Wirths, presented the problem, and its potential devastating impact, to the *SS* hierarchy beyond the Auschwitz wires. Wirths felt strongly that full remediation of the health crisis could not be accomplished without replacing the current wooden structures with ones constructed of concrete. Rats cannot chew through concrete, he pointed out. Wirths wrote a memo to *SS Sturmbannführer* Bischoff, of the Construction Inspectorate of the *Waffen-SS* and *Police Schlesien* on March 20, 1943, in which he raised his concerns about the brewing health crisis, and pleaded that it was an urgent issue requiring urgent attention. Bischoff responded on August 4. He did not agree.

"*. . . the construction of dedicated morgues in the individual subsections of the POW camp, as per the aforementioned*

request of the SS garrison physician, will not be carried out . . .
the corpses are to be removed twice daily, in the morning and in
the evening, into the morgues of the crematoria; in this way, the
separate construction of morgues in the individual subsections
can be avoided." [130]

Dr. Wirths and his staff were left to deal with the health issue as best they could, and the *Sonderkommando* continued to pile bodies in a morgue area in back of the barrack, vermin or no vermin.

Basha was familiar with the area; she had seen many girls go there before. Now, it was her turn to join them.

Notes

120. "The Geneva Convention," The Wikimedia Foundation, last modified December 2, 2022, https://en.wikipedia.org/wiki/Geneva_Conventions.

121. Bess Freilich interview by Marc Seligman, 21.

122. Ibid.

123. Bess Freilich interview by Josey G. Fisher, 2-2-27.

124. Bess Freilich interview by Marc Seligman, 21.

125. Bess Freilich interview by Josey G. Fisher, 2-2-27.

126. Bess Freilich interview by Marc Seligman, 22.

127. Ibid.

128. Bess Freilich interview by Josey G. Fisher, 2-2-28.

129. Ibid.

130. Carlo Mattogno, "The Morgues of the Crematoria at Birkenau in the Light of Documents," CODOH, accessed November 2, 2021, https://vho.org/tr/2004/3/Mattogno271-278.html.

Railroad line for prisoner transport into Auschwitz.

Courtesy of United States Holocaust Memorial Museum Photograph Archives.

**A transport of Jews is taken off the trains and assembled
on the ramp at Auschwitz-Birkenau.**

Courtesy of United States Holocaust Memorial Museum Photograph Archives,
Photograph Number 77354

Jews await selection on the ramp at Auschwitz-Birkenau.

Courtesy of United States Holocaust Memorial Museum Photograph Archives,
Photograph Number 77319

**Jewish women and children await selection on the ramp
at Auschwitz-Birkenau.**

Courtesy of United States Holocaust Memorial Museum Photograph Archives,
Photograph Number 77255

Auschwitz women inmates sort through a huge pile of shoes.

Courtesy of United States Holocaust Memorial Museum Photograph Archives,
Photograph Number 77394

**Prisoners in the Aufräumungskommando (order commandos)
unload the confiscated property of a transport of Jews at a
warehouse in Auschwitz-Birkenau.**

Courtesy of United States Holocaust Memorial Museum Photograph Archives,
Photograph Number 77386

View of one of the warehouses in Auschwitz, which is overflowing with clothes confiscated from prisoners.

Courtesy of United States Holocaust Memorial Museum Photograph Archives, Photograph Number 85750

Women in the barracks at Auschwitz concentration camp.

Courtesy of United States Holocaust Memorial Museum Photograph Archives Photograph Number: 31450B

Jewish women and children who have been selected for death at Auschwitz-Birkenau, wait to be taken to the gas chambers.

Courtesy of United States Holocaust Memorial Museum Photograph Archives,
Photograph Number: 77312

A row of ovens in one of the crematoria at Auschwitz.

Courtesy of United States Holocaust Memorial Museum Photograph Archives
Photograph Number: 19444

Basha's Displaced Person's identification Card.

Courtesy of Renee Harper.

Dora and Basha after liberation, 1945.

Courtesy of Evelyn Kaplan.

Group Photo at Feldafing, 1948. Basha is in the Front Row, Second from Right.

Courtesy of Evelyn Kaplan.

Photograph of Basha taken at Feldafing by a woman DP who was studying photography.

Courtesy of Evelyn Kaplan and Renee Harper.

Basha enjoying post-war freedom.

Courtesy of Evelyn Kaplan.

Bess with daughter Evelyn Kaplan.

Courtesy of Evelyn Kaplan.

Bess and Samuel had a successful business and an active social life.

Courtesy of Evelyn Kaplan.

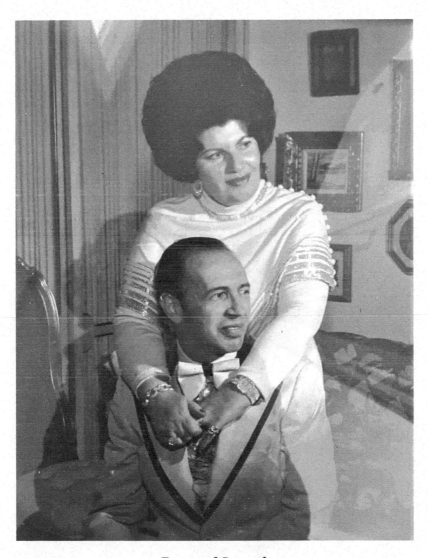

Bess and Samuel.
Courtesy of Evelyn Kaplan.

CHAPTER 7

The Crematorium

The *Sonderkommando*

Basha was ordered to sit on the ground while the *Sonderkommando* (Special Command Unit) unloaded the dead from the truck with the red crosses on it and stacked them nearby. She immediately recognized the *Sonderkommandos* in their black-and-gray-striped uniforms and caps. She had seen them many times before. The *Sonderkommando* consisted of male, primarily Jewish inmates who were ordered to take their fellow prisoners, both dead and alive, to the crematoria. In exchange for this grim task, they were allowed to live—at least for a while longer. They also had slightly better accommodations, separated from the other prisoners so they could not tell them what was going on, better food, and a ration of cigarettes. For those so inclined, they could also steal the belongings of incoming prisoners and trade the items to the *SS* for things useful to them. Even though they had no choice in accepting the position—other than immediate execution—for many the perquisites only increased their feelings of guilt. But the job was only temporary. Regardless of their physical or emotional willingness to work, most *Sonderkommandos* were sent to the gas chambers after a few months of labor and replaced with new arrivals. They knew too much about the systematic murder, and death was the only way the *SS* could ensure their silence. [131]

The Birkenau Death Factory

The first time Basha came to Auschwitz II–Birkenau in February 1943, she marched in on the main road through the gate on the southeast side of the camp. To her left were four large barracks for women. The rooms in the corner of the women's barrack next to the gate were reserved for Mengele's medical experiments. On the right side of the road were two large barracks that housed a smaller number of women, a family camp, men's barracks, and a section of barracks for Gypsies. A medical barrack was at the far west side of the building. A rail line ran between the south and north barracks compounds alongside the road, and there was a long platform on which new prisoners disembarked the transports. The crematoria were on the west side of the barracks compounds. The prisoners would be sent to the ovens, but first to the gas chambers, where they would be killed with the chemical Zyklon-B. Basha knew how it all worked. When she was previously assigned to Birkenau, she had been close enough to watch. In fact, there had been no way for her to escape it.

"When I was in Birkenau before, our barrack was not too far from the crematorium. And we heard the cries and the shots through the night, and people screaming. So loud. The sky was so red from the flames of the crematorium. [132]

"And once we were standing there, me and my girlfriend . . . and we saw a whole bridal party. The bride and groom and all the guests. They [the SS had] *surrounded them when they had this wedding, and they brought them all—the bride and the groom— to the crematorium. I was standing* [there] *because it was right there, our barrack was right there. I was standing not too far from the wires so I knew where I was, and those people that came from the other side, from the free world, they couldn't believe it. Who could believe that people would take innocent people and*

kill them just for no reason at all? Babies. Old people, young people, rich people, poor people, very well-dressed-up people. Some from France came all dressed up beautifully. They all went. Who could believe that they would do something like this?"[133]

When Basha had overheard her mother sharing stories with her Zionist friends in their home, she could not believe what she heard. They had to be distortions, she had thought. But what she was witnessing now was likely far worse than anything Chava had heard and repeated back in Pruzhany. All disbelief was dispelled. The stories played out in front of her, and worse, she knew it would only be a matter of time before the *Sonderkommando* loaded her into an oven. On the other side of the wire, the *Sonderkommandos*, forced into the soul-crushing job, were also horrified. Some fought back.

The *Sonderkommando* Uprising

In 1944, a group of *Sonderkommandos* formed a resistance movement within the camp, enlisting aid and support from inside and outside of the unit. Most of the concentration camps were set up to have a great deal of self-sufficiency. Maintenance was done by the prisoners, and that meant prisoners had access to tools. Stolen tools could be used to create, or become, weapons. At Birkenau the resistance movement had a special and very important asset. Many of the female prisoners were assigned to a *kommando* working at the Weichsel-Union-Metallwerke, a munitions plant that manufactured artillery fuses. They had access to gunpowder, which they wrapped in cloth or paper and smuggled out of the factory in small quantities, right under the noses of their captors. The task took painstaking care and extraordinary courage. The penalty for being caught would be immediate execution. [134]

Although accounts of the uprising vary, likely due to the chaos and small number of survivors, the execution of the revolt began, perhaps somewhat prematurely, on October 7, 1944. A group of about three hundred Greek and Hungarian Jewish *Sonderkommandos* were told they were going to be transferred to a nearby town to clear away rubble. In the world of the concentration camp *Sonderkommando,* the word "transferred" was usually a euphemism for "executed." Fearing that their time had run out and they were about to be killed, the *Sonderkommandos* attacked their guards with fists, hammers, and stones, killing three of them, and set Crematorium IV on fire with oil-soaked rags they had accumulated. At Crematorium II, the *Sonderkommandos* heard the commotion and believed the uprising had started. One of them calmly, according to witnesses, approached an SS officer and struck him with a hammer. The rest of the unit leaped into action, catching their *Oberkapo* (supervising *kapo*) and throwing him into the crematorium oven. Alive. The revolt spread to the *Sonderkommandos* at the other crematoria, who quickly retrieved their hidden weapons, tools, and explosives and joined the fight. Unfortunately, the insurrection did not become the mass revolt that had been planned. Nevertheless, a group used the chaos to cut the perimeter fence with stolen wire cutters and make a run for freedom. They made their way to the town of Rajsko where they hid in a granary. [135]

Basha was present during the revolt but did not participate. Her testimonies state that she was not aware of the planning of a revolt, much less who and what was involved. She was as surprised as the *SS,* and when the uprising ended, she pieced together enough information to have a vague understanding of what had transpired.

"The girls that worked in the ammunition factory gave somehow

the man from the men's camp ammunition, and somehow this
ammunition got to this Sonderkommando *whose men helped in*
the crematorium. They made an explosion in the crematorium,
a few of them. [Then] *they ran out and started* [to yell]: *'Run,*
everybody.' They took the Germans and pushed them in a hole. It
was an uprising . . . all this happened in all the four crematoria
at once, and a few of them exploded. And somehow, they cut the
[communications] *wires, but the Germans started an alarm and*
there was so much shooting, and I don't think anybody survived
[of] *those people. They killed them all."* [136]

The results of the revolt were dismal. The SS guards recovered
from their shock and counterattacked with automatic weapons,
killing many. They discovered the escapees in the Rajsko
granary and set it on fire. Many of the women who had helped
by smuggling explosives were uncovered and executed. SS
injuries were plentiful, but only three were killed versus 451 dead
Sonderkommandos. Although the revolt was a failure, there was
one positive outcome:

"Then the crematoria, one of them or two of them, didn't function.
So, they stopped a little bit the burning then, because two of them
didn't work." [137]

The damage to the crematoria, and subsequent decrease in
executions, brought hope that Allied air intervention would end,
or at least slow down, the continuing genocide.

"That's why we prayed. That finally the Russians or American
airplanes would come and bombard those crematoria, to stall
those shipments of thousands of people, to stop the burning.
Had they bombed the crematoria at that time, I'm positive that
it would have been stopped and so many people, so many more
people, would have survived and so many lives would have been
saved." [138]

Basha and her fellow prisoners knew German trains were prime targets for Allied aircraft, but neither the trains to Auschwitz nor the crematoria buildings were ever attacked. They could not understand why.

". . . and this is what we can't believe: if they don't know what's happening to us, that they're shipping innocent people, civilians, and mothers, and children, and old people . . . if those planes don't know those are civilian people, they probably think that [they are] military trains coming constantly. But why don't they bombard them? They were after the German trains . . . they usually bombed the German trains, but they didn't bombard them, so they knew . . . they knew about Auschwitz, but nothing happened. They just let us bleed to death, that's all." [139]

The trains continued to run. The ovens continued to burn. The prayers continued to be unanswered.

Only about one hundred of the estimated two thousand Auschwitz *Sonderkommandos* survived the war, but the stigma of the job stayed with them forever. Some Jewish camp survivors understood that the *Sonderkommandos* had little or no choice in their assignment, other than immediate execution, and viewed them as a different kind of victim. Others viewed them as Nazi collaborators and ostracized them. Between their personal guilt and public shaming, they never truly escaped their wartime nightmare. Whatever Basha's personal feelings may have been about the *Sonderkommando,* during or after the war, she did not express them in her testimonies.

On the day she stepped from the truck with the red crosses into the Birkenau crematorium courtyard, she likely was not thinking about the *Sonderkommando* at all, other than recognizing their uniforms and knowing what their presence meant for her. She knew they would be taking the other victims in the truck, those that were already dead, directly to the ovens. She did not know how long it would take them to get to her, but she knew they would eventually. She sat in pain and contemplated her imminent death.

Maybe it came as a surprise to her and maybe it did not, but Basha was far from the only living person forced to sit on the ground and wait. Squinting her eyes to adjust to the light, she could see that the crematorium courtyard was filled with prisoners of all ages who had just arrived on the transports and were terrified, many having absolutely no idea what was happening. Basha saw young mothers breastfeeding their babies, and heard elderly people expressing hopes and prayers that they were merely being relocated. That was exactly the way the *SS* wanted it. The less the victims knew, the more smoothly the executions would go. After all, a multitude of prisoners were in the courtyard and relatively few guards. The last thing the *SS* needed was mass panic that sent prisoners running in all directions. The *SS* machine guns would quickly cut them down, but the whole process would be messy and an affront to the Nazi sense of order.

The prisoners were assembled in something intended to be a straight line, but it twisted, turned, and bulged in places where families gathered. As victims passed from life to death through the crematorium, Basha's group was commanded to stand, move forward, and then sit again. The line was moving forward, but it was not getting shorter. New arrivals continued to take their place at the end, fearfully asking the same questions as those who arrived before them.

While they waited, the selection process continued at Auschwitz I in the same manner as when Basha and her family first set foot off their transport train. Men and older boys were forced into one column, and women and children into another.

They underwent a cursory visual inspection by functionaries and doctors to quickly weed out prisoners who had no potential for hard labor. Children under the age of sixteen—unless they appeared particularly healthy and strong—and the elderly were immediately selected for death. Those who appeared to be borderline cases were questioned by the medical team, who asked their age and occupation. If they were deemed useful, they lived. If not, they became part of the selection. *SS* guards took those chosen for labor to the induction center where they received instructions, were tattooed, and taken to their barrack. Those selected for death were marched to Birkenau, or driven by truck if they were incapable of walking. The *SS* guards told them they were being admitted to the camp, but first had to bathe and be disinfected.

The victims disrobed at the crematorium and were herded into the gas chamber, believing it was a shower. They were locked in and the Zyklon-B gas was dropped in from above. The last minutes of their lives were a terror-filled realization of the truth. After they were all dead, the *Sonderkommandos* shaved their heads—the hair, an industrial commodity, would be weaved into fabric—and removed all gold dental work. Stripped of their useful components, the bodies were moved to the crematorium. Then the process began again. [140]

Basha did not state in her testimonies what she was thinking as she sat in the crematorium line. Maybe she was too physically and emotionally exhausted to think, or maybe she chose not to record, and mentally relive, her thoughts later. What she did record was the experience of the new arrivals continually probing her for information.

"So, I was sitting there and there were an awful lot of people, thousands of thousands, sitting like this on the ground, waiting

for the alarm to go into the crematorium. And there were people that they just brought [in on] the transports from different countries, and they were in [civilian] clothing. They didn't come from the camp or anything.

"*They didn't know where they were. They saw me, and they saw that I looked different, that my [hair] was shaved off. I didn't have no hair. The way I looked, they knew that I am coming like from a different place, a different world. And they thought maybe I knew something, and they all started to ask me questions. And mothers were standing and giving pieces of bread to their children and begging me, 'Tell us that they'll let us live, tell us, assure us, if we are going to live.' And I just could not move my mouth. I just lost my voice. I just sat there and couldn't tell them the truth, and I couldn't deny. I couldn't tell them a lie. I was just sitting and waiting for what they'll do with us [in] the next couple of minutes. And there were thousands of Jews, thousands and thousands, waiting . . .*"[141]

The assembly line of death moved on. Gas, cremate, clean up, repeat. Basha's group eventually moved from the courtyard into the crematorium building. The SS guards continued to create the illusion that the crematorium was a hygiene facility by passing out bars of soap and towels. The frightened prisoners continued to ply Basha with questions.

"*I was the only one that looked the way I looked. They all came from the free world, they looked still like human beings, and they saw me the way I was, and they thought that I am from a camp and maybe I could tell them something what's going to happen to them. Like I said, I just didn't know what to say. Mothers were trying to comfort their children, and some of them were feeding them. And some of them were talking and saying that really, they're taking us to give us a bath, and if they wanted to kill us, they would kill us another time. While they were talking, they were moving closer, and closer, and closer to those open doors."* [142]

A guard eventually made his way to Basha with the soap and towel. He paused, looked at her battered body, and asked a question.

"And there came down a Nazi, and he said, from where do I come from? And I told him from Budy. He said, 'We don't have no room. First, we have to get rid of this.' [Indicating the room of Jews.] *He didn't want that the people should ask me questions, because he saw that they were talking to me. They were afraid that I might say . . . the whole idea with them was* [that] *. . . the people shouldn't know, because there were incidents when some people grabbed the Nazis' guns and they were killing them. When they* [prisoners] *really smelled the burning flesh, they knew where they were going. But they wanted to avoid those incidents."* [143]

Basha was what we might today call a public relations problem. The story of her abuse was written all over her body with blood. There was nothing about her presence that would lead the other prisoners to expect lenient care from their captors, and the guard needed to get her away from them before she caused panic. The logical solution to the problem would be to get rid of her by taking her to the crematorium immediately, but surprisingly, he had a different idea.

"You go to Birkenau. Your next [in line to die] *will come some other time."*

The guards pulled her out of the crematorium line and pushed her out the door. Again, the Nazis had failed to kill her, but that did not mean they would stop trying.

Historical Perspective
on Chapter 7

The Gas Chambers

The first gas chamber and crematorium were located at Auschwitz I and were capable of gassing 340 people every twenty-four hours with Zyklon-B gas. Originally developed for pest control, Zyklon-B is based on hydrogen cyanide and can cause death in as little as two minutes. The *SS* found that the previous methods of prisoner execution—shooting and carbon monoxide poisoning—caused stress in some of the troops, particularly when the victims were women and children. Using Zyklon-B in the gas chambers improved troop morale, and since the *Sonderkommando* took the victims into the crematoria and removed their bodies later, guards had an emotional buffer from the dirtiest part of the process. Troop morale and killing efficiency were the foundations of the Zyklon-B program. As usual, the only consideration for the victims was to kill as many as possible as quickly as possible.

As the extermination policy against the Jews became more aggressive and victims arrived from throughout Nazi held territory, the number of executions increased dramatically, stressing the capacity of the body disposal facilities. Gas chambers and crematoria were added to the Birkenau camp, and Crematorium I was converted to storage.

Four crematoria were eventually constructed at Birkenau. Two capable of incinerating 1,440 bodies per day, and the other two 768 bodies per day. [144] The *Sonderkommando* had plenty of work. Crematorium II was adjacent to Basha's former barrack on the west side. There had been no way for her to escape the sounds of the constant horror that went on all day and night on the other side of the barrack wall.

Notes

131. "Sonderkommandos," *Holocaust Encyclopedia,* United States Holocaust Memorial Museum, September 17, 2020, http://encyclopedia. ushmm.org/content/en/article/sonderkommandos.

132. Bess Freilich interview by Marc Seligman, 22.

133. Ibid, 23.

134. "The Great Sonderkommando Revolt of 1944," Sky History, accessed November 3, 2021, https://www.history.co.uk/article/the-great-sonderkommando-revolt-of-1944.

135. "Auschwitz-Birkenau: The Revolt at Auschwitz-Birkenau" Jewish Virtual Library, accessed November 4, 2021, https://www. jewishvirtuallibrary.org/the-revolt-at-auschwitz-birkenau.

136. Bess Freilich interview by Josey G. Fisher, 3-2-38.

137. Ibid.

138. Ibid.

139. Ibid.

140. "The Extermination Procedure in the Gas Chambers," Auschwitz-Birkenau Memorial and Museum, accessed November 4, 2021, https://www.auschwitz.org/en/history/auschwitz-and-shoah/the-extermination-procedure-in-the-gas-chambers/.

141. Bess Freilich interview by Josey G. Fisher, 3-1-30.

142. Ibid, 3-1-31.

143. Bess Freilich interview by Marc Seligman, 23.

144. "Auschwitz-Birkenau: Crematoria and Gas Chambers," Jewish Virtual Library, accessed November 4, 2021, http://jewishvirtuallibrary. org/crematoria-and-gas-chambers-at-auschwitz-birkenau.

CHAPTER 8

Something Like
Medical Care

Basha painfully stumbled back out into the sunshine where the truck with the red crosses on it was waiting. The guards opened the rear doors and roughly pushed her onto the floor inside, amid the olives, for the short drive to Birkenau. Rather than the prisoner barracks, the truck delivered her to a facility for convalescing prisoners.

Not surprisingly, prisoner healthcare in the concentration camps was not at the forefront of the minds of the *SS*. Considering everything else that was going on, one could be surprised that any healthcare was provided at all. In Basha's case, the crude medical care offered was far superior to the other option, death, but prisoners took substantial risk when reporting sick. Anyone attempting to dodge their labor detail by feigning illness might find themselves selected for execution by poison.[145] Those who were truly ill and had no choice but to seek medical care had to gamble that they would receive attention rather than execution. The arbitrary selection process was based on the medical officer's assessment of the prisoner's potential value for future labor. Frequently, the officer's personal feelings about the prisoner's nationality, religion, sexuality, or social habits also played a role.

In camps and sub-camps that were large enough to have medical facilities, there was generally an outpatient/convalescent clinic, along with a hospital barrack for longer-term patients. To report sick, prisoners had to first get permission to leave their labor detail or barrack. If permission was granted, the prisoners were subjected to a strict process for getting care. At Auschwitz, prisoners reported to the outpatient facility at night where they received a cursory examination by a prisoner medical provider— hopefully one who had been a prewar doctor, or who at least had adequate training in basic healthcare. Those who were obviously injured or very ill were admitted to a reception ward. No effort was made to separate those with communicable diseases from the others; they were parked for the night at the first convenient bed. Prisoners who were less ill were granted permission to return the next day. [146]

The following morning, the prisoners in the reception hall were ordered out of their beds and into the outpatient lobby, where they were joined by the prisoners who had been sent back to their barracks the previous night. They were organized by nationality rather than medical condition, and told to strip naked, including shoes, and stand waiting on the stone floor until an *SS* medical officer arrived. There was a notorious lack of urgency on the part of the *SS* doctors. They showed up at the clinic when they got around to it. When the doctor arrived, he individually called the prisoners before him, who presented the sick card they had been issued the previous night. After a brief, superficial examination, the medical officer would indicate whether they were to step to the left or the right. On one side, the prisoners were admitted to the medical facility. On the other, they were admitted to the crematorium. [147]

The concentration camps generally had only one *SS* medical officer, but at times in some of the bigger camps, there were as many as three. Frequently, there were several *SS* noncommissioned officers working in the medical wards. The prisoners themselves carried out the bulk of the medical work. By the end of the war, there were approximately seventy medical doctors who had been imprisoned in the concentration camps, primarily for being Jewish, as well as hundreds of nurses.[148] Postwar testimonies indicate that the prisoner medical staffs were generally caring and compassionate toward the prisoners and did their best to provide the best health care possible with the limited resources available. Some of the imprisoned doctors went to extraordinary lengths to save lives, not only of the sick, but also of political or other vulnerable prisoners. At risk healthy prisoners were sometimes put on the sick list to spare them from the hands of SS guards, who were intent on brutalizing or killing them. Prisoner doctors would occasionally assign and record the name of a living prisoner to the body of one who had died so they could continue to live using the dead prisoner's name. Not infrequently, prisoner doctors took advantage of the disinterest of the SS medical teams by hiding prisoners in the tuberculosis ward of the hospital where the SS medical staff rarely went. Some prisoners lived there for months, and even years.[149]

In another classic example of irony, the SS medical teams were often better at taking lives than saving them. In addition to their nonchalant attitude about who would be admitted for healthcare and who would be sent to die, the medical teams themselves frequently became involved in the execution process. The hospitals were chronically short of beds and drugs, so some prisoners who were relatively healthy found themselves receiving poison instead of medicine. Overpopulation of inmates outside the camp hospital could also be a problem. At times when the prisoners were not dying quickly enough to satisfy the camp management, medical teams were called in to help remedy the problem. At evening roll call, a guard or *kapo* would demand that the prisoners roll up their trouser legs. A medical noncom would walk down the ranks of prisoners, looking for anyone with swollen ankles. They would be declared medical patients and marched to the hospital, specifically, to the morgue. There they were injected in the heart with 10 mL of carbolic acid, immediately, and neatly, ending their lives. [150]

Despite her appalling injuries and appearance, Basha slipped through the random net of death selection at Birkenau and was admitted to the convalescent clinic.

"So, I [lay] there in the hospital. It wasn't actually a hospital— the camp for the real sick—the barrack for the real sick." [151]

Being in the convalescent clinic was certainly better than being in a labor barrack, but not necessarily by much. Any resemblance between a concentration camp medical facility and a modern hospital was slight, and almost coincidental. Nevertheless, being in the convalescent clinic freed Basha from assignment to a work *kommando,* and her bunk, inferior as it was, allowed her to sleep and regain her strength. Still, she could not completely escape the lurking *kapos.*

". . . there were Germans too, women that beat us and hit us, and I remember just lying there, and I didn't know what happened to me. I was lying on this so-called bunk—it wasn't even a bunk—and I didn't . . . just in complete confusion . . . I woke up and probably was in a coma, or whatever, and I asked another girl which was lying near me, 'Oh,' I said, 'do they give you so much bread now in Birkenau?' So, she says 'No, so many days they gave you the piece of bread and you were just completely [unconscious], and that's how it accumulated.' This girl, she saved me. Fourteen pieces of the bread that they gave to us, and she saved them for me. Like I was talking to the girl and she was talking to me, and a minute later I see something is lying on me, and it's so heavy, and I turned around and she was cold already. Yes, she spoke to me and she died already." [152]

Basha drifted in and out of consciousness. When she was awake, she found herself in the care of an older Jewish woman who was very concerned about her. It would be years before she learned it, but the older Jewish woman, Lola, was the mother of Kitty Hart, a friend from the camp, who would later write the book, *Return to Auschwitz*, which would become the basis for the documentary film, *Kitty: Return to Auschwitz*. [153] Lola was not only devoted to Basha's health, but to keeping her safe from the *SS*.

"I remember her [Kitty's] *mother because she worked for the hospital, and I remember I saw* [her] *picture* [in the book and film], *and I remember her mother because her mother was old, and very few older women were there. And while I was lying there, her mother used to come and tell me, 'Get up, get up, because you passed already a few selections, and the next one you might not pass and they'll take you to the crematorium. Get up.' I remember her mother's hair started to grow out. She had dark hair. She stands like before my eyes; she had white skin, and I see her before my eyes. It didn't click on me right away, but afterwards I saw a picture of her mother exactly. I remember she used to come and tell me. She said, 'Please don't push your luck. You go out* [back to the labor camp]. *Here they'll take you away, and over there maybe you'll have a better chance. Get out of here,' she told me all the time."* [154]

Regaining sufficient strength to return to a labor *kommando* was not the only problem that Basha faced. The convalescent clinic produced almost as much disease as it cured. Malnutrition and a lack of medications continually plagued the prisoner medical facilities. That, compounded by incredibly poor sanitation, not only slowed the healing process but presented a very real and serious risk of subjecting patients to an additional variety of diseases. Access to sufficient clean water was a problem in many of the camps, leading to issues with personal hygiene and the inability to wash uniforms.

Prisoner turnover in the camps was continual, and the new arrivals were generally unclean and infested with vermin. Disinfestation with chemicals was rigorously pursued in most camps, and some, such as Buchenwald, maintained sanitation officers who inspected the barracks for cleanliness, or at least infestation, and even provided some immunizations for prisoners. In other camps, the medical officers were content to contain the infestation and contagion to the prisoner areas while working diligently to prevent outbreaks of disease from infecting *SS* troops. Typhoid fever and typhus ran rampant along with a variety of other diseases. Major outbreaks of streptococci plagued most camps, causing skin and eye afflictions, and cellulitis. Prisoners who had been in the camps for a while understood that a moderate illness could become a death sentence in the camp medical facilities, but many newcomers naively sought medical attention, frequently to their demise. Unless a prisoner had a good relationship with the hospital *kapos* who wielded enormous power—frequently the power of life or death—a prisoner might be better off to continue working and take their chances of dying outside the hospital rather than in it. [155]

Basha slowly began to regain her health and became more aware of her environment. Lying in her bunk one day, she saw a sight that initially confused her.

". . . I was just lying there and looking at the ceiling [over] this bunk, and there wasn't a centimeter of wood that wasn't filled with lice. The whole thing was moving, moving, moving, moving, one on top of the other, and then I started to come to myself and I noticed that I had here, on my breast, a big hole, and it was completely filled up to the level, my breast, with lice. They came and they went, and they went out and they came back." [156]

The wound in Basha's breast, literally a hole, was the result of the beating she had received when she had been caught with the blanket under her dress. Although significant time had passed since the beating, her malnourished body was slow to heal.

"When I came back to Birkenau, all these wounds, they filled up with lice. The lice just laid in heaven there. They came and they left whenever they wanted. I remember a sweater they gave me, a little sweater, and it was itching me terribly, and I threw the sweater down, and the sweater was picking itself up from the floor, up and down . . . the lice were picking the sweater up; it was moving like it was alive. It was moving, actually, because [it] *was the lice picking the sweater up. It was unbelievable.* [157]

"They [the lice] *go in and fill the whole hole, and then they came out. Everything was moving. They were all colors, some thick. On everything, you couldn't see nothing but lice."* [158]

The result of the constant lice infestation was predictable.

"In the hospital I was very, very sick. I had typhus. And I was incoherent, I was . . . I didn't know where I was. I was unconscious most of the time . . . I was lying near the girls. Here I'm talking to them, and they are cold already. They're lying near me on the bed . . . gals, sixteen and seventeen years old. They're blue already, and they had died. Of dysentery. Other people were vomiting blood and . . . and typhus. Everybody was sick with typhus. Because of the lice and the congestion." [159]

Whether or not the *SS* had any concerns about the impact of the lice on the prisoners is debatable, but they clearly understood the danger they posed for their troops. In December 1944, they conducted an *entlausung* (delousing) of the camp's barracks. Since the vermin had infested even the most minute cracks in the walls and floors, they chose to explode chemical bombs in the buildings, creating a disinfectant fog that penetrated everything. The inmates also had to be deloused—another painful experience for them. They were stripped of all their clothing, which was placed in large, boiling cauldrons of water. After what they deemed was sufficient time to kill the lice, the troops pulled the clothing from the boiling water and tossed it on the roofs of the barracks where it froze. Throughout this process, the inmates stood outside, naked, among four and five-foot drifts of snow for an entire day. They finally were allowed to retrieve their frozen garments, each of which bore the inmate's number. When the prisoners attempted to manipulate the frozen clothing to finish drying and wear it, many of the frail garments fell apart, leaving the owner with a jacket missing a sleeve, or pants missing a leg. The *SS* showed little concern, although they did find sufficient clothing to cover those who were left with virtually nothing to wear. [160]

In addition to the lice, lack of medication, lack of hygiene, and a general lack of care, there was a foreboding and uncontrollable specter in the clinic. Daily, Dr. Mengele strode through the ward looking for new victims for his experiments, or to put patients to death for no other reason than that he could.

"Every day, Mengele came and picked as many as he wanted, and he burned them, every day. I passed through three selections already." [161]

Mengele's prisoner selections could be arbitrary, but his process was also systematic. As he and his men prowled through the medical facility looking for victims for the ovens, a truck would back up against one of the building doors. The rear doors of the truck opened before it backed up, so when it touched the building there was no opportunity for anyone to escape around it. Mengele's men forced their victims into the trucks, closed the doors, and took them immediately to the crematorium. Basha repeatedly escaped from the selection, sometimes through her own ingenuity, and sometimes with help.

"They told me there was a Jewish nurse down at the hospital [162] ... [She] told me that I should go down to the bottom of the beds, and she covered me up with the blankets. And they didn't notice me. I went through a few selections, and they took those people, [other prisoners] *cleaned up* [removed everyone from] *the whole hospital."* [163]

Aside from occasional help and her strong determination to live, forged by her promise to her mother, some of Basha's ability to dodge death can be attributed to nothing more than luck. She had pulled away from Mengele's men once through her determination and strength. Now her strength was nearly depleted, and determination alone could not save her. Her survival became a matter of chance.

"They always knew how many they wanted, and [when this number] *was filled, that's when they stopped. It was just my luck that I wasn't in that* [number]. *And the same thing in the crematorium. They had so many people there they couldn't burn fast enough, and that was my luck, that they brought back. If I didn't have to wait, if there weren't so many people, they would have put me in there right away."* [164]

As her fever, and her mind, slowly cleared, Basha did not need Lola's urgent warnings to understand she was in dire danger. However, she had been in the clinic for weeks, mostly bedbound. Combined with a lack of nutrition, her muscles had severely atrophied.

"One day I knew that I must leave or else I would die, that he [Mengele] *will take me away, so I learned how to walk.*

Actually, I couldn't see how a person could stand up on his two feet and move his feet forward. I just could not understand that something like this could happen. I mean, where [can] *a person get the strength and stand up? I just couldn't stand up."* [165]

Basha's determination kicked in again. It was blatantly clear to her that she had already had more than her share of luck, and if she wanted to live, she must push herself physically and mentally. Slowly, she began to walk around the clinic.

"I finally learned how to walk [by holding onto things] *and stop crawling.* [I] *started walking, and while I was trying to make my everyday walk, which was a few steps, I heard someone on top of the bunk crying, 'Aren't you the girl from Pruzhany?' And I said yes."* [166]

Basha looked at the girl questioningly. With their shorn heads and emaciated, battered bodies, it was difficult to recognize people they had known from the past, but in a couple of seconds Basha realized the girl was Dora Golubowicz. Dora was also very sick, with a hole in her leg that had rotting flesh around it. Despite their terrible condition and circumstances, it was a moment of happiness that became the foundation of a lifelong friendship. Only another prisoner could fully understand what they had been through, and that created a special bond. They did not have to talk about it; their shared experience existed on a level few could understand.

Knowing time was working against her, Basha continued to push herself physically.

"After about six weeks, or two months, exactly I...don't remember, something like [that], *I knew I had to walk out the hospital* [or] *I wouldn't last too much longer, so I went out, and they took me to a different barrack, and they put me in a kommando . . ."* [167]

Basha walked out of the clinic under her own power. Dora soon would follow. They had escaped death once again, but their problems were not over. Far from it.

Notes

145. Kogan, 144.

146. Ibid, 140.

147. Ibid, 144.

148. Ibid, 142

149. Ibid, 145.

150. Ibid, 143.

151. Bess Freilich interview by Josey G. Fisher, 3-1-31.

152. Ibid, 3-1-31.

153. Kitty Hart, *Return to Auschwitz: The Remarkable Story of a Girl who Survived the Holocaust* (New York: Atheneum, 1982).

154. Bess Freilich interview by Josey G. Fisher, 3-1-31.

155. Kogan, 136-38.

156. Bess Freilich interview by Josey G. Fisher, 3-1-32.

157. Ibid.

158. Bess Freilich interview by Marc Seligman, 24.

159. Ibid, 25.

160. Dora Freilich, interview by Helen Grossman, 3-1-35.

161. Bess Freilich interview by Josey G. Fisher, 3-1-32.

162. Bess Freilich interview by Marc Seligman, 24.

163. Ibid.

164. Bess Freilich interview by Josey G. Fisher, 3-1-33.

165. Ibid, 3-1-32.

166. Ibid, 3-1-33.

167. Ibid, 3-1-34.

CHAPTER 9

Work or Die

Basha was again sent to Auschwitz-Birkenau. She had gone "out of the frying pan and into the fire" and back more than once, when most prisoners just went into the fire. Literally.

Originally created as a means of dealing with opponents of Nazism, the KL system had grown dramatically, along with its scope. Had it remained only a means of dealing with Hitler's political enemies, Basha would have been safe. Any political opinions she may have had about Germany were irrelevant. As a teenage Polish girl, she was certainly not a likely candidate to participate in the overthrow of the Third Reich. However, the Nazi philosophy branded all Jews as enemies of the state; in fact, as enemies of the world. Basha's life, and the lives of hundreds of thousands of other Jews, were meaningless to the Nazis unless they could be productive for Germany. Moving from job to job and camp to camp was all that kept Basha alive.

Work to Live or Worked to Death

After all Basha had been through, being alive was a remarkable achievement. Staying that way, however, would remain a difficult, often seemingly impossible, challenge. Basha was assigned to a new barrack and labor *kommando,* and knew full well that if she did not work, she would not live. The policy of "no useless mouths" applied to everyone. The chances of the *kapos* giving a prisoner a day or two to recover their health before returning to work were slim. If they were not forcing prisoners to work, they were not doing their jobs, and if they were not doing their jobs, they were useless mouths. They knew how that would end.

The labor policy was simple: work or die. Every morning, Basha would be required to march with her *kommando* to the work site where they would pick weeds for a full day, and then march back. This would be her first new problem to overcome. She could barely walk. Again, strangers provided life-saving assistance.

". . . I remember two German women, and they were very nice. They were from Germany, and they carried me . . . in the basket. Two girls that carried the baskets in this kommando *and they put me in the basket going to work, and somehow, the German kapo let them do it. I don't know, it was sheer luck, and that's how they carried me back and forth . . ."* [168]

Apparently, the *kapo* did not care how she got to the work site as long as she could work when she got there.

Basha's assignment to weed-pulling had nothing to do with camp neatness. The weeds they pulled were carried in the baskets to the camp kitchen and cooked as food for the prisoners. Basha had just enough strength to pull the weeds and thereby escaped a beating, or worse, from the *kapos*. As her *kommando* worked its way across their assigned area, Basha overheard bits and pieces of a conversation between two of the women guards watching over them. She did not hear enough of it to understand what they were discussing, but there was something in the tone of their voices and their body language that gave her a strong feeling that the conversation was more than just idle gossip. She eventually found out.

"I heard the German officer, that was an SS *woman, and the German* kapo *as they were talking very quietly between them, and I overheard it, and I was thinking to myself, what is all this here, the talk between them? Soon I found out . . . they took us,*

[to the place the *SS* woman and *kapo* were discussing]. *We were not too far from there. and they were very anxious to see it for themselves. What I saw before my eyes I will never forget it: there were mountains and mountains of human ashes. That was the remains of most of the European Jews that lay there. The cemetery of ashes, just mountains and mountains of it. It's like I found myself in the desert with these mountains of it. They used to burn them, and that's where they kept the ashes, and they were talking, the* kapo *and the German Nazi woman, and they joked about it, and they were laughing, but we knew what it was and, in my heart, I felt that those were the remains of my brothers and my mother. Then I knew that there was no hope. That nobody was alive, that I'm left all by myself in this world, and in order to survive, to fulfill my mother's wish actually, I had to take care of myself and try to live like this alone."* [169]

Circumstances added insult to injury:

"Mountains and mountains of ashes. They threw it in the fields to make their crop grow better." [170]

With the kind help of the two German women, Basha continued to recover and slowly regained her strength. She was soon able to walk without assistance and, eventually, help carry the baskets.

Even with her improved health, Basha was plagued by one burning question. At this point, was life was still worth living?

Historical Perspective
on Chapter 9

Growth of the KL

Hitler and Himmler's concentration camp system had been in a growth cycle for a decade. The *SS* initially built the camps to house political opponents. Germany had a constitution that safeguarded the rights of the population, but it was relatively new. Germany was a monarchy through World War I, when the Weimar Republic replaced it from 1919 to 1933. Many citizens wanted a return to the monarchy and others were opposed to democracy. With this political schism, Hitler dismantled the German constitution with remarkable ease.[171] After that, if a Nazi policy was against German law, they solved the problem by eliminating the law. In the case of political prisoners and others that were perceived to be a threat to the Third Reich, or even just an annoyance, *Schutzhaft* (protective custody) [172] became a catchall law to incarcerate those known as anti-social malefactors. It was part of a package of laws initiated on February 28, 1933, which, for all practical purposes, dispensed with the civil liberties previously guaranteed by the German constitution.

Between forty thousand and fifty thousand political opponents were ensnared in the net of the Gestapo in the next two months. After receiving an aggressive lesson in political compliance, many were released, reducing the number in protective custody to roughly twenty-six thousand by the fall of that year. However, the criteria for imprisonment were eventually broadened to include those who would otherwise not be considered criminal or undesirable, such as Freemasons and pacifist Jehovah's Witnesses. The population of the camps increased by roughly thirty-five thousand in 1938, when the regime began imprisoning Jews. The situation for the Jews was not entirely hopeless at that point. The regime offered to release any Jewish prisoners who would agree to emigrate from Germany, providing they leave their wealth behind. For the politically perceptive, being alive and penniless was far superior to wealthy and dead. Unfortunately, the process was complicated by the fact that emigrating Jews needed to find a country that would accept them, which was not easy in a frequently anti-Semitic world. The picture was bleak for those who remained in the camps under *SS* control. Theodor Eicke made his position clear to his troops at Dachau when he stated, "pity for enemies of the state was unworthy of an SS man. There was no room for weaklings in his unit and they would do well to lock themselves in monasteries as soon as possible. He had a use only for hard, determined men who would carry out any order ruthlessly; they did not wear the death's-head badge for nothing." [173]

By the end of 1933 there were roughly fifty camps in Germany devoted to the "re-education" of German citizens who not only failed to welcome Nazism but had the courage—or questionable judgment—to speak against it publicly. Although the death camps had not yet been created, some prisoners were murdered anyway, generally at the whim of camp supervisors. For the rest, a brutal series of beatings was standard procedure and, if possible, a ransom was extorted from the prisoner's family. After the Blood Purge of June 1934, in which rogue elements of the *SA* were murdered by the *SS* on Hitler's orders, many felt that the concentration camps would be dismantled. *Reichsführer-SS*, Heinrich Himmler, staunchly opposed closing the camps. He had risen steadily in the Nazi hierarchy, and controlling the camps was a significant power platform which he was unwilling to relinquish. The argument he made to Hitler focused on the specter of terror the camps presented to anyone who considered opposing the Third Reich.

This argument was soundly grounded in humankind's instinct for self-preservation. Dissenters knew that under *Schutzhaft* the road to the camps was fast, horrifying, and increasingly more frequently, one-way.

Rather than diminish, the concentration camp system grew rapidly. Conquered territories became prime real estate for the construction of new camps and sub-camps, particularly in the east, where Hitler envisioned eliminating the indigenous *Untermenschen* (subhumans) and, seizing their property for the *Lebensraum,* he sought for his new Greater Germanic Reich that would first envelop Europe and then, perhaps, the entire world. On February 21, 1940, in conquered Poland, *SS Oberführer* Richard Glücks, head of the Concentration Camp Inspectorate, found a marshy plot of land in the vicinity of Kraków, Poland, and informed Himmler that he felt it would be a good site for a new "quarantine camp." This would become Auschwitz I, from which many sub-camps were eventually created. It was originally envisioned as a place of harsh treatment for political prisoners, but its role expanded later that year when German chemical giant IG Farben determined that the area was suitable for the construction of a new synthetic coal oil and rubber plant. Auschwitz became a source of slave labor for the facility.

Still later, as the Nazis stepped up their program of Jewish genocide, the first crematorium was built. At the war crimes trials in Nürnberg on April 15, 1946, Rudolf Höss, Commandant of Auschwitz from May 4, 1940 to May 8, 1944—during the period Basha was imprisoned there—testified that he had supervised the extermination of 2.5 million prisoners and allowed another half million to starve to death. He was later turned over to the Supreme National Tribunal in Poland, found guilty of war crimes, and sentenced to death. He was hanged on April 2, 1947. Fittingly, the gallows were constructed next to the crematorium at Auschwitz.

Despite the stirring music performed by the Women's Orchestra of Auschwitz—created by the notoriously cruel, but musically sensitive *SS-Lagerführerin,* Maria Mandl—arriving at the train station at Auschwitz was anything but a pleasant experience for the frightened prisoners. *SS* troops were abusive, but generally maintained the facade that the camp was for labor, or a step toward eventual resettlement. There was one notable exception. Auschwitz deputy camp commander, *SS-Hauptsturmführer* Karl Fritzsch, likely indulging in a bit of sadism for his own amusement, bluntly addressed the first 758 inmates of Auschwitz with his perverse version of a welcoming speech.

> *"You came here not to a sanatorium, but to a German concentration camp, from which there is no other way out but through the chimney. If someone doesn't like it, they can go straight to the* [electrical] *wires. If there are Jews in the transport, they have the right to live no longer than two weeks. If there are any priests, they may a month; the rest three months."* [174]

Fritzsch disappeared in 1945 during the Battle of Berlin and is assumed to have been killed while attempting to flee the Russians.

The Two German Women

There is a discrepancy between Basha's two testimonies regarding the nationality of the two women. In the Fisher interview (3-1-34) Basha states the women were German. In the Seligman interview (25) she states they were French. The author has chosen to use the Fisher transcript because it was conducted fifteen years prior to the Seligman interview, closer to the time of the actual event. There is now no way to be entirely certain which is correct.

One thing which is certain, however, is that at that point in time, the history of Auschwitz was likely of little interest to Basha. All that mattered was that she was back and still alive.

Notes

168. Ibid, 3-1-34.

169. Ibid.

170. Bess Freilich interview by Marc Seligman, 17.

171. "Why was Hitler Able to Dismantle the German Constitution so Easily," History Hit Podcast with Frank McDonough, accessed March 15, 2023, https://www.historyhit.com/why-was-hitler-able-to-dismantle-the-german-constitution-so-easily/.

172. "Protective Custody (Nazi German)," https://en.wikipedia.org/wiki/Protective_custody_(Nazi_Germany).

173. Höhne, 203.

174. "Karl Fritzsch," Wikipedia Foundation, last modified March 15, 2023, https://en.wikipedia.org/wiki/Karl_Fritzsch#cite_note-2

CHAPTER 10

The Will to Live

Everyone suffered in the camps. Everyone was malnourished. Everyone was beaten. Everyone was worked to exhaustion. Everyone lived in filth and was constantly subjected to vermin infestation and disease. Everyone. Yet some lived and some did not. The persistent will to live was, no doubt, a factor in survival, although one that would be difficult or impossible to quantify. How much will was enough, and where did it come from? Basha survived while many young girls, who appeared no worse off than she, did not. A few died even as she was talking to them. They were equally abused, but at some point, the others gave up. Like the girls who jumped into the well at Budy to escape the "show," they no longer had the will to live.

In her testimonies, Basha freely admitted that she felt like giving up many times during her imprisonment, but in the back of her mind there was always the memory of her mother and the promise she made to her. With all her heart, mind, and body she would live to tell the story. Maybe that was the difference. Perhaps she might have given up on herself, but she would never give up on her promise.

There was also another type of prisoner; those with a burning determination to fight back. As with the *Sonderkommandos* who revolted, they would fight for their freedom, or at the very least, just fight. Successful or not, they were an inspiration to the other prisoners and an aggravation to the *SS*. Basha vividly remembered one of these young women and the impact she had on the prison population.

"There was a girl that did escape. Her name was Katyah, and they brought her back. [Basha's memory conflicts with the documentation of this event. The correct name is Mala Zimetbaum.] *She was a* schreiber [writer/secretary] *they called her. The Germans used her to write down the numbers* [of those] *they wanted to send to the crematorium . . . then came the truck, and then they called the numbers and then they took the people. And she was the one that* [they] *used to write down the numbers, a lot of numbers, and she did it intentionally . . . she wrote them down wrong and those people didn't exist. That's how these people, that really the Germans told her to write* [down], *remained alive. And we knew what she was doing. And she escaped somehow. She had contact because she was like, you know, the Germans. She had a better job and she looked a little bit different than the rest of the girls, and she had contact with the men. And she knew a man* [non-Jewish political prisoner Edward Galiński], *and he helped her and somehow they escaped, but they brought them back. They found them in a little place, and from what I found out later, the Germans just walked up to her. She was supposed to meet that fellow in this place that she escaped with, and while she was sitting and waiting, the Germans approached her. They just picked up her sleeve and they noticed she was branded* [tattooed with her prisoner number], *and they took her out of the place and brought her back."* [175]

Mala was taken to the infamous Block 11, which was used exclusively for prisoner torture and executions. Adjacent was the Death Wall, also called the Black Wall, where thousands of prisoners were shot to death. Exactly what Mala was subjected to in Block 11 is not known, but typical treatment consisted of being locked in a small space in total darkness for days on end, or forced into standing cells. The standing cells were roughly one square yard of floor space, with a roughly two-square-inch breathing hole in the wall. Four prisoners would be crammed into each cell. [176] Mala's brief taste of freedom earned her unspeakable punishment.

". . . and they tortured her for weeks and weeks, they tortured her and then they finally brought her back to the camp, and the whole camp had to stand and watch it [as] they tried to hang her, and she screamed out, 'Long live freedom!' Those were her last words."

In the last seconds of her life, she spit in the face of the executioner and died on her own terms.

"She slashed . . . she had a razor, and she slashed her arm and she was bleeding, but she was still alive. They took her to the crematorium, and the whole camp had to stand and watch it . . . she was really a Jewish heroine. She was a beautiful person." [177]

Her companion in the escape, Edward Galiński, was later captured and executed.

Reunited

In the midst of all the misery, Basha had a bit of unexpected luck.

"And as I got better, I somehow got into a Schuhkommando, *and that was inside."* [178]

The job was to repair shoes, or dismantle them to recycle the leather. It seemed like an innocent enough task, but nothing in Auschwitz was entirely innocent. The used shoes had once belonged to Jewish prisoners, most of whom had been sent to the gas chambers.

The war caused a worldwide shortage of consumer goods. Even families outside the war zones had to learn to prepare meals by cooking with minimal amounts of meat, flour, and sugar; and gasoline rationing limited driving. Since most automobile factories had been converted to the production of military equipment, there were no new cars to buy anyway, gasoline or not. Existing stores of leather and rubber in Germany had been depleted by the production of military boots and leather accessories, leaving a sparse selection of shoes for citizens of the Reich. German wartime shoe production relied on the use of synthetic materials, which were generally considered inferior by German consumers. In the broader scope of things, inferior shoes may not sound like much of an inconvenience, but added to all the other inconveniences, it made for an unhappy population. The German government responded as best it could. One response was to turn to the concentration camps as a resource for military and consumer raw material.

Prisoners coming into the camps had to surrender their personal possessions, including their shoes. Those who were immediately sent to the crematorium would not need them. Those selected for labor were issued clogs, which were constructed by nailing a small leather loop onto a wooden sole. No consideration was given to comfort, but the clogs were certainly better than bare feet, particularly in the winter. The clacking sound of the wooden soles on concentration camp floors remained a persistent sensory memory for camp survivors.

The possessions of the Jews were confiscated immediately, alongside the railroad tracks when the prisoners exited the incoming transport trains. Jewish prisoners loaded the items onto trucks, which delivered the goods to an area of Auschwitz nicknamed, "*Kanada.*" [179] There, other Jewish prisoners sorted through the items, separating the useless from the useful and stacking like items together. *Kanada* became a prime area for looting by the *SS* and *kapos,* particularly jewelry or other valuables. The confiscated Jewish items became the property of the Reich and stealing them was a crime against the state. Some looters were caught and prosecuted, but other than the threat of punishment, there were few, if any, qualms about stealing the confiscated possessions. The prevailing attitude—the one promoted by the Nazi government—was that the Jews had stolen all of their wealth, so it was fair to steal it back. Many items that escaped theft were sent to Germany. In the case of shoes and leather goods, they remained in the camp for recycling.

"It was all the shoes that they took away from the people that they brought to Auschwitz, and we had to take them apart, and somehow, they recycled the leather and made German boots out of the leather. There were millions and millions of pairs of shoes, and we had to take them apart, and that was the work I was doing." [180]

As sad as the totality of the circumstances were, the *Schuhkommando* provided a job where Basha would work indoors, out of the elements, and free from the backbreaking labor she had previously endured. The job also came with a big, emotionally uplifting surprise.

Decades after the incident, while driving her mother home from an appointment, Evelyn and her mother were caught in a sudden snowstorm. The snow apparently took Basha's thoughts back to Auschwitz, and she told Evelyn a story with such emotion that Evelyn wrote it down when she got home. Evelyn recalls:

"One experience that she recounted to me happened after Roll Call. Roll Call occurred extremely early every morning, no matter what the weather, in bitter cold, wind, ice, snow, pouring rain, or unbearable heat. The Nazis kept meticulous records, and

every inmate had to be accounted for. If someone was missing or the count was incorrect in some way, the inmates were forced to stand for hours until the count was correct. If someone faltered, stepped out of line, or collapsed, they were either beaten or shot.

"*One day after an unusual, uneventful Roll Call, my mom went back to her barracks to prepare to go to her forced-labor assignment. On her way she encountered a former schoolmate and dear friend. They were so excited to see each other, and her friend had some great news to share with my mom. She saw my mom's father—my grandfather—going to work in the camp. My mom was in total disbelief. She thought her entire family had perished. Her father was alive! The friend related to my mom the time and place that she saw my grandfather, Isaac Anush. He would walk to work along a fence that separated the women's camp from the men's camp. It took much planning and plotting on my mom's part to get herself near that fence at the perfect time to catch a glimpse of her father.*

"*Being fearless, brave, and courageous, as well as possessed with an indomitable spirit, she ventured as close to the fence as possible. She searched the faces of the worn and shattered souls that walked in front of her and suddenly screamed with recognition: 'TaTe, TaTe,' she cried. 'It's me, Basha!'*

Many heads turned in her direction, then turned back and continued their downtrodden march to work. My grandfather stood for an extra few seconds as she called out again, 'It's me, Basha!' He looked at this emaciated child, shivering in torn rags, head shaven, hollow eyes with black circles around them. Her skin was scratched raw from lice bites and she was covered in oozing scabs. This child could not be his beautiful daughter with her auburn hair always styled in thick, intricate braids;

with lovely skin like a porcelain doll and hazel-green eyes that twinkled like stars. 'Du bist nicht meine tochter,' [You are not my daughter] *he called back and turned to catch up with his group."* [181]

Basha remembered the sad moment in her post-war testimonies.

"He was standing right before me and I was wearing an apron, a small apron like you wore in the kitchen, and I wrapped myself with it three times, that's how much was left of me, and my head was, of course, shaved. Dead people looked better than me. I was a real Muselmann. I was a walking skeleton and my father said, 'No, it's not her, it's not her! I don't recognize her; it couldn't be her.' I didn't look like a human being at all, and he couldn't bring himself to believe that it's really me, and I screamed, 'Yes, I'm your daughter. I'm Basha. You're my father.' He didn't look any better. He didn't see it in himself [but] he saw it in me. I was fifteen years old and he didn't recognize me." [182]

Evelyn continues:

"Mom felt defeated, disappointed, saddened, and heartbroken. Her bubble had burst. Did she change so much that her own father didn't recognize her? He had changed too. Isaac was a butcher. He was strong, always carrying huge slabs of meat over his shoulder. He raised chickens, milked cows, grew vegetables, and plowed his small garden to support his wife and seven children. They all helped out. Isaac always stood tall like a general at attention and he was a deeply religious man. Now he was no longer the same. He was a broken soul, defeated and meek. He was thin, beaten and covered in bruises. Mom also noticed a dent in his forehead that was never there before. He had no socks, and while he walked, she noticed the wooden

clogs he was wearing caused him to sink in the snow and mud of Auschwitz. Every step he took was a major struggle.

"Saddened that her father didn't acknowledge her and worried about his feet in the bitter cold, Mom decided she would try somehow to get her father a pair of socks. This was quite a quest to try to achieve in Auschwitz. She knew of a woman in her barracks that had the most elite job . . . she worked in Kanada, the warehouse where the belongings of the inmates and those murdered in the gas chambers were sorted. Many of the belongings were sent to Germany to support the war effort. Inmates would barter with this particular woman for something they desperately needed: cigarettes, a hat, scarf, etc. Although quite risky, this black-market-type business was prevalent in the camp. Being caught meant instant death; yet this woman managed to smuggle many items for a price. My mom had nothing to bargain with except her small cube of bread. Mom didn't eat for three days surviving on snow. She wanted to exchange her three cubes of bread for a pair of socks for her father.

"In the evening when all of the women were back in their barracks, Mom approached the woman who worked in Kanada. She asked if she could get a pair of socks for her father and gave the woman the three cubes of bread. The woman shoved the bread back at my mom sarcastically saying, 'Your bread isn't good enough' and started laughing.

"Again, Mom felt defeated, but she was determined and relentless in her effort to keep her father alive. She decided that she would go back to the fence hoping for another encounter with her father. This time she would attempt to throw him the three cubes of bread that she had saved in her unsuccessful barter for the socks. She felt her father needed the bread more

than she did. She knew this would be a risky endeavor. Getting caught meant a severe beating or death; but she was selfless. She innocently strolled over to the fence searching the shallow faces and the empty, hollow eyes. She spotted her father and yelled out, 'TaTe,' and threw the bread over the fence. Miraculously, the bread landed right at his feet." [183]

Getting a brief glimpse of her father, speaking to him, and throwing him a piece of bread when the *kapos* were not paying attention, were precious moments for Basha. The hope of seeing him was something to look forward to every day. One day, however, another prisoner whispered a disturbing comment to her as she passed by the fenced male compound.

"So, a man told me that my father is not going to last long because he's taking his bread and he is selling it for cigarettes. It was like a black market. They [smokers] *were selling* [their bread] *for a cigarette . . . because my father was smoking, and to him the cigarette was more important than a piece of bread.*" [184]

Basha's joy at the possibility of seeing her father turned to deep concern. Now if she did not see him, she would wonder if she had just missed him, or if he had died. Her options for helping him were limited, almost to the point of being nonexistent, but just as she had risked death before, slipping through the ghetto fence in Pruzhany to get food for the sake of her family, she now risked her life again, this time to get food for the sake of her father. Throwing bread to him took on supreme importance, overshadowing any personal fear of being caught by the guards.

"I felt very bad about it [her father's declining health], *so I used to take my bread and give it to my father. I was working. I was already swollen, swollen from hunger because I took my portion, this tiny piece of bread, that's all they gave us, and some brown*

water, like with the weeds and everything, that you couldn't really drink it. It was sickening. It tasted like vomit, and so only this piece of bread sustained us. But I gave my bread to my father. I was eating nothing at all. I threw it over the fence where he worked." [185]

The process of getting the bread to her father required a substantial amount of courage and, perhaps, an even greater amount of luck. Basha had to constantly be aware of the position of her guard and where she was looking. It was nerve-racking, at the very least. The tension of deliberately risking her life day after day was beyond what most people could endure, but she did it for her father, the last person in her life. Typically, her *kommando* was escorted by an *SS* woman. Perhaps the woman was lax in observing Basha's actions, or perhaps she figured out what was going on and chose to overlook it. Perhaps there was a small bit of humanity left in her. Basha never knew. But one day Basha's luck ran out. The *SS* woman was absent, replaced with a male *SS* man. Evelyn continues:

"As he [her father] *bent down to pick it up, his face suddenly flushed and the expression in his eyes was that of sure horror. A Nazi officer was standing directly behind my mother. He had witnessed the entire event of throwing the bread. Looking at her father's countenance said it all . . . she knew she was in deep trouble. As she turned and saw the Nazi officer, she realized she was no longer trembling from the bitter cold. He was tall, with a strong jaw and steel blue eyes that penetrated her very being.*

'What you just did is forbidden,' he said, staring at her.

She tried to swallow the lump that had suddenly clogged her throat, and in perfect German she replied, 'if you were in my shoes and it was your father, wouldn't you have done the same?'

The Nazi officer continued staring at her, possibly shocked that she had the courage to reply. My mom's shivering turned into cold sweat. What was he going to do to her?

She turned to look at her father, wanting her last vision of life to be his face and not that of a Nazi. Her dad's eyes were shimmering pools of tears with a few escaping down his cheeks, forming white frozen streaks on his ruddy skin. He knew of the death of his wife, youngest daughter, and five sons. Now he feared he was going to witness the murder of his only remaining child. Turning away from her father, the Nazi ordered her to go back to her group and get back to work. She feared turning her back, knowing that many times the Nazis played games like this and shot inmates in the back. She turned back one more time to catch a last glimpse of her father.

He yelled out to her, 'You are my daughter, my Basha!'

She turned and walked back with frozen tears on her cheeks, fearing a bullet would penetrate her shivering body at any moment. Was she protected by the arms of Hashem, or did she touch a soft spot in the heart of a Nazi officer? There was no bullet, no beating." [186]

Was it a miracle? Perhaps, and Basha may have very well believed that. She was unquestionably aware of how close she had come, once again, to death, particularly with this man. She said, "He was actually the worst murderer between all the Germans, I think. He was the sickest."

Being considered the worst in a group that regularly engaged in unconscionable acts of cruelty stretches the boundaries of one's imagination. This man was vying with a cadre of morally bankrupt brutes to occupy the lowest possible rung on the ladder of human decency. Worse, he clearly enjoyed inflicting pain and terror on his innocent victims. In fact, he turned it into sport. His usual assignment was the Weichsel-Union-Metallwerke ammunition factory in the industrial complex at Auschwitz III-Monowitz.

As with all *kommandos*, the girls at the ammunition factory received a brief midday break to eat their meager lunch, a small piece of bread and some water. For a few minutes they could go outside, rest in the sun and fresh air, and engage in conversation. In their bleak world, those few minutes were something to look forward to.

The Nazi guard also looked forward to this time. While the prisoners walked outside to escape from the noise, dust, and smell of the factory, he periodically took his rifle and climbed to the roof of the building, where he had an unobstructed view of the yard. There, he engaged in sniper practice. As his rifle shots rang out, some girls fell and the rest fled back inside the factory in confusion and terror. He kept shooting until he ran out of targets. Shortly thereafter, the *Sonderkommando* would arrive and take his victims to the crematorium. Everyone else went back to work.

Basha knew the man's reputation and understood that on this day she should remain unobtrusive, stay quiet, and draw no attention, but she also feared for her father's health.

Her common sense told her one thing, but her heart told her something else.

"That was the day that, somehow, he was assigned to our company, and he was walking with us, and I threw that time the bread. I shouldn't have. I made a mistake. Like Sunday, they gave us a day off and I was afraid that my father would be hungry. I threw the bread, and he [the guard] caught me. I thought it was the end then, and he, like I said before, he was the worst murderer of them all, and I knew I didn't have no other choice. I tried to

talk to him, to this crazy man, and I opened up my mouth and I told him, I said, 'I just gave him only a piece of bread,' and I said, 'It was my bread, I didn't eat it myself.'

"He said, 'What was in the bread? Did you put a letter in the bread?'

"I said, 'No I didn't put nothing in the bread.'

"That was the time when the Jewish girls [working in the ammunition factory] helped the men [during the Sonderkommando revolt]. From this ammunition factory . . . they gave them explosives, and they tore up the crematorium, and that was a bad time to do what I was doing, because the Germans were very suspicious. [107]

"I threw in the bread, and I knew what he was going to do to me, this Nazi. My fate was already sealed because I figured the minute we come [back] to Birkenau, he's going to take me straight to the crematorium. But to this crazy murderer . . . I started talking and somehow, I don't know what happened, he let me back into the compound everybody jumped on me.

"They said, 'My God, you're like reborn.'

"I mean, the girls couldn't believe their eyes, and I used the last tool that I have, which was, I used my tongue and begged him and prayed. And I told him, I said 'If you would have a father someplace and you would see him starving, I think you would give him your last piece of bread, too.' That's what I told him, and somehow this murderer's heart, maybe, was touched. Who knows what he thought? Maybe it was a miracle. Maybe, I don't know, just maybe, [but] I remained alive to tell the story, that's all. That he let me go back into the camp and he didn't kill me then, it was something that he never did before."[188]

It was astonishing, since this guard notoriously had a special ritual for committing murder, which apparently gave him delight.

"Because this guy used to take barrels, put the gals in the barrel, and roll them straight to the crematorium and throw the barrel in the oven. That's what he did all the time. How I survived that day I'll never know." [189]

No one else in the camp knew either. None of the other girls had ever seen anyone escape once they caught the attention of the Nazi madman.

"They were all afraid that he was going to put me in a barrel too, that I was finished. The Stubenältester [barrack section leader kapo] *was a gal from Kraków, and she was taking care of the kommando. A Jewish girl. She came in and she said, 'Basha, you don't know how lucky you are. I thought I'd live to see you being rolled to the crematorium.'"* [190]

Perhaps it was not entirely luck. Evelyn has strong feelings about this pivotal, life-changing event in her mother's tragic youth.

My mom was a woman of courage: a huge risk taker. The risks she took involved life and death. Hope permeated every fiber of her being. Despite all her life challenges in the concentration camp and after, she never lost hope. Her spirit was so strong, defying hate and fear. [191]

Contrary to the *Stubenältester's* statement, Basha was painfully aware of how lucky she was. It was during this period that she began to obsess about all the girls she had seen killed, girls around her who had been selected for death while she survived. Perhaps due to her suffering from survivor's guilt, the persistent memories of the murders of her fellow prisoners began to take a toll on her.

"And I worked like this and . . . Budy was still on my mind. It

just, I just couldn't live a day without thinking [about] *what I saw there. Because I always saw that picture of gals, young gals, pushed in between the wires of the camp. They took out the electricity, and they put in . . . let's say, if they put fifteen gals* [in], [they] *put fifteen German Shepherds* [in], *and* [the dogs] *used to rip them apart. And we all had to watch it. And this year, with what I was doing, I was losing my mind. I felt that I was losing my mind."*[192]

Nevertheless, when the female guard returned, Basha resumed throwing the bread to her father.

<hr>

The former schoolmate from Pruzhany had more news for Basha. Elated that her father was still alive, she began to have hope that her brothers may also still be alive. Combined with feeling better physically, and again working and mingling with the other prisoners, things seemed slightly better. She mentioned her hopes to her friend, but the friend had withheld some information from her. Confronted with Basha's hopes, she told her the rest of what she knew. It was not good—not good at all.

"She said, 'Basha, your brothers were on a truck. And they were hollering to me, make sure to tell [our] *sister Basha that instead of taking us to a different camp like they promised, for the young kids to go where they'll have it better, they're taking us straight to the crematorium.' And it was near the crematorium that they told her.* [After the war] *when I met my father, I asked him about my two brothers, what happened to them after all? They were in the camp for the first six weeks,* [which] *were the worst. What happened to them? And he said . . . he couldn't talk. At first, he said, 'Please don't bring it up because I'm going to go berserk, I'm going to go crazy.'*[193]

Basha eventually learned the entire story and understood that her father's profound anguish was not based solely on the loss of his sons, but also that he felt he played a role in their demise.

"Two of them [her brothers Berel and Hillel] *got into the camp. Two of them . . . they took* [them] *with the men, with the younger men, and they took them to Auschwitz, to the camp for men;* [her father was] *with two of my younger brothers. They were younger than I.* [Berel] *was thirteen and* [Hillel] *was twelve. They took them, and they were already about six weeks in Auschwitz, and this was the hardest time because if you survived a little bit mentally, like if you didn't go crazy, maybe you had a chance to live a little bit longer.*

"So, they lived six weeks already in the concentration camps, and then the Germans gave the order that they wanted all the young kids to register, that they were taking them into a camp where they'll have it a little bit easier, especially for the children. Then my father said that it's so hard because they take all the youngsters and they killed them in this camp [Auschwitz], *and they* [the sons] *asked him what they should do. He encouraged them* [to register]. *What did he know? And my poor father had to live with it, and they took them, and there was no chance for young children. They took them straight to the crematorium one day."* [194]

For the rest of his life, Isaac Anush was tormented, wondering if his sons would have lived if he had told them to stay with him.

Systematic Medical Mass Murder

Working in the shoe *kommando* was a respite from the back-breaking work on the outdoor labor details, but no guarantee of safety. The guards and *kapos* were just as vigilant and cruel as ever, and Dr. Josef Mengele continued to prowl the camp looking for victims. Worse, Mengele was not the only one.

At this time Basha was unaware of the quasi-medical nightmare that was unfolding near her. Just steps from her bunk, two Nazi doctors, Professor Carl Clauberg and Dr. Horst Schumann were locked in competition to develop a special medical procedure; one they hoped would evoke the praise they so passionately sought from their boss, *Reichsführer-SS* Heinrich Himmler. In what became the largest series of experiments in the camp—one that saw hundreds of girls in Auschwitz butchered—the goal was to create a fast, inexpensive means of eliminating the Jewish race through mass sterilization of young girls.

Young girls exactly like Basha.

Although Basha knew nothing of this new medical atrocity brewing, she knew that nothing good ever happened when Mengele arrived. With his coterie of underlings, he regularly strode through the camp and its work facilities looking for prisoners appropriate to fulfill whatever their current need might be. Sometimes they looked for victims for their medical experiments, other times they needed prisoners to transfer to another work facility. Frequently, the selection was solely to reduce the prisoner population by sending weaker inmates to the crematorium to make room for new, stronger inmates to exploit. There was a significant element of luck involved in evading the Mengele mob, but Basha and the other girls did their best to not look like candidates for whatever he was up to. This was a risky proposition. If one attempted to look weak or unhealthy to avoid a medical or hard work detail, they ran the risk of looking useless and being sent to the crematorium. Basha had already once escaped the grasp of Mengele's men, literally, when she pulled away from him and ran to safety, but they came back, over and over.

"I was a lot of times in front of Mengele. So many times. Right after [the incident with the guard who caught her throwing bread], *there was a selection and then somebody told us we're going to work in the ammunition factory. I didn't want to work there, because this way I used to fix the pairs of shoes for Gentile girls that worked in the kitchen, and I learned to be a shoemaker . . . that's how they gave me an extra piece of bread and I could help my father, and I knew that this would stop once I worked in the ammunition factory. I didn't want to go to the Union factory and everybody said that we're standing before Mengele and he's going to pick for the Union factory."* [195]

Basha was determined to make herself look unsuitable for work in the ammunition factory. However, Mengele's qualifications for that job were initially unknown. Soon the rumors spread.

"They said he was picking only the stronger ones. Everybody was covered with all kinds of tumors and open sores . . . all kinds of sores, and I tried to make it worse. I was scratching myself. I should look terrible that he shouldn't take me to the Union factory." [196]

Basha's efforts to make herself look too weak and sickly to work in the Weichsel-Union-Metallwerke ammunition factory were successful. Mengele, like the Angel of Death in the Book of Exodus, passed over her. Unfortunately, in Mengele's case, he came back. His next selection was not for labor; it was to remove the weak and sickly and send them to the crematorium. Basha's solution to one problem had created another that was potentially far graver.

"And here was this a selection to the crematorium, and I could have [been selected based on the way she had made herself look], *so . . . somehow, he put me to the right* [side with those who were to live], *and I remained alive and went through so*

many selections, stood before Mengele so many times, but it was fate, and maybe it was meant somebody from my family should remain alive. And who knows, maybe to continue to live, [and] that's why I have my grandchildren. Had he pointed to the left, I wouldn't be here and have such beautiful children and their grandchildren. And God, if He would have saved a million and a half children, can you imagine what they would contribute to this country, what they would do to this world? A million and a half kids they killed." [197]

Death was everywhere and age was not a factor. The Nazis had chosen the Jews for extermination, and there appeared to be nothing to look forward to except more suffering and eventual death. The prisoners had no knowledge of what was going on in the world, or the progress of the war. Every day brought more hopelessness and misery.

And then one day things changed. The camp guards told them they were going to move.

Historical Perspective
on Chapter 10

Medical Mutilation – Clauberg and Schumann

Thc two doctors vying for attention and, presumably, rewards from Himmler were Professor Carl Clauberg and Dr. Horst Schumann. Driven by their ardent Nazi beliefs, they intended to play a major role in the anticipated Greater German Reich.

Hitler's goal was to conquer Eastern Europe and Russia through military force, dispossess the indigenous peoples of their lands, and resettle the areas with what they considered racially pure Aryan Germans. He felt that some of the former land owners could be useful, serving as little more than slaves to the new German property holders, but the rest, the *Untermenschen*, deemed racially inferior and subhuman, presented a problem. This is where Professor Clauberg and Dr. Schumann came into the picture.

Clauberg proposed his theory for eliminating the Jewish race to Himmler over a pleasant lunch one day in 1942. He described a process for injecting a chemical agent into the cervix of the victim, which would cause sterility by closing the fallopian tubes. However, he admitted, there were a couple of drawbacks; it caused the victim excruciating pain and many women died. Nevertheless, with Himmler's approval he continued the experiments despite the enormity of the suffering.

Schumann took a different path in his informal competition with Clauberg for the goodwill of Himmler. He began sterilization experiments using extremely high doses of radiation on his victims, even though he had no training in radiology. This process also had hideous side effects. Patients received severe burns to their sexual organs, which were often followed by infection and death.

After destroying the lives of a multitude of patients, Schumann had to admit that surgical intervention was more effective than radiation. Clauberg emerged the victor of those two medical atrocities, but Schumann convinced Himmler to allow him to continue experimentation at the Ravensbrück concentration camp. He was positive that with the right equipment he would be able to sterilize up to one thousand women a day with a chemical injection.[198] Himmler was likely not particularly interested in the process, but rather focused on the outcome—the Final Solution to the Jewish Question. He was more than willing to provide the lab specimens.

Notes

175. Bess Freilich interview by Josey G. Fisher, 3-1-35.

176. "Block 11," Wikimedia Foundation, last modified July 2, 2022, https://en.wikipedia.org/wiki/Block_11.

177. Bess Freilich, interview by Fisher, 3-1-36.

178. Bess Freilich interview by Marc Seligman, 25.

179. "*Kanada* Warehouses, Auschwitz," Wikimedia Foundation, last modified March 11, 2022, https://en.wikipedia.org/wiki/*Kanada_* warehouses,_Auschwitz.

180. Bess Freilich, interview by Fisher, 3-1-36.

181. Evelyn Kaplan, email to author, April 7 2022.

182 Bess Freilich interview by Josey G. Fisher, 3-1-35.

183. Evelyn Kaplan, email to author, April 7, 2022.

184. Bess Freilich interview by Josey G. Fisher, 3-1-37.

185. Ibid.

186. Evelyn Kaplan, email to author, April 7, 2022.

187 Bess Freilich interview by Josey G. Fisher, 3-1-37.

188. Ibid, 3-2-38.

189 Ibid.

190 Bess Freilich interview by Marc Seligman, 26..

191. Evelyn Kaplan, email to author, April 7, 2022.

192. Bess Freilich interview by Marc Seligman, 26.

193. Bess Freilich interview by Josey G. Fisher, 2-1-22.

194. Bess Freilich interview by Josey G. Fisher, 2-1-21.

195 Ibid, 3-2-39.

196. Ibid.

197. Ibid.

198. Wachsmann, 438.

CHAPTER 11

In the Middle of the Noose

By fall of 1943, the Russians had gradually pushed the Nazis back to Germany. Basha, entirely cut off from news, or even reliable rumors, had little idea about the true progression of the war. She could tell by camp activity that something was going on, but she certainly did not know that Russian troops were only days away from liberating the camp. Had she known, she might have been slightly cheered (if one dare to use that word under the circumstances), figuring they certainly would not treat her any worse than the Germans had.

Hitler's grandiose plan for the prompt conquest of Russia failed miserably. In 1941, his *Wehrmacht* troops were well-led, well-trained, and well-equipped. That, combined with continued military successes, fueled his burgeoning ego and sense of invincibility. He was certain he was unbeatable, and perhaps, even divinely chosen to rule the world. His assessment of his assets was reasonable, but his assessment of his enemy, colored by his innate socio-racial prejudice, was deeply flawed. He viewed the Russians as a mongrel subspecies of humanity, living in an intellectual backwater with neither the resolve, leadership, nor weaponry to prevent his hasty conquest. His underestimation of the Russian people and military was a deadly mistake, as was his underestimation of the vast expanse of Russia and its seasonally brutal climate.

Hitler, supremely confident of a quick victory, had not provided for the possibility that his troops would have to endure the extreme Russian winter. As temperatures plunged to forty-five degrees below zero in January 1942, weapons froze, and without winter clothing, so did his army. Things were going very badly for the German troops, and they would get worse.

On the morning of January 17, 1945, Basha turned out for the last roll call for all the Auschwitz camps and sub-camps. The count was 66,020 prisoners. Not all could be moved; some were simply too physically debilitated. The sick, weak, and dying were left behind, approximately nine thousand of them at the time of withdrawal. The rest were assembled and ordered to march east. Himmler's directive to the camp commanders in charge of the evacuation was a typically cold, blunt threat that the Führer would hold them personally responsible to ensure that not one living prisoner fell into the hands of the Allies.

If there was one thing Basha was particularly good at, it was remaining alive.

Although unaware of Himmler's order at the time, it would not have surprised Basha, nor did the order to move.

"A little while later, they said they're going to evacuate us. Well, we knew already. There was artillery, we saw the bombs. And the planes were going back and forth. One time they bombed the Union factory and quite a few people were killed. Those days the Germans went into the camp to hide because they thought the camps wouldn't be bombarded. But a few times they bombed the SS barracks and a lot of them died. And we prayed, we prayed. 'God, please make them throw a few bombs at our camps. Then everything would be finished.' Because we couldn't take it no longer." [199]

The Death March

In the summer of 1944, the Russian Army launched a massive offensive that destroyed the German Army Group Center. Charging across a front 558 miles long, their western attack appeared unstoppable. After the successful landings in Normandy, France, Allied troops rapidly advanced from the west. The result was a noose around the throat of Germany. Unfortunately, the noose that tightened to choke the life out of Nazism also encircled the innocent like Basha.

In complete disregard for common sense and facts, Hitler would not consider releasing the concentration camp prisoners. He believed he could still win the war, and that the prisoners would still be of use to him. Contrary to characteristic German efficiency, the evacuation of the camps was late and somewhat haphazard. Only the strong prisoners made the march; the rest were left behind to fend for themselves. When Russian troops finally entered the camp on January 27, 1945, they found approximately seven thousand emaciated, living prisoners as well as hundreds of unburied corpses. Auschwitz survivors stated that the first Russian troops to enter the camp appeared stunned into silence. They had seen a lot of things, but nothing like that.

The evacuation of Auschwitz began on January 17, 1945. A day later, Basha received the order to begin to march. It was almost two years to the day since her family was rousted from their home in Pruzhany and forced onto the sleds into captivity. Unlike the first evacuation, Basha's testimonies say nothing about fear or anxiety. The two years of abuse she had endured appear to have become something of an emotional anesthetic. Death was no longer a threat. Death would bring relief from suffering.

This was a tragic emotional state for a sixteen-year-old girl and, unfortunately, her physical state was about to be equally challenged.

"[The Germans] started a march. They [the Russians] were chasing us deeper into Germany and we had to walk in the snow, and so many of us died. So many. By the thousands we died from exhaustion, from pain." [200]

Hungry, weak, and sick, the prisoners also lacked the adequate clothing to stave off one of the harshest winters in recent years. Temperatures reached -4°F, and there was nowhere to stop and warm up. Only the body heat generated by the constant walking fought off the cold. The snow that clumped on the bottom of their wooden clogs added to the instability inflicted by their weak muscles. Many wrapped rags around their feet. As with the girls at Budy who positioned themselves in the middle of the group to avoid being selected for the "show," the girls attempted to stay near the middle of the march to avoid being viewed as stragglers. Those who fell behind from cold and fatigue were promptly shot by the *SS* execution squads that followed the prisoners, leaving a miles-long trail of bodies. Historians believe that as many as 25 percent of the prisoners did not survive the march.

"We were walking for days. We were marching, and they marched after us, screaming 'Faster, faster.' And who was left behind, who couldn't walk anymore, they killed. And while we were walking, so many people walked before us. So, we were walking on dead people. We were walking on dead people who were still laying there. We were walking, the march, we were walking on bodies, thousands of bodies. We didn't walk on the road actually; we were walking on the bodies from people that walked before us, from all the camps. There was an evacuation going to Germany because the Russians started to come already." [201]

Basha did not know what happened to her father, which added another layer of emotional misery. She believed, and prayed, that he was on the march somewhere, but she did not know the current status of his health. The frozen bodies on the road were a constant reminder of what happened to those who lacked the strength to continue.

Adding to the chaos and congestion, hordes of German immigrants also fled. Their piece of *Lebensraum,* seized by the Nazis from Polish citizens, made them targets for hateful, returning Poles. The fleeing German troops left them unprotected and vulnerable to the inevitable retaliation brewing around them. Worse, the retreating Germans troops would be replaced by Russian troops, and there was absolutely no doubt they would be ruthless. They had the choice to lose their homes or lose their lives. The choice was not difficult. With their animals and wagons, they desperately raced west for safety behind the American lines. Those who did not flee regretted it.

The local Polish peasants, caught in the midst of the human storm, continued to try to live as best they could, transporting their goods and produce to market. This could be a blessing or curse for the evacuees, depending on fate.

"While the peasants . . . I don't know . . . whether they passed by just for us [to] grab [a] potato. Why they took that road with the peasants passing by with carrots and potatoes. But they didn't do us no favors, because some gals—I didn't—but some gals went over and grabbed a potato, and they were killed. They were laying with the potato in their hand . . . And then they took us to trains that were waiting for us. And they were pushing and shoving . . . hitting and beating, and the bombs [grenades] they were throwing. It was chaos . . . and the trains were half full of snow. We stood like this in the snow traveling from camp

to camp. Nobody wanted us. Then finally, finally, we came to Ravensbrück and they accepted us." [202]

Approximately fifty-seven thousand prisoners began the march from Auschwitz. Only about forty-one thousand made it to the end. Basha had survived another horror.

Unfortunately, there were many more horrors to come.

Historical Perspective
on Chapter 11

Germany's Early Victories

Hitler's abundant confidence was not unfounded. Since the first shots of World War II were fired in 1939, his troops had won an impressive series of victories. He had hoped to reach an agreement with Great Britain to avoid war with them, but the British made it clear they had no intention of cooperating with him. Convinced that the British were immovable on the subject, Hitler used France as his platform to attack England. The Battle of Britain commenced on July 10, 1940 and continued until October 31 of that year. Primarily an air battle, the vaunted German *Luftwaffe* was surprisingly unable to defeat Britain's struggling Royal Air Force. An invasion of Great Britain across the English Channel without air superiority was a move too risky for even Hitler's supercharged ego. Instead, he turned his attention to the east. Greece and Yugoslavia fell to Nazi troops in early 1941. He had never intended to keep his treaties with Russia for long, and now the vast lands of Russia appeared to be his for the taking, providing him with the *Lebensraum* he needed for the German Empire he envisioned.

On June 22, 1941, German air and ground troops violated their pacts with the Russians, launching a surprise attack to the east. Russian troops fell back, and the German military enjoyed five months of successes. *SS Einsatzgruppen* (mobile killing units) followed closely behind the *Wehrmacht,* cruelly abused the population, and gathering political commissars and Jews for mass execution. The Russians found the German actions unforgivable and unforgettable. When they eventually counterattacked and marched into Germany, they returned the abuse in kind.

Germany's invasion of Russia stalled when they reached the city limits of Moscow in October 1941. The assault had been costly; five hundred thousand German troops had become casualties, and the Russian roads, or lack of them, had disabled as much as 40 percent of German trucks. Many of the mighty German Panzer tanks also failed in the hostile terrain, unlike the rugged, wide-track Russian T-34 tanks, which were built to withstand the land and climate. Russian troops, fighting for their homeland, dug in, forcing the Germans to a standstill.

Resolved to fight for their homeland, and with support from the Western Allied supply chain, the assault reversed. By fall of 1943, the Russians began slowly pushing the Nazis back to Germany, and by January 1945, Germany's Eastern defenses had collapsed. After the enormous abuse Russian citizens had suffered at the hands of the Nazis, the Russians set out for revenge.

Destroying the Evidence

With the Western Allied troops advancing toward Germany from one direction and the Russians from the other, the German military had more than its hands full; however, the problems for Nazi Germany were not all military. Perhaps they had never considered the possibility that they might lose the war, and believed their crimes would go undiscovered. That was not turning out to be the case. Enemy troops moved within range of the concentration camps, and evidence of their atrocities would soon be made public if they did not act. An apparently delusional Heinrich Himmler positioned himself for a postwar role in the new German government when Germany lost the war, while at the same time carrying out Hitler's orders. Around November 1, 1944, as enemy troops approached Auschwitz, Himmler ordered the gassing of prisoners to cease, and by the end of November he had ordered the dismantlement of the crematoria. *Sonderkommandos* and prisoners removed the evidence of mass murder, and cleaned the camp as much as possible. Destroying or cleaning structures was a big enough problem on its own, but there was a far greater problem. The three Auschwitz camps and related sub-camps still housed thousands of prisoners. Something had to be done with them, and quickly. By the close of 1944, it was clear they would have to be relocated, so in January 1945, Himmler gave the order to evacuate the complex, along with the other Polish concentration camps, and send the prisoners to camps in Germany. The Death March was about to begin.

The Bombing Controversy

Basha's anger at the Allied failure to bomb Auschwitz remained with her long after the war ended. It was not a matter of military neglect, contrary to her observations and feelings. In fact, it was a very contentious issue at Allied headquarters. Since 1942, they had been aware that the camp was used for the systematic extermination of Jews, but there was no consensus on what to do about it. Most in air operations command felt the safest way to free the prisoners was to win the war quickly. Others felt that, at the very least, Allied aircraft should attempt to bomb the crematoria. The obvious problem was collateral damage. There was no way to bomb Auschwitz without killing prisoners, perhaps a great many of them. Allied air chiefs were well aware that, at that time, only about 34 percent of their bombs landed within one thousand feet of their target. Auschwitz was a relatively small area–approximately twenty thousand acres–and crowded. Any Allied attempts at precision bombing of individual buildings were unlikely to be precise enough.[203] Allied air chiefs balked at the prospect of killing those who had survived the Nazis. How that would be viewed in the hindsight of history was a legitimate concern.

Escape of the German Settlers

Even the Nazi government, loath to do anything that implied defeat, recognized that the German settlers on Polish lands were in danger. Nazi officials in Berlin created an evacuation plan, but were slow to implement it. The Nazi government evacuated a few German citizens in the furthermost Eastern regions as early as the summer of 1944, but more German families simply used common sense and fled on their own. As expected, the Russian troops horribly abused captured German citizens. The Russian commanders focused on pushing forward to Germany and disregarded the rape and murder inflicted on civilians. The Russians staged a civilian massacre in the town of Nemmersdorf, East Prussia.[204] The Nazis spread the news of the massacre as a propaganda tool, but for many fleeing Germans, confirmation of Russian brutality only turned worry into panic. German citizens packed all they could carry and fled west. When the Russians eventually marched into Germany, many German citizens of the Eastern areas also fled, hoping to escape into American-controlled territory.

Notes

199. Bess Freilich interview by Marc Seligman, 28.

200. Bess Freilich interview by Josey G. Fisher, 3-2-40.

201. Bess Freilich interview by Marc Seligman, 28.

202 Ibid.

203. Andrew Roberts, *The Storm of War: A New History of the Second World War,* (New York: HarperCollins Publishers, 2011) 247.

204. "Nemmersdorf Massacre," Wikimedia Foundation, last modified November 15, 2022, https://en.wikipedia.org/wiki/Nemmersdorf_massacre.

CHAPTER 12

A New Ordeal

Surviving the march was no small accomplishment. It was three weeks of fighting starvation and fatigue. The groans of the prisoners were continually punctuated with the sound of rifle shots, a reminder of how the SS handled stragglers. All of this took place during one of the coldest winters in recent years.

> *"From Auschwitz, deeper into Germany they took us to many camps, and they were full of people, and I remember they took us to Ravensbrück. They took us, and they let us sit before we could enter the barracks. I remember the dress that I was wearing froze to the ground. When I stood up. the dress was torn up. I was sitting like this the whole night. Then we could walk into the barracks. The barracks were filled with water, filled with water, and that's how we sat . . . in the water."* [205]

Ravensbrück

Ravensbrück was unusual In the KL system. Located 50 miles north of Berlin, roughly 425 miles from Auschwitz, the camp was originally intended to be exclusively for female prisoners. Beginning operation in 1939, a chauvinistic Heinrich Himmler viewed women as less dangerous than men. Since most inmates were political prisoners at that point, he felt women could more easily "be reformed." He was adamant that the women not be whipped except for the most severe acts of misbehavior. [206]

Initially, conditions at Ravensbrück were good compared

to other camps. A prisoner who transferred there from another facility in 1940 was surprised to receive her first meal, which included fruit porridge, bread, sausage, margarine, and lard. Prisoner functionaries changed linens regularly, and the camp was cleaner than others in the system. Instead of the brutal manual labor of other camps, the task assigned to Ravensbrück prisoners was to manufacturer garments.[207] Aside from the senior camp management, the guards were *Weiblichen SS-Gefolges,* female civilian employees of the *SS.*

As the war progressed, the marginal advantages of Ravensbrück over other camps gradually ebbed. Prisoner populations grew as Germany conquered new territories. In 1941, the KL system built a men's camp adjacent to the Ravensbrück women's facility to contain the latest victims of successful Nazi aggression. Food rations became meager, and the weak and injured were selected to be killed. At first the selected prisoners were shot, but by 1942 the common methods were either lethal injection or the gas chambers at Auschwitz-Birkenau. Roughly six thousand women died in the gas chambers by the end of the war. [208]

The original prison population of nine hundred in 1939 grew to fifty thousand in 1945, creating overcrowding, disease—particularly typhus—and the wretched squalor that was typical of the camps.

That is when Basha and her group arrived.

The days when Ravensbrück was slightly less awful than the other camps were long gone. Prisoners who arrived in the winter of 1945 found no food or water. Toilet facilities consisted of open holes in the floors of the barracks. There was no place to sleep, partially due to overcrowding, and partially due to the miserable circumstances overcoming some prisoners' moral sensibilities.

The impact their actions had on their fellow inmates was no longer important. Dora remembered:

"... there were no places where to sleep, and we stood there in the barracks where once there were some bunks, but the girls [that] were there before, the women that were there before, took it [wooden support boards for bunk mattresses] *out and burned it outside to keep a little warm, so there were no boards left anymore. If you wanted to lay down, you kept the boards inside the back of your pants, and I was with another girl* [apparently Basha], *so she kept one and I kept one, so we put two boards together if she wanted to lay down for an hour, and then I would lay down for an hour, and they would be stolen every minute of the day from you. Someone could run up in the back and take it away from you because that was the only way of survival."* [209]

The reality that Russian troops were closing in fast had no discernible impact on how the prisoners were treated by the guards. Himmler may have been concerned about his image in the postwar world, but at this point, camp guards and *kapos* continued their relentless cycle of cruelty. Basha continued to be victimized.

"One German woman grabbed me, she punished me, and I had to stay in a hole filled with water, and she put two bricks on top of me. I had to hold it like this [with her arms horizontal]. *And she was beating me. I couldn't let my hands down for a second. I lived through this, too. It was like it was meant for me to survive, somehow. I believe it."* [210]

It was apparent that the war would be over soon, and the prisoners, near starvation, became increasingly more motivated to survive. All they had to do was stay alive a little longer and they might again be free. Their actions reflected their desperation, anxiety, and hunger.

"They gave us pieces of bread at Ravensbrück, and we went to sleep and put the bread under the pillow, and in the morning, it was gone. I mean, one inmate stole from the other. So, I didn't have nothing to eat. And the camp was huge, it was so many people. They brought them from all over. [211]

"Once I was standing . . . I saw gals carrying the big soup kettle. And some gals grabbed this and the soup spilled, and the gals were laying on the ground to lick it up. I just stood and watched. From the back came the Nazi. I didn't see him; he ran from the back. And whoever was in the way, standing and watching, they hit from the back. He hit me unexpectedly from the back. It's a miracle he didn't break my skull. But I had headaches for a long, long, while, even when I was in the displaced [persons'] camp." [212]

Many guards got away with these abuses. Others would eventually stand before a jury. Few got what they deserved.

In coming years, the abused girls would be hungry for revenge, but in the spring of 1945, they were just plain hungry.

Basha did not need a newspaper to understand how the war was progressing. The perimeter of Ravensbrück marked by thin barbed wire did nothing to obstruct her view of the pandemonium just steps from her. The roads were clogged with German families in flight.

"We saw already [the German civilians]; *we saw them, the horses and wagons with big hoods* [covered wagons], *and they carried everything they owned. They were running, they were running, the Germans, they didn't know where they were running. They were running one on top of the other. They were running away from the Russians. They wanted to go closer where the Americans are coming. They were very afraid of the Russians."* [213]

The sight of fleeing German citizens was not the only evidence of impending German defeat. The sounds of Allied aircraft in the sky above her were a constant reminder that the noose was tightening.

"We knew the end was coming because we saw the planes constantly. You know, going over the camp. But they didn't do nothing. They didn't throw no bombs."[214]

Basha was partially correct. Allied aircraft did not deliberately bomb the camps, but pilots traveling overhead at three hundred miles per hour in heavily armed aircraft, such as the P-47 could, and sometimes did, mistake the prison camps for military facilities. A three-second burst from its eight .50 caliber machine guns, sprayed the target with over 2,500 bullets. Hopefully, the target was the enemy. If not, the results were tragic.

"One day, you know the [unintelligible on recording—probably Red Cross] *gave them* [camp administration] *packages. Constantly, we were sent packages, but the Germans never gave* [them] *to us. But one day, they gave us the packages and it was dry milk, and the gals sat down and mixed it with water and they were sitting on the ground when a plane came. He probably didn't know what it* [the camp] *was and* [he strafed the compound, and] *he killed a few, quite a few gals."*[215]

Russian pilots often did not attempt to make a distinction between German troops and German civilians. After what the Germans had done to their civilians and country, many Russians considered all Germans the enemy. German civilians moved slowly and crowded the roads, which made them attractive targets for some Russian pilots' revenge. The Russians dropped bombs on the disorganized mass, and strafed them with machine-gun fire as soon as German stragglers came within striking distance. Sometimes the Russian tankers saved their ammunition and simply drove over the German civilians with their heavy-tracked vehicles. It is impossible to accurately estimate the number of dead, but Polish historians Witold Sienkiewicz and Grzegorz Hryciuk placed a broad range between 600,000 to 1.2 million total civilian refugee deaths from Russian attacks. [216]

As the war raged on around them, Basha and the other inmates could do nothing but wait and wonder what was coming next for them.

The imminent defeat of Germany was obvious to all, except possibly Adolf Hitler. The KL prisoners were now more of a liability to Germany than a potential asset working in war plants. Allied bombers had destroyed much of Germany's war industry, and it was unlikely—probably impossible—to rebuild and refit the factories quickly enough for it to matter. It seemed illogical to guard, feed, and move the prisoners away from the advancing Russians. Releasing the prisoners and using the troops and funds to prop up the defense of Germany would have been considerably more advantageous. Nevertheless, Hitler was immovable on his position. His demonic hatred of Jews superseded logic and he would not let them go. As overcrowding at Ravensbrück became untenable, Basha received word that her two-month imprisonment had concluded and she would be transferred to the sub-camp of Malchow. Any benefits created by the move for the *SS* were not reflected in their treatment of the prisoners.

Malchow

Malchow was opened in the winter of 1943 as a sub-camp of Ravensbrück intended for female inmates. Ten barracks were built and equipped to house one hundred prisoners each, for a total population of one thousand women. When Basha arrived in the spring of 1945, the prisoner population had grown to five thousand. Overcrowding and lack of sanitation created the usual concentration camp problems, and many prisoners died from starvation, exhaustion, tuberculosis, and typhus. Among the cruelest in the KL system was *SS* wardress, and later camp commandant, Luise Danz.[217] She always left prisoners on near-starvation rations and deliberately mistreated them with cruelties, like forcing them to kneel for long periods on the sharp stones of the compound grounds. She regularly beat them, and constantly threatened them with the attack-trained *SS* German Shepherd dogs. (Danz was convicted of crimes against humanity after the war and sentenced to life imprisonment, but released in 1957 as part of a general amnesty.)

Malchow served as a transit camp for Death March prisoners from various camps in the east, so most prisoners moved through the camp rather than staying there. However, a few received jobs. *SS* administrators never told prisoners what they intended to do with them, so Basha did not know what to expect.

> "... *they took us to Malchow, south of Ravensbrück. A different camp, closer to Berlin. And there they took me to work. There was camouflage and trees, pieces of wood. We had to put plastic branches to make it look like it was trees to cover up the road.*"[218]

Regardless of the attempts to carry on business as usual in the camp, Basha saw further evidence of Germany's collapse. It was impossible to conceal.

> "*We saw that the end is coming, that the Germans were cutting their electrical poles, the electricity and telegraph, and the telephones, and we knew that something was happening. Swedes came, a whole delegation, and they looked at our camp, and they observed everybody with tears in their eyes, and a couple of weeks later huge buses came by. Buses, I remember. And some girls ... the Germans just took off their numbers from their dresses, and they told them they were free, and those buses took those girls*

to Sweden. To Sweden actually, from this hell. From an inferno, to life in just a few minutes. But when our time came, we were supposed . . . our barracks were supposed to go on those buses. [But] the previous buses from the day before were bombarded, and the whole thing stopped . . . they were bombarded somehow. Somebody made a big mistake, and they thought it was soldiers or military buses. Some of them did remain alive, yes, some of them, but a lot of them got killed. It was buses, and those buses stopped, they stopped coming, and we still remained in the camp . . ." [219]

As the sights and sounds of war continued around them at Malchow, Basha and the other girls sat and waited. They did not know if the Germans would kill them, move them again, or leave them to starve. They knew the Russians were close, but after all they had been through, they did not know for certain if they would rescue them or harm them. They did not know anything, so they sat and waited. The girls were in terrible physical condition, as Dora remembered:

"Still shaved, and we are in the striped uniforms, and we can barely walk. Each and everyone has boils all over because we are so thin, and the lice are so thick that they sucked out the blood, and our infections are unbelievable. Everybody has a blood infection. Everybody has diarrhea." [220]

Eventually, the Germans cleared up the uncertainty, at least to a degree. Anxious camp administrators ordered the guards to move the girls out of the camp, but apparently did not tell them where to send their prisoners. Dora continued:

"They say that they are going to take us out of the camp, and that we are going to march into the nearest town. They don't know the reasons themselves, but they are already changing their [civilian] clothes [to escape capture]. Now, the highway

is just Calamity Jane. Trucks, horses and buggies, motorcycles, cars, open trucks, closed trucks, German people with children. It is the end of the war, but they don't know where they are going." [221]

The guards, uncertain as everyone else about what was going on, still understood how to point their rifles at the prisoners and shout orders. Basha recalled how the guards herded her and the others to join the disorganized, frantic masses on the road.

". . . we still remained in the camp until around May 5, 1945. Then they chased us out of the camp, and we were marching again farther. And we saw a camp kommando *in civilian clothes passing by with a bicycle and we knew this was it, and he just plain walked away. We saw the Germans* [soldiers] *getting undressed* [and into] *civilian clothing in the forest, and they just mixed with the military and they left. And we knew that, somehow, it looks like it's really coming to the end. All of this, and we walked away and nobody looked* [at us.]*"* [222]

Some of the young male prisoners, with their striped camp uniforms in shreds, picked up the discarded German uniforms and put them on for warmth. For a few, this was a fatal mistake. Approaching Russian troops mistook them for German soldiers and shot them. [223]

SS guards who had shown such intense devotion to tormenting them now totally ignored them. This realization was telling. Looking around at the bedlam, it was clear to Basha that the German Army had fallen into the every-man-for-himself mentality. Nothing was of interest to them except their own escape.

"The [German] *Army on the road, they were going one on top of another. They didn't care. Trucks were going on top of horses,*

horses on top of trucks. Its [Germany's] *mighty army . . . it was like destruction completely."* [224]

Basha may have felt some satisfaction at the fear she saw in the faces of the fleeing German troops, but that did not solve any of her problems. They continued their apparently pointless march until a prisoner came up with a potential solution.

Throughout Basha's imprisonment, a few older girls always tried to be helpful and supportive to the younger ones. Now as they marched in the midst of the growing pandemonium, one of the older girls—probably in her early to mid-twenties—decided they likely would be no worse off on their own than if they remained in the confused mass. She suggested they slip away into the forest when they had a chance. At the very least, no one would be around to point rifles at them. Several of the girls agreed, so Basha, Dora, two other girls from Pruzhany, and six other young prisoners joined the older girl, and they ran into the trees at their first opportunity. The Nazis either did not see them, or they no longer cared.

Hunger had been Basha's constant companion since the war broke out in 1939. Food was scarce under the Russian occupation, but at least there was some. The tiny scraps of bread the guards gave her in the camps had barely kept her alive, but at least she could rely on receiving it. When they fled the *SS* troops on the march, Basha feared the ration she received from the *SS* at the beginning of the march would be the last food she could expect to see for an unknown period. Even that had been a problem.

"On the march they gave each gal a little can of sardines. What could you do with sardines? We took a nail, and we made a hole and we drank it. That was the worst thing to do for our stomachs, so we were terribly sick." [225]

As they made their way down the road and through the forest, it became apparent that the only source of food available was what they could forage from the countryside. Desperately hungry, they grabbed anything in sight. The result was the same as before.

"We grabbed a few potatoes and we cooked them, and we all got terribly sick. Terribly sick. Diarrhea . . . and it was coming out from both sides. Blood . . . and we got terribly sick. We were lying . . . we were more dead than alive. Everybody was suffering so much. We thought, when we are liberated, we won't stop eating, but from the first bite—one bite was all—our stomachs weren't used to food." [226]

Although they had escaped their *SS* captors, they were anything but safe and secure. The war was not quite over, and their flight was taking them directly into its path. Under the cover of darkness, they slipped out of the forest and over a little bridge that led to the German town of Barkow on the other side of a lake, about sixteen miles west of Malchow.

"We came to a little school, and that's where we stayed in the middle of the night. One girl—I don't know whether she went berserk or something—but she told us that we can't stay in this place, that we should leave this place. And she started walking in the middle of the night . . . actually walking to the front. I mean, there were Katyushas firing, machine guns and explosions all around us. Everything was burning, and we were in the middle of it all. We saw what we were doing—we were going to the front—the front was right there. It was a terrible experience. We saw what we were doing and we said, 'No, we can't go farther because we're all going to be killed.' And we turned around and went back to the same place. [227]

"At ten o'clock we saw the first Russian soldier, a young kid, and we knew the ordeal was almost over." [228]

Knowing the war was over, the girls felt free to leave the school and explore the town. The streets filled with a mix of displaced persons. Men, women, Jews, Gentiles, and even a few former prisoners of war were wandered the streets, trying to figure out what to do next. German citizens, fearing the approaching Russian troops, abandoned their homes and fled deeper into Germany. This turned into a mixed blessing for the girls, as Dora remembered:

"A lot of Germans that were hiding, they were running. They didn't know where to go. And we occupied a big house that was beautiful; there were still pots standing on the oven and cooking. People left the house; they were running away. We stayed in that house. We were eleven girls, eleven friends that survived together. And we were very hungry, and we started eating everything that was in sight, and we got very, very sick. Very, very sick." [229]

Fortunately, the older girls stepped in once again to take charge of the situation.

"We were the youngest ones; we had a few that were like ten years older. They were more clever than we were, and they started taking command over us. And they said, 'We are not frying anything. We are not eating anything that is fat.' We have been without food for the last three months, barely having anything, one bread for a week for ten people, just a slice of bread, undernourished, full of lice crawling all over, beaten up, blistered. I don't know what you call it here, but it was like boils. It was from dirt, and it was from undernourishment." [230]

When the Russians occupied Barkow, they were initially very kind and sympathetic toward the girls. The Russian troops saw the emaciated girls dressed in rags, and genuinely seemed to want to help them. They told the girls to ask them for whatever they wanted, and the soldiers would get it for them. They provided food, including freshly slaughtered sheep.

However, the Russian attitude toward the Germans was the exact opposite. They had witnessed what the German troops had done in Russia, and they not only had no sympathy for German civilians, but the Russian troops engaged in an enraged, open program of revenge. They raped all the German women they could find, regardless of age, and seemed to have the same attitude as the *SS* when it came to randomly shooting and killing people.

Basha and the girls remained in the house for about four weeks recovering their health. They found decent clothes to wear and began to look much better. That is when the trouble started. The young Russian soldiers began taking an interest in them and coming around at night. The girls became uneasy. They did not want to be victimized like the German women. The girls boldly sought out the Russian commanding officer and told him of their concerns. He was sympathetic, but also realistic. He informed the girls of the Germans' raping and pillaging of the Russians, and told them about all the suffering his troops had been through. He could not guarantee the girls would remain safe from his young, deprived soldiers. He offered to give them sufficient protection to get out of town, the faster the better. There was no need for discussion. If a Russian general could not control his troops, eleven girls certainly could not. The general provided them with two horses and a covered wagon, and the girls packed it with all the food they could find. [231]

Now that they were no longer captives, each girl was faced with turning her dreams of postwar life into postwar reality, and that came with a set of difficulties. Dreams generally do not include hunger and physical pain, nor people who wish to curse you or harm you for no other reason than that you are Jewish. There were eleven girls and eleven dreams. They stayed together until the dreams began to separate them. Basha vividly remembered:

"We kept ourselves together, a few girls together, and we spent the rest of the time together before everyone went on their way. Actually, we found out that the liberation didn't solve all our problems. That we were all alone in the world without family, without anybody to care for us. No place to go, and everything . . . so much confusion. And we didn't know whether to go back. The Americans were on one side, the Russians were on another, and we wanted so badly to go back to our house[s] to see if anybody is alive, [but] then going back meant going back to the Russians. Everybody advised us not to, because within a few steps of this place, the American Army was stationed. We could walk into the Americans and could save so many heartaches that we had afterwards, but we chose to go see what happened to our homes and to the rest of our family. That we chose to go back to Russia—and I went back to my house, to my home, to my hometown—that was a big mistake." [232]

It was a mistake that would take years to rectify.

Historical Perspective
on Chapter 12

Nazi Guards and the War Crimes Trials

Many of the Nazi guards who had inflicted brutality on the prisoners would claim they had nothing to do with it, or had no knowledge of what was going on. The process of finding war criminals began a few months after the conclusion of the war and continuing throughout their lives. Between 1946 and 1949, roughly 1,000 former Auschwitz guards were investigated for war crimes, with only 673 receiving indictments. Relatively few of the worst offenders were hanged, but for the rest convicted, the average sentences were three or four years in prison. [233]

The White Buses [234]

The prisoner evacuation vehicles Basha saw at Malchow, the white buses, also went to many of the KL camps. They became known simply as the White Buses, and were part of a rescue effort which began in the fall of 1944. The Germans invaded Denmark and Norway on April 9, 1940, and the Gestapo arrested many citizens of those countries, imprisoning them in concentration camps. Several humanitarian agencies visited Scandinavian prisoners, bringing them food and mail, while other agencies discussed plans for negotiating a release of Scandinavian prisoners. They were initially unsuccessful, but Norwegian diplomat Niels Christian Ditleff continued to aggressively press for the release of Scandinavian prisoners. He contacted Swedish Count Folke Bernadotte in September 1944. Bernadotte was the vice president of the Swedish Red Cross and enthusiastically joined in the planning. Bernadotte and Ditleff successfully opened negotiations with the Germans, eventually expanding their plan to include all concentration camp prisoners, not just Scandinavians.

As negotiations continued, a strange, almost bizarre, circumstance occurred that worked in Bernadotte's and Ditleff's favor. Heinrich Himmler's masseur, a German named Felix Kersten, lived in Stockholm, and functioned as a quasi-diplomat between Himmler and the Swedish foreign service. Kersten's massage skills had brought greatly appreciated relief to some of Himmler's physical ailments, and in the process, he became Himmler's confidant, free to discuss topics that would be forbidden to anyone less trustworthy. The masseur had Himmler's back, but more importantly at this time, he also had his ear. Bernadotte worked through Kersten to negotiate a prisoner-release deal with Himmler. Himmler could plainly see that the end of the Third Reich was in sight, and by working with Bernadotte, Ditleff and the Red Cross, the victors might see him as a humanitarian—or at least human. With Himmler's tacit approval, the rescue effort began in March of 1945 and continued for a period postwar. The release of approximately thirty-one thousand prisoners of many nationalities was eventually negotiated, with over fifteen thousand transported on the buses.

Basha missed an early release by days.

The Dachau Massacre [235]

The prisoners were not the only ones anxious to get away from the KL camps. The crimes of the SS guards were obvious, and it became a priority for them to flee the fast-approaching Allied troops. Most escaped. Many were arrested after the war. Some were punished. However, a few were caught in the camps, surrounded by the horror they created, and the sight was more than their captors could take. There would be no arrest and trial for these guards; their captors took the matter of punishment into their own hands.

In general, the *SS* had earned a reputation for brutality, but as far as the prisoners were concerned, the *SS-Totenkopfverbände* (*SS-TV*) troops who had viciously operated the camps, earned a special place in hell. The appalled liberating Allied troops agreed, and a few decided to send them on the trip personally. All *SS* troops wore the *Totenkopf*—Death's Head—symbol on their hats, but *SS-TV* troops wore an additional Death's Head symbol on their right collar. It marked the wearer as one who would gladly abuse or murder victims. With the changing fortunes of war, things had reversed. Now it marked them as the ones to be abused and, yes, even murdered. *SS-TV* troops had no illusions about what would happen to them if they were captured by the Russians, so capture by the Americans was preferable. As it turned out, that choice was not entirely foolproof.

On April 29, 1945, the United States Army's Forty-Fifth Infantry Division marched through Bavaria on their way to Munich. Dachau was not an objective, but their route dictated that they march past the camp that afternoon. The first hint that something unusual was happening in the camp was the nauseating stench that surrounded the area. Forty railroad boxcars were parked at the entrance to the camp, so the GIs cautiously moved in, opened the doors, and inspected them. The sight horrified even the most battle-tested and callous of them. The boxcars were filled with the emaciated, rotting corpses of Jewish prisoners piled on top of each other like abandoned freight. Officers ordered some unfortunate GIs to count the bodies, which totaled 2,310.

Proceeding through the gate and into the camp, the Americans discovered thousands of what Basha referred to as *Muselmann*—walking dead. All troops were enraged. Some became physically ill. A few sought immediate revenge. Despite an investigation and sworn testimony from witnesses, many details of what transpired that day remain murky. What is certain is that American troops lined up an unknown number of *SS* officers, guards, and attack-trained German Shepard dogs against a wall and shot them to death. They may have killed others in other areas of the camp and in other ways, but the record is unclear. Liberation released years of pent-up rage in the prisoners. Those physically able attacked *SS* guards, striking them with shovels, stones, or their bare fists. One prisoner, Walenty Lenarczyk stated, "They caught the *SS* men and knocked them down, and nobody could see whether they were stomped or what, but they were killed." [236]

The murder of *SS* POWs (Prisoners of War) by American soldiers was a clear violation of the Geneva Convention; therefore, it presented a difficult and embarrassing problem for US military command. Transcripts of the investigation were marked "Secret." Brigadier General Felix Sparks, who was present at Dachau that day, stated that the American troops who were questioned about the matter claimed the *SS* troops were attempting to escape, a story that few, if any, believed. Sparks acknowledged the deaths, but stated not more than fifty *SS* troops had been killed and the figure was probably closer to thirty. Writing in 1986, Colonel Howard Buechner, also present at Dachau that day, stated that the event involved the "deliberate killing of 520 prisoners of war by American soldiers." Obviously, a great discrepancy.

When General Dwight D. Eisenhower spoke of the Dachau liberation, he stated that U.S. troops liberated 32,000 prisoners and quickly neutralized approximately 300 *SS* guards. Exactly what he meant by "neutralized" may be open to interpretation. It was assumed he meant "taken prisoner," which is certainly possible. But speaking about a war crime committed by your own troops would clearly be uncomfortable, particularly after the outrage expressed a few months earlier at the *SS* execution of eighty-four

American POWs at Malmedy, [237] during the Battle of the Bulge. Now the shoe was on the other foot. Perhaps "neutralized" was a euphemism for something else. Since the complete truth of the matter remains unknown all these decades later, it is likely to stay that way.

General George S. Patton wrapped up the problem when it hit his desk. He dismissed all charges. Patton, known for his strict military discipline, had become physically ill when he toured a concentration camp with generals Eisenhower and Bradley, and he had frequently expressed his contempt for the *SS*, so it is not beyond the realm of possibility that he felt the guards had gotten what they deserved and dropped the matter. Again, the record is unclear.

For *SS-TV* guards, the best chance for survival was to shed their *SS* uniforms and blend into the local population. The search for them would go on for decades.

For the prisoners, things changed rapidly and for the better. They suddenly had food and medical care, but one change was emotional. Former prisoner Jack Goldman remembered that the GIs learned the prisoners' names and used them: "For the first time, we were no longer numbers." [238]

In the midst of all the chaos and horror, that simple act restored their humanity.

Notes

205. Bess Freilich interview by Josey G. Fisher, 3-2-40.

206. Wachsmann, 227.

207. Ibid.

208. "Ravensbrück," Holocaust Encyclopedia, accessed March 26, 2022, https://encyclopedia.ushmm.org/content/en/article/ravensbrueck.

209. Dora Freilich, interview by Grossman, 3-2-39.

210. Bess Freilich, interview by Fisher 3-2-40.

211. Bess Freilich interview by Marc Seligman, 29.

212. Ibid.

213. Ibid.

214. Ibid.

215. Ibid.

216. "Flight and Expulsion of Germans (1944–1950)," Wikimedia Foundation, last modified December 1, 2022, https://en.wikipedia.org/wiki/Flight_and_expulsion_of_Germans_(1944%E2%80%931950).

217. "Malchow Concentration Camp," Wikimedia Foundation, last modified May 26, 2021, https://en.wikipedia.org/wiki/Malchow_concentration_camp.

218. Bess Freilich interview by Marc Seligman, 30.

219. Bess Freilich, interview by Fisher 3-2-40-41.

220. Dora Freilich, interview by Grossman, 3-2-45.

221. Ibid, 3-2-44

222. Bess Freilich, interview by Fisher 3-2-41.

223. Dora Freilich, interview by Grossman, 3-2-45.

224. Bess Freilich interview by Marc Seligman, 29.

225. Bess Freilich interview by Marc Seligman, 30.

226. Ibid.

227. Bess Freilich, interview by Fisher 3-2-41.

228. Ibid.

229. Dora Freilich, interview by Grossman, 3-2-46.

230. Ibid, 3-2-47.

231. Ibid.

232. Bess Freilich, interview by Fisher 3-2-41.

233."Trials of SS Men from the Auschwitz Concentration Camp Garrison," Auschwitz-Birkenau Memorial and Museum, accessed March 26, 2022, https://www.auschwitz.org/en/history/the-ss-garrison/trials-of-ss-men-from-the-auschwitz-concentration-camp-garrison/.

234. "White Buses," Wikipedia Foundation, last modified February 16, 2023, https://en.wikipedia.org/wiki/White_Buses.

235. Kara Goldfarb, "How Dachau Concentration Camp Guards Got Their Comeuppance," *All That's Interesting*, March 1, 2018, http://allthatsinteresting.com/dachau-reprisals.

236. Ibid.

237. "Malmady Massacre," Wikipedia Foundation, last modified April 6, 2023, https://en.wikipedia.org/wiki/Malmedy_massacre.

238. Kara Goldfarb, "How Dachau Concentration Camp Guards Got Their Comeuppance," *All That's Interesting*, March 1, 2018, http://allthatsinteresting.com/dachau-reprisals.

CHAPTER 13

Unwanted

Near Barkow, Germany
May 8, 1945

Germany's surrender brought an end to the European War, but it would be years before any sense of normalcy was restored. Families would mourn their dead and care for their wounded, and shortages of goods would continue in some countries for years. For roughly one million people in Europe, former Jewish KL prisoners as well as non-Jews who had lost everything in the devastation of war, their lives had been reduced to little more than the clothes on their backs. Their homes, and even their entire towns, had been destroyed, and many of their family members were dead or missing. They had no idea where to go, or who to turn to for help. Finding enough food to live for one more day became a priority.

One would think that a small group of homeless teenage girls would engender sympathy from the population, but that was not the case. For many, years of war had drained people of sympathy and replaced it with an emotional numbness. The girls walked through a populace who had seen and experienced so much terror and ugliness that it did not phase them anymore. Basha felt the numbness, too.

"I knew I was liberated, but there was no joy in it. There was nothing. We walked to a city. See, I was liberated actually on the Elba, where the Americans and the Russians met. Where they

met. And I walked to the city that belonged to the Americans.
[City name unintelligible on recording.] *I could have stayed
there, but I wanted to go home. I wanted to be on the Russian
side. I could have stayed with the Americans. And the town was
celebrating, and the people were dancing from joy. And there
were so many people, and they were drinking Coca-Cola. I'll
never forget, the Americans gave it* [to them]. *And I thought to
myself, why are those people so happy? What's awaiting me now?
Where am I going to go? What am I going to do? I'm the only one
from my family left. I didn't know whether my father was alive.
Father told us if anyone should remain alive, we should come
back to Pruzhany. And that's where I was determined to go. So,
I didn't remain with the Americans, but stayed on the Russian
side."* [239]

After the German surrender, the objective of the Western
Allies quickly changed from waging war, to establishing new
governments and providing humanitarian support. It was a noble
attempt, but initially only marginally successful. The enormity
of the task was daunting. In addition to feeding, clothing, and
housing their occupation troops, the Allies were also confronted
with a massive influx of new POWs. Occupation troops cared for
their former enemies with the limited resources available. The
Allied powers did not consider the average German soldier a
postwar threat; however, it took time to investigate the prisoners
to determine whether any of them had committed acts which
could lead to prosecution for war crimes. Former *Reichsführer-
SS*, Heinrich Himmler, had escaped Berlin disguised as a German
Wehrmacht sergeant and successfully evaded capture until
May 21. A British captain was conducting a routine prisoner
interrogation of him when Himmler admitted his true identity.
While undergoing a medical examination later, he bit into a

potassium cyanide capsule hidden in his mouth and successfully committed suicide. When one considers that Himmler, one of the most recognizable people in the world at that time, had managed to travel undetected for almost two weeks, the problem of finding lesser-known criminals among the tens of thousands of POWs is obvious. As the slow interrogation procedure progressed, the mass of waiting prisoners required food and supervision. The task was immense.

People were not the only problems. Bombers attacked Germany almost every day, but not all of the bombs exploded. Working in the rubble of bombed cities always brought the potential risk of hitting—and detonating—unexploded ordinance. Clearing debris could be fatal.

In the Russian-controlled territory, the care and feeding of German POWs was indifferent at best. Some were sent to Russia to work in slave-labor camps, and most were never heard from again. Former concentration camp prisoners and Displaced Persons (DPs) did receive some assistance from the Russians, but they had the same supply-and-demand problems as everyone else.

In the post-surrender logistic nightmare, it is likely that few former concentration camp prisoners or DPs received the highest standard of attention, but under the circumstances, most got the best available. Consequently, in the bigger picture, Basha and her friends were one pathetic looking group among thousands just like them.

Even with rudimentary care, the difference between their initial treatment by the Russians and that of their former Nazi captors was enormous. Their stomachs slowly adapted to food and their wounds healed. They also experienced something they had not seen for a long time. They were treated like humans.

"Six weeks later, we got a little bit of strength, the three gals of

us. The Russians gave us two horses and a wagon, and [we] *went on a trip back to Pruzhany."*

Some kind people had given the girls items to put in the wagon, hoping they would be useful later, perhaps for bartering.

"From Berlin, we traveled to our town. On the way . . . some Ukrainian gal stopped us. She told us to leave the horses here and to come in. We can wash and we can bathe. My God, to wash and bathe! We didn't do that for years! So, we listened. And we took from Germany some materials just in case. People said in Poland you could sell it. You would be able to survive. Sell it for bread. So, we had this on the wagon with the horses and we went to wash. It didn't take too long. When we came out, [they had taken] *away our clothing. They took away the material* [in the wagon.] *They took away the horses too, and we had to stay the whole night and try to cover ourselves up with some rags."* [240]

They had started their journey with nothing but the clothes on their backs. Now they were gone too.

Despite this latest infliction of malicious misery, Basha and the girls were not deterred in their determination to reach their hometown. Someone provided them with enough clothes to cover themselves decently, and then, without the horses and wagon, they had to devise a plan to continue their journey. They had recovered much of their strength, but they did not have any money or baggage. The lack of belongings was an odd blessing. They decided they would travel by hopping on a passing freight train. They were strong enough to lift their bodies onto the cars, but probably not while carrying a suitcase.

Hopping a freight train would have been a brash act before the war, completely out of the question for young girls. Things were different now. After their treatment by the Germans, there was little fear left in them. They wanted to go home. They wanted to see their city. Most of all, they wanted a miracle that would put them in contact with their families. The daring and uncomfortable train ride worked out well for them, but as they continued to learn, nothing was foolproof.

They did not get far into the Russian sector before trouble arose again. The European War may have ended, but suspicion remained, and for good reason. Young German men—predominantly die-hard Nazis who had been indoctrinated in the Hitler Youth or served in the *SS*—formed a guerrilla group known as the Werewolves. They were intent on killing Allied troops and destroying their equipment. They did not last long or do a great deal of damage, but the threat kept occupation troops on their toes. In the Eastern areas, the Russians remained vigilant for potential anti-communist partisans, or others who might be disruptive or dangerous. There was also tension among the Allies. The Western powers were wary of communism, and the Russians, having been stabbed in the back by Hitler, were wary of friends who could suddenly become foes. The alliance remained, but the Western and Eastern Allies kept a careful watch on one another. Their occupation forces were fully armed and it would take little more than a telephone call on one side or the other to set them at each other's throats.

Under normal circumstances a few homeless teenage girls would not draw suspicion as guerrillas or troublemakers, but in those tense times, no one was above suspicion. Trust was a rare commodity, and the Russians knew how to deal with people they did not trust.

The railroad journey was fairly quick, certainly much quicker than it would have been with the horses and wagon. When the train stopped, they had to get off and wait to jump another train that was going closer to their final destination. They were filled with anticipation as well as a degree of anxiety. Despite the obvious signs of the aftermath of war all around them, they clutched onto the hope that some family and friends in Pruzhany, and perhaps even their homes, had survived the devastation. They pushed back their anxiety and fought to retain a sense of optimism. That was crushed only a few steps from the train when it stopped near Warsaw. Basha saw familiar faces, but their conversation was not what she would have hoped for.

> *"The train . . . when we came to the Russian side, we met a few partisans from our town—Jewish people. And they said, 'You just destroyed your life. You should have never come here. You should have never come here.' Well, little did we know. We spoke to them and they left. We were just walking into the city. It was Brest-Litovsk, right near the border between Poland and Russia."*

They were quickly spotted by the Russian Secret Police who wanted to know who they were and what they were doing.

> *"The Secret Police, they asked us where is our certificate?* [Basha replied,] *'We were in the camps,' and I showed them my number* [tattooed on her arm]. *'What kind of certificate do you want from us?'"* [241]

The Russian Secret Policemen did not waste a lot of time talking to the girls. The attitude seemed to be that everyone, even a small group of teenage girls, would be considered a spy or criminal until they could prove otherwise. The Russians took the girls to a prison facility for questioning.

Imprisoned Again

Compassion, sympathy, and even basic humanity were things Basha and her former prison companions had seen little of since the war broke out in 1939. Even in the hands of their supposed liberators, that was not going to change. The Russian Secret Policemen ordered the girls to come with them.

"The Russians took us into a concentration camp. The minute we entered, we were right near our town, and they kept us there for a long while, questioning us, and they kept on saying that we were spies. The Germans killed the whole Jewish population and they found we were alive, [so] we must have been spies. They questioned us, and of course they questioned us separately, and each girl told a different story. Like, they asked, 'What time did you go to work?' and we didn't know what time, we didn't have watches. Each girl gave them a different time, and this they [held] against us because they said our conversations didn't match . . . what we told them. That means that we probably were spies, and therefore we had to stay in this camp, and we stayed in that camp. Then they kept on questioning us and torturing us and torturing us. 'Just how come we are alive?' That was their only question, 'how come you're alive, how come they killed everyone and they left you. I mean why?' And it was sheer torture. They were questioning us, they were humiliating us, they didn't give us no food, no nothing." [242]

The Russians held them captive in the concentration camp for about two months. Then, without explanation, the situation changed.

"Then all of a sudden came an order that we can go on our way. Later, we find out that those three partisans, they bribed the [Unintelligible on recording; probably the Russian name for the secret police], those three Jewish partisans." [243]

The chance and brief encounter with the Jewish partisans when Basha and the girls had stepped off the train may well have been the difference between their life and death. These frequent coincidences reinforced Basha's belief that her survival seemed to be foreordained.

The Painful Return Home

After two months of Russian confinement and neglect, Basha and her companions were on their own once again. They were back to being malnourished and weak, but they were free and just as determined as ever to get to Pruzhany. They returned to the railroad yard, found out which trains were going in the right direction, and hopped on one that was heading toward their home.

One of the disadvantages of hopping random trains, as opposed to having a ticket, is that the itinerary can be somewhat uncertain. As the train approached Lenovo, Poland, the train station nearest to their home, it quickly became apparent that they were going to have a problem.

> *"We went on a train, and we thought that the train would stop at Lenovo, near our Pruzhany, but the train, we could see, was going at its usual speed, and it* [was not going to] *stop. So, me and the other two gals* [from Pruzhany], *we jumped from the train."*

Jumping from a moving train is extremely dangerous under the best of circumstances, but it is worse when your strength and coordination are compromised by malnutrition. If any of the girls broke a bone, it is unlikely that anyone would help, or perhaps even care. Nevertheless, they had to get off the train one way or another.

> *". . . we jumped, so . . . we were children, but we were wise. We went through so much. So, we jumped forward, and that saved our lives. We couldn't jump straight with* [unintelligible on recording]*."* [244]

By jumping forward in the direction the train was moving, they hoped to reduce the speed at which they hit the ground. Remarkably, no one was injured. Despite the horrors of the last two years, they were continually blessed by these moments of good luck. Landing safely was one thing, but remaining safe would continue to be a challenge. After gathering together and checking for injuries, the girls started to walk toward Pruzhany.

"And I had there a little piece of bread in a kerchief. And I find my friend [Dora], *and we both were going to the station, to Lenovo. There was a soldier staying right near the train station, and he only had one arm. A Russian soldier, and he said, 'I lost my arm in the war, and you brought . . . '* [something in Russian that Basha could not understand]. *He thought, God knows what I have in the kerchief. He didn't know it was bread, he thought it was . . . God knows what I had there. So, he said, 'Why don't we change? I'll cut off your arm, and I'll take away your* [indistinguishable on recording].*' This was in my own city where every stone I knew. It was Lenovo but it was right near my town."* [245]

The uncomfortable situation diffused when Dora saw a familiar face. She remembered:

"I see a guy coming over to us, and comes over, and he looks at me and he says to me, 'Are you the girl from Pruzhany? Did your parents have a bakery?'

And I said, 'Yes,' and he recognized me.

He said, 'Are you alive?'

I said, 'Well, I am.'

He said, 'I used to work for your father. You don't know me, but I used to deliver bread for your father. What are you doing here?'

And I tell him the story. I say to him that my father had jumped out [of the train], *and I came back looking for him, and maybe he knows if my father is alive. He didn't hear about it. I said, 'Is there Jews in my home town?'*

He said, 'Yes, there are a few, but they are all from the forests that came back.'"

The man warned the girls to stay away from the Russian. "Get away from him because he is a murderer. He is so miserable because he lost his arm in the war." Then he helped the girls get away. [246]

Basha picks up the story:

". . . [T]he guy . . . used to take passengers from the station with his horse and wagon, to our city, to Pruzhany. So he said, 'Listen, you sit down, not all of you, not all three of you. Some will have to walk, and one I'll let [ride on the wagon]. *You'll have to rotate. One will sit on the wagon, because the horse is too weak.'*

So, he took us—I'll never forget this—the sun was going down. It was a beautiful sunset, entering my town. I cried so many nights to be back here at home, and see my town once again in my lifetime. I saw only ruins and ruins.

So, the guy said, 'Listen, there is a Jewish family right near the river, and I'm going to drop you off there so you can sleep over the night.' So, we were happy.

"He dropped us off, and a woman came out, and I knew the woman because I was friends with her daughter. Her daughter was my age. And her son was my brother's age. The mother was very pleasant, a nice lady. She saw us and she started crying, 'My God, my God.' And we said, 'Listen, will we be able to sleep over the night in your house?'

And she said, 'No.'

I couldn't believe it. It was summertime, so I said, "Can we sleep over on the porch?" She had a porch, open porch.

She said, 'No, you have to go away from here.'

I said, 'Why?'

She said, 'I don't have my children. I don't want to look at you.'

Because they [her children] *were hiding in the woods, the children, the boy and the girl. They went out to find some food* [among] *the peasants, and the Germans caught them and killed them. So, she said she doesn't have her children and she can't look at us. I remember the peasant said, 'See, even your people change.'* [347]

———— ✦ ————

The girls walked into their beloved hometown after over a two-year absence. They did not see a familiar face. No family, no friends. Instead, they found hatred. The Jews had been run off or killed, but the anti-Semites were still there in full force.

"The goyim kept on looking at us, and they didn't like our presence there. They were afraid we had come to take back all the things that they had robbed from us. We stayed in a little broken house there, and every time during the day and in the night, they threw big stones, and they broke all the windows, and kids went after us, tearing our clothes, and said in Polish, 'Look, the Jews are coming back.'

"I remember passing by a factory once, and the people . . . I saw the windows full of people that ran to the windows to look at us like we were some kind of people landed from Mars. Just to look at us because they weren't used to seeing a Jew anymore, and they couldn't believe that somebody survived. And of course, they didn't like it because they knew that maybe we'll want our things

back, but we weren't interested in it. We didn't want nothing back. We didn't have no place to put it, even if they gave us our things back, and we came to see if anybody was alive. Nobody was there." [248]

As the anti-Semites gave her cold stares and hurled insults at her, Basha made her way to the ghetto. Most of it had been destroyed—including her house.

"That I knew once it was my home, where I spent my happy childhood, and we were such a close family. Even though we didn't have much, we didn't need much, and we had each other, and this was everything for us. There was so much love and devotion to each other, and there was nobody now. I was only by myself sitting there, and it was dusk already, sitting in a place where once my home was, and I was torn to pieces, torn to pieces. That's when the old woman came that told me that her son-in-law was the first one to empty our house of the furnishings." [249]

That was all Basha could take. She sat on the ruins of her childhood home and wept.

Notes

239. Bess Freilich interview by Marc Seligman, 29.

240. Ibid.

241. Ibid, 31-2

242. Ibid, 32.

243. Ibid.

244. Ibid.

245. Ibid.

246. Dora Freilich, interview by Grossman, 1-1-49.

247. Bess Freilich interview by Marc Seligman, 32.

248. Bess Freilich, interview by Fisher 3-2-42.

249. Ibid.

CHAPTER 14

Homeless

Basha had dreamed of joyfully celebrating her return to Pruzhany, but the reality of the event was more like a nightmare.

"I was living after the war in my hometown, in the town of my childhood. I recognized the streets, and sometimes I would walk where the Gentiles lived, and everything looked just the way it was before. The gardens were tended, the houses looked nice and neat like there was no war, like nothing happened. But the Jewish Quarter—the ghetto—was all wiped out, and I knew that, somehow, I was living like in a cemetery. We wanted to get out, and we couldn't already. The Russians didn't let us." [250]

The heartache Basha felt at the destruction of her childhood home and neighborhood was exacerbated by the jubilation all around her.

"We came to the center of the city. People were dancing in the middle of the street. They built, like, a platform, and there was music, and they were showing films there at night. We couldn't find a familiar face. I couldn't find a place to put my weary body down. Then we find also a guy who came from the woods, from the partisans, and he said, 'Come, you'll sleep over the night in our house.'" [251]

After all the girls had endured, the few hours of peace and respite were a great help. The partisan had survived the war living in the woods and fighting. He had also suffered severe privation and stress from the specter of death that had continually lurked in the shadows around him. Coming from that perspective, one much different from that of the Gentiles, perhaps showing kindness and compassion was his way of celebration. Whatever his motivation, the girls received some much-needed rest and then reentered their city with no contacts, resources, or plan other than the single obsession that had drawn them back to Pruzhany since their imprisonment began.

". . . [W]e just wanted to see if somebody remained alive and came to the town, because before we left, we promised each other once we remained alive, that's where we were going to meet, and that's why. I could have stayed on the American side and avoided all this trauma that I went through after the war, but I felt like something was pulling me. I had to know. I had to know if somebody was [still] *alive."* [252]

The desire to resolve the question of the fate of family and friends overpowered everything else in her life except the bare minimum of existence. Basha intended to keep searching as long as she found hope. To do that she would need to figure out how to stay alive on a day-to-day basis as she progressed. Although few people were willing to come to her aid, the chaos that remained after the German retreat created some opportunities. Just as she and the girls had foraged in the woods for edible vegetables and plants after the Death March, there were still opportunities to forage, only now within the city itself. Polish properties seized by German citizens after the German occupation, and abandoned during the retreat, now sat empty with whatever goods had been left behind in the frantic withdrawal. Curious citizens searched them for whatever they might contain. Some took what interested them. Basha and the girls focused on what could help keep them alive.

"I walked into German homes where I could just pick anything up, but I didn't reach for that much, because I never knew [what] I would need some day. Something that I'll require for anything, that I would live a normal life. It never dawned on me that I would be a human being again." [253]

Although her physical world had expanded enormously, her emotional world remained very small.

"I only kept on looking [to see if] a German with a gun [was] in back of me ... even when I was free, I really couldn't adjust to it. I thought I was still in camp. I just couldn't believe that it ended, it was constantly with me even though the concentration camps were already empty of us." [254]

Her newfound freedom was difficult for her to grasp.

"I passed by the school that I used to go [to]. It devastated me. I was thinking about the good times [I had when] I used to go there." [255]

The taunts of the anti-Semitic citizens were painful, but the girls just walked away. The Russians, however, were another matter. They continued to harass the girls, but walking away was not an option. The Russians took control of them again, this time putting them in a place Basha described as a concentration camp.

"And the Russians kept on after us. They said, 'They killed the whole city. How come you [are] alive? You probably collaborated with the Germans.' Every day there were investigations." [256]

The Russians were as persistent in their harassment, intimidation, and bullying of Basha as they had been previously, over and over again dwelling on the question of her survival. She was powerless against the intelligence officers and soldiers who continued to grab her and the other girls off the streets and hold them under their control. Facing abuse from all directions, Basha retaliated the only way she could: verbally.

"Once I [pushed] *myself* [for] *the courage to tell them: '*[You are] *investigating us because I think that you are the biggest anti-Semites. You're just like the Nazis were. What bothers you, actually, is that you saw from a whole town that a few from so many thousands of girls, a few of them remained alive, and they came back to pick up the pieces, to see what happened to their homes and to their families, and it bothers you that they came back and that they remained alive. I think this is really in your heart—why you're questioning us—because there's no other reason for you to torture us like this.'"* [257]

The Russians finally released Basha from the room, bruised and crying, in a freshly torn dress.

Basha quickly learned that, considering the circumstances, a torn dress was mild punishment. Basha soon met the custodian of the Russian facility, Mr. Rosenbaum, the husband of the woman who refused to let them stay in her home. He had information and advice.

"And there was a guy there that was walking in the corridor, and he took care [of *the facility.*] *He was a Jewish fellow from our town. And he worked there . . . he got a job there. And he told me, he said, 'Basha, you had the worst of them all. He's worse than the Nazis, this here guy.'"* [258]

But, as had happened when Basha spoke up to the vicious Nazi who had confronted her about throwing bread to her father, she had talked back to authority and survived.

Since her imprisonment began over two years previously, Basha continued to have insufficient information to help her understand her plight. Mr. Rosenbaum had access to the facility and kept his eyes and ears open. There was also a young boy from their town who worked for the Russians and had witnessed the girls being tortured. He, too, became their ally.

"There was a Jewish boy that worked with the NKVD from our town [People's Commissariat of Internal Affairs: a form of secret police]. *He worked there like an orderly, and he came one night to us in the middle of the night. And he said that they gave him—the Russian NKVD—gave him a letter to throw in the mailbox, and he knew somehow that it had something to do with us. And he opened it up and he read it, and it was* [written in the letter] *that every girl says a little bit different to the stories, the stories don't match. Which they couldn't match because, like I said, nobody knew the time exactly. Those were the things that, actually, every girl said different. I thought that when they woke us up to work it was two o'clock. Another girl said two-thirty."*[259]

The letter writer asserted that the conflicting stories of the girls were evidence they were lying. Basha had no way to refute the statements of the unknown letter writer, but she was now aware that their treatment may not be solely based on Russian hatred. The Russians may have genuinely believed the girls were lying and intended to keep intimidating them until they were satisfied, one way or another, where the truth lie. With no proof to offer in her defense, and nothing to say that she had not already said, the future looked like an endless continuum of threatening interrogations. The Russian intelligence officers could appear at any time.

"We wanted the night to go on forever, but we slept only a few hours. So they woke us up, [in the] *pitch black, in the nighttime, so they said we are not telling the truth."*[260]

The girls had only the clothes on their backs, and the food the Russians provided. They had a roof over their heads and there was no lock on the door, but Basha had to consider whether their dismal situation was better than walking out onto the streets with nothing. Rosenbaum and the young NKVD orderly helped with her decision. They learned the Russians had a plan for suspicious DPs, which included Basha and the girls.

"[The Russians would send] *us to Siberia, to Chelyabinsk. That's where the coal mines are. For us to work there after the concentration camp. We should work in the coal mines.*[261] *We knew that after all we had lived through . . . the war . . . we lived through so much, and we lost our families, and there was a chance for us to remain alive. Once we go there* [to the coal mines] *it would be the end . . .*[262]

"*So he* [Rosenbaum] *said, 'You must leave right away.' He paid a few peasants . . . paid a few peasants that they should take us to Lenovo, to the* [train] *station. And he gave us some money. We should have that in case we needed it.*"[263]

Basha and the girls fled while they still had a chance. At that point in time, as far as Basha knew, only she, Dora, and the other two girls with them from their town had survived, but when they ran from Pruzhany they found themselves among hundreds of thousands of survivors—none of whom had anywhere to go. In their march across Europe, the Nazis had deliberately sought out, imprisoned, and killed Jews, but Gentiles also fell victim to the assault from the East and the retreat to the West. Bombs and artillery do not ask a person's race or religion before they detonate. The result was a never-before-seen humanitarian crisis.

Fleeing Again

Basha had attained her goal of returning to her hometown, but after two or three months of hopelessness, there was clearly no reason to stay and every reason to leave. She had no intention of surviving the cruelty of the Nazis only to suffer the cruelty of the Russians, and then die in a coal mine in Siberia. With only the clothes on their backs and the money that Mr. Rosenbaum had given them, the girls fled Pruzhany immediately, with no plan other than to try to reach a place that was under American control. This would involve crossing the border into Poland, and the borders were closely guarded. They would either have to sneak across or talk their way across. They would not know which option to take until they got there.

They decided to leave the area the same way they had come: by train. The money from Mr. Rosenbaum allowed them to buy tickets and sit in a coach rather than jump on and off boxcars, as they had before. The rail line ran through a small adjacent town, so they walked there immediately. In another of the small miracles that continued to materialize in her life, Basha saw a man she knew. At that time, the man was engaged in the business of printing counterfeit identification and travel papers, and he made a set of documents for each girl. Basha and the group climbed aboard the next train heading west and hoped for the best. The counterfeiter was apparently quite good at his new craft, and the counterfeit documents passed the critical inspection of the border guards without issue. Basha and the girls soon found themselves in Łódz, Poland, where a local took them from the station into the city in a horse-drawn wagon. The experience was initially uplifting, not just because they were free from Russian oppression, but because after years of torture for being Jewish, they suddenly saw Jews free to celebrate their faith.

> *"Around Rosh Hashanah it was yomtov* [a holiday] [when] *we came to Łódz. It was* erev yomtov [the eve of the holiday] *and people were rushing to the synagogue, and we came with no place to go . . . we didn't know nobody. It was a strange city, but we saw . . . Jews.* [264]

"We came to Poland, and that was on Yom Kippur. I'll never forget. And we came and we saw people going to the synagogue. With the long coats, and they were orthodox people, and there weren't too many Jews, but you could feel the holiday, you could feel it." [265]

Basha could feel the celebration, but suddenly felt strangely detached from it as she watched the families enter the synagogue.

"We were sitting like this in a wagon, in a horse and wagon. No place to go again, no home, no parents, no nobody. And a guy passed by, and he was from our town. This was in Łódz, we came already. And he was from our town. And he gave us the keys to his little room where he lived, and he said he was going to live with a fellow he knows. And he gave us the room, and that's where we stayed." [266]

She had a roof over her head and saw her people openly practicing their faith, but at no time did Basha feel the illusion of safety. She had seen and experienced too much in her short life to be easily comforted. More importantly, unlike in the camps, news and information was constantly available, and the news was rarely good for Jews.

"This [Łódz] *was the center of the survivors in Poland, all concentrated in one city. Because if you lived in the small towns, the goyim used to take the survivors . . . used to cut out their numbers* [tattoos], *and they killed so many of us after the war. [There] was a pogrom in one city where they killed so many girls that survived Auschwitz. They just ran in at night and just massacred all of them, and so everybody was afraid to live in the small towns. They all concentrated, whoever survived, in Łódz, and we saw that we are* [among] *Jews, and somehow we wanted somebody* [to] *help us with something to get a roof over our heads.*

"There was . . . a committee, [and] we went there, and [it] was helping, and they gave us, I remember, like chopped herring and Crisco [fried with] some flour. We got very sick from the Crisco, but this was our diet, and they used to give this to us constantly. And a lot of the Israeli agents were after us; we should join the kibbutz because they saw we were single young girls, that this was no way for us to wander around without family. That nobody should live like this. But my desire was to go back on the American side and see if somebody was still alive. Somehow, in my heart, I hoped that my father is alive, and that's the only reason I didn't join the kibbutz." [267]

The *kibbutz* would provide a sense of family that she sorely missed, and likely result in relocation to Palestine, where her family had long dreamed of emigrating. The trade-off for the new life would be giving up the search for her father, and perhaps never knowing if he had survived the war. If he had survived, she might never see him again.

The decision was fateful, in more ways than one.

Historical Perspective
on Chapter 14

Eight Million Homeless – The Plight of the Displaced

The guns had silenced, but hunger, homelessness, and poverty continued. There were many good people around the world who wanted to help. Others were indifferent. Some were hostile. No matter what one's stance on the situation, it was a problem that would not go away on its own.

Frequently, the issue was not as simple as going back to their homelands and rebuilding their properties. Political boundaries and regimes had changed. For many, as much as they may have wished to go home, the place they knew and loved no longer existed as they remembered it. As the Allies divided Europe into different areas of influence, many Displaced Persons (DPs) were reluctant to live under a new political system. Specifically, many whose towns now fell under Soviet control had no desire to live under another authoritarian system. For them, going back was not an option, and moving forward presented questions and challenges that were difficult for them to face physically, emotionally, and financially. Nevertheless, within a year, 75 percent of the displaced had returned to their former homes or established a new home elsewhere. [268] That was certainly an improvement, but far from a solution given the number of people affected.

The displaced Jews faced those problems, plus an additional significant one. The war had not resolved the issue of anti-Semitism. As Basha discovered when she went back to Pruzhany, those who hated the Jews before the war generally continued to hate them afterward. Those returning from the concentration camps could encounter hostility, and possibly even danger. On July 1, 1946, forty-two repatriated Jews were killed and over forty wounded in the town of Kielce, Poland by Polish soldiers, police, and citizens. Anti-Semitism had been strong in the city prior to the war, and under the influence of the Nazis, anti-Semitic hatred had been promoted by the government and even the clergy. On July 4, 1946, approximately 160 displaced Jews who had returned to Kielce were quartered in a single building administrated by a Jewish relief organization. A Gentile local child charged that he had been kidnapped by a man in the building—a charge that was later proven false—but the initial anger fueled by anti-Semitism manifested in an attack on the Jews. A Polish court later sentenced nine Kielce citizens to death for the murders, but news of the event was a stark warning for Polish Jews who wanted to return to their homeland. [269]

Notes

250. Bess Freilich, interview by Fisher 4-1-44.

251. Bess Freilich interview by Marc Seligman, 33.

252.Bess Freilich, interview by Fisher 3-2-43.

253. Ibid.

254. Ibid.

255. Bess Freilich interview by Marc Seligman, 33.

256. Bess Freilich, interview by Fisher 3-2-43.

257. Bess Freilich, interview by Fisher 4-1-44.

258. Bess Freilich interview by Marc Seligman, 34.

259. Bess Freilich, interview by Fisher 4-1-44.

260. Bess Freilich interview by Marc Seligman, 34.

261. Bess Freilich, interview by Fisher 4-1-44.

262. Ibid.

263. Bess Freilich interview by Marc Seligman, 34.

264. Bess Freilich, interview by Fisher 4-1-44.

265. Bess Freilich interview by Marc Seligman, 34.

266. Ibid.

267. Bess Freilich, interview by Fisher 4-1-44.

268. "World War II: Displaced Persons," Jewish Virtual Library, accessed May 8, 2022, https://www.jewishvirtuallibrary.org/displaced-persons.

269. "Kielce Pogrom," Wikimedia Foundation, last modified November 10, 2022, https://en.wikipedia.org/wiki/Kielce_pogrom.

CHAPTER 15

A New Family

The little room the man provided for the girls would allow them to survive the upcoming harsh Polish winter in warmth; however, some of that warmth was generated because the room was extremely overcrowded. The man, a cap maker, apparently had a soft spot in his heart for homeless young girls, and Basha's group was not the first to whom he generously offered accommodations. When the girls arrived they brought the total occupancy of the small space to twenty. By comparison to what they had already been through, the tight quarters were an inconvenience, but certainly not a hardship. They talked, planned, and dreamed of their future. Every moment of every day was clouded by uncertainty, but they pushed forward with the persistent hope of finding other surviving family members. They had come a long way physically and emotionally. Their health improved, their hair grew out, and their self-image and confidence progressed, although slowly. There was no quick recovery from the horror they had experienced; in fact, they would never totally recover. The emotional scars would be lifelong, but they had also developed an increased level of emotional strength. They would spend the rest of their lives balancing the two.

Reentering Life

With the shred of stability their little room provided, the girls had to figure out how to make a living. A growing number of ambitious refugees, like the cap maker, had worked themselves to a position where they had a reasonably dependable source of income. The girls had nothing to invest in a business of any kind, but some of their new roommates who had been around longer were making money buying used items and reselling them for a profit. They would leave Łódz and travel to surrounding areas where things were less expensive, buy things, and bring them back into the city to sell with a markup. A length of fabric that could be made into a suit, or an attractive piece of jewelry, could yield a few *zlotys*—money that could be reinvested in more items to make increased profits. Since other girls were successful in this endeavor, Basha and Dora felt they could do the same thing. The girls who traveled outside Łódz helped them get started by selling some of their items to Basha and Dora at a price low enough to resell the items at a profit. The other girls made a little money, and Basha and Dora made a little money. They certainly were not becoming wealthy, but the money kept them fed and the business was a tangible symbol of the progress they were making.

One afternoon in the little room, one of the other girls suggested she and Basha go for a walk to relieve the tedium. Basha rejected the idea. She had not yet made much money, and her clothing was little more than rags. She was ashamed to be seen. On the other hand, she was also tired of constantly sitting indoors, so she suggested they wait until night and walk in the darkness when no one would see how shabbily she was dressed. The other girl agreed and they waited until sunset.

It was autumn and beginning to get chilly. As they walked through Łódz, the other girl recognized three young men standing on a street corner. They were in the same business as Basha, trying to make a little money by selling a used coat. The other girl engaged the young men in conversation, but Basha was uncomfortable and remained silent. One of the young men was obviously interested in her. Basha remembered the brief conversation:

"And he asked me if I'm single, and I said yes. And he said, 'Such a pretty girl and you're single.' I kept quiet. The other guy said, 'She's very pretty but she doesn't talk, she doesn't speak.'" [270]

This first meeting probably would have led to nothing, but a couple of days later Basha went to the market and ran into the young man again, whose name was Samuel Freilich. This time she felt more comfortable talking. She agreed to go out on a date with him, and soon they were seeing each other regularly. Basha suddenly had a small bit of normalcy in her life.

As the weeks passed, Basha and Dora began making enough money to set a little aside toward things they especially wanted. In Dora's case, it was a pair of shoes. She had not had a proper pair for a long time, and she saved for them diligently. One day they sold a watch at a good profit, and with her share, Dora finally had enough money to make her long-awaited purchase. To most, that would seem like a small item, but to Dora, buying those shoes was a big moment. She, too, now had a small bit of normalcy.

Basha and Samuel continued to enjoy each other's company, and as Dora remembered, one day Samuel had an idea.

"And she [Basha] had met a guy, you know, we were young, and he started taking her out, and he said to her, 'You know, I have a brother too; maybe your girlfriend would like to meet my brother.'
"And she said, 'Well, why don't you come up with him sometime and we will get acquainted?' "So, they came up one evening, and they were doing the same thing, the two brothers: they were also selling and buying, but [to a] bigger extent than we did. "And we got acquainted, and he said, 'How about we go out one night to the movies?'

"You had to start living again. You had to connect things, you had to somehow start mingling with the world, and the free world. And one day he made a date with me, and he came to pick

me up and I was looking for my shoes. I told him that I bought this week a pair shoes; we had a very good sale. And I couldn't find the shoes in the room. And we started joking around and he said, 'You probably don't want to go and you hid the shoes.'

"And I said, 'No, I didn't.'

"Anyway, somebody stole the shoes and sold them." [271]

Another inauspicious moment, but one saved by a mutual sense of humor. From that point on, Dora began dating Bernard Freilich. Ironically for the shoeless Dora, Bernard and Samuel were just going into the shoe business.

More Persecution and Flight

Things were certainly much better for Basha than they had been a year previously, but they were far from perfect. The other girls who left Auschwitz with her slowly began to establish new lives and scattered across Europe and the world. Basha had some newfound stability in her life with Samuel, and they married after a brief courtship. Dora and Bernard were married in the same ceremony, along with a third couple, all intending to build new families. But unfortunately, there was nothing they could do about the anti-Semitism that raged throughout Poland. Samuel and Bernard had also been imprisoned during the war, and were the only two survivors of their family. Under no circumstances could any of them forget the persecution they had endured for being Jewish, but in Poland it was not just a memory. The persecution— and even murder—of the Jews continued.

Jewish survivors congregated in a neighborhood of Łódz and were relatively safe together there, but were unwelcome in other areas of the city and country. They spent their time searching for family members who had disappeared during the war, and contacting family members they knew had survived. Many sent letters to family in other countries pleading for help getting reestablished, but even if there were offers, it was extremely difficult to emigrate. The Polish borders were controlled by vigilant guards who demanded travel papers, which were not easily obtained. Countries around the world established tight immigration quotas, and severely restricted the number of Jews they would accept. The survivors were trapped in Poland, and Poland was not safe. Not safe at all.

The July 4, 1946 anti-Semitic attack in Kielce, Poland,[272] resulted in the murders of forty-two repatriated Jews. This was an outrage to all Jews, but it was particularly distressing to Basha. She had friends among the victims.

"We tried to escape from Poland after the Kielce pogrom that they killed survivors in Kielce, forty of them. Some of them that I knew, they were in Auschwitz. They cut out their numbers [tattooed on their arms]. And that made the atmosphere very terrible. Couldn't stay in Poland no more." [273]

The random atrocities were reminiscent of the Gestapo.

"After the pogrom at Kielce we knew we had to leave Poland, that it was very dangerous for us to stay there. There were a few Kibbutzim that went to a wedding, to a different town, and on the road, they [an anti-Semitic Polish group] *stopped the trucks, and they killed all the young people, they killed all of them on the road, and we knew that the whole thing is starting all over. They were anti-Semites, and we knew that the Polish soil is still wet with our blood, but still we knew that it was time to leave this place. We felt it was the cemetery for us, and the sooner we leave the better it will be.* [274]

It was an attractive idea to emigrate to Palestine to be among Jews in an optimistic and energetic new society, particularly to

Samuel and Bernard. The area had its problems, to be sure, but compared to what they had already been through, it looked like an excellent option.

When newsreels exposed the horrors of the concentration camps to audiences in cinemas around the world, many felt that a Palestinian country of Jews governed by Jews looked like a good idea. It did not look like a good idea to everyone, however. The indigenous Arab population in the area was predominantly Muslim and opposed to the Jews in general, but particularly to their moving into the land they considered their own.

The British had taken control of Palestine after World War I, and under the Balfour Declaration of 1917, agreed in principle to set up a Zionist state, triggering an immediate anti-Zionist backlash. Also, many Arabs believed the British had promised them a self-governing, Arab-Palestinian nation as a reward for their help against Turkey during WWI. That never happened, so they found the idea of the Jews getting their own nation instead of them to be particularly galling.

The British, trying to govern and appease both groups, had their hands full and dragged their feet on Jewish immigration and statehood. In fact, they limited Jewish immigration. The Jews found themselves being prohibited from an area that was supposed to be established for Jews, an equally galling situation. However, for the daring and resourceful, there was a way around this problem. Jews, including Basha, Dora, Samuel, and Bernard, could be smuggled into the country. As the word "smuggled" implies, this required a certain amount of subterfuge.

In 1920, an organization called *Aliyah Bet* formed for the purpose of moving Jews to Palestine. *Aliyah Bet,* loosely translated from Hebrew, came to stand for "secret move to Palestine." The primary mode of transportation was by ship, but British sea patrols did their best to intercept the ships, and the passengers were frequently taken to the island of Cyprus where they were interned.

The trips were dangerous and sometimes included fatalities, but Jewish refugees continued to want to emigrate with the help of *Aliyah Bet*. The four registered with the organization as Greek Jews. They were given false names and coached on how to speak and behave to carry off the ruse. Polish authorities were every bit as aware of *Aliyah Bet* as the British were, and paid careful attention to anything that looked like illegal emigration. Just as Basha and her group were ready to flee to Palestine, they were caught by Polish authorities and taken to Katowice, Poland, to be searched and interrogated. Basha's group had to account for their actions, and the Polish authorities had to account for a questionable arrest. For expediency's sake, both sides lied. The police said they were looking for guns, which they were not, and the group said they were searching for lost relatives, which they also were not. The group was released without punishment or further interference, but the trip to Palestine was off. [275]

The group had virtually nothing but determination, but that they had in abundance. They continued to cross the border and continued to be sent back. Finally, they succeeded in a one-way crossing into Germany. They still had nothing, but now they had nothing in a safer place.

Hordes of Homeless

Ideally, now that the war was over everyone would just go home, but for approximately 40 million people of the displaced, home no longer existed. Roughly 11 million of them ended up in areas controlled by the Allies. The war military crisis had become a postwar humanitarian crisis. The DP were a diverse group which included Jews from the concentration camps, anti-Nazi political prisoners, former POWs who had not been repatriated, and average citizens of various faiths and ethnicities who had the bad luck to be in the way of a war that annihilated everything in its path. Primarily Eastern Europeans, they were from Armenia, Poland, Latvia, Lithuania, Estonia, Yugoslavia, Ukraine, Hungary, and Czechoslovakia, among other countries. They did not share a common language or culture. What they did share was human frailty. Many were ill, some dying. Virtually all were malnourished. Refugee programs did their best to provide for them, but it took time to gear up to care for the immense number of victims. Some Allied soldiers shared their personal food and supplies; it was just too difficult for them to witness the suffering and do nothing. That helped, but not nearly enough.

Some of the DPs managed to find family members, friends, or sympathetic citizens who took them in until they could get reestablished. However, for an enormous number of DPs, there was no place to live except the streets. Allied authorities turned to the United Nations Relief and Rehabilitation Administration (UNRRA) to care for these people. Finding accommodations for so many people in homes and small buildings was virtually impossible, so the UNRRA began the construction of displaced persons camps where thousands of DPs could be housed in one location. Between 1945 and 1952, more than 250,000 Jewish DPs were given shelter in these facilities, [276] along with many more of different ethnicities. The plan to congregate the DPs in camps was very good in theory, but the execution of the plan was enormous, complex, and slow to reach the level of care intended.

Finding locations for the camps was the first problem. Any vacant property became a potential site for a DP camp, and in 1945, occupation forces found hundreds of sites in Germany, Austria, Italy and other European locales. There was no time for extensive planning; they had to act immediately using whatever was available. The result was a broad spectrum of quality in the camps. Hotels, youth summer camps, and former German military facilities provided reasonable, if overcrowded, shelter. On the other end of the spectrum, some DPs were housed in partially bombed-out structures, and to add insult to injury, some were placed in former concentration camps, such as Bergen-Belsen. Whatever their physical surroundings, the DPs were chronically short of food, clothing, and personal toilet articles. [277]

Another familiar problem reared its head. Anti-Semitism was present among the victors just as it had been among the vanquished. Some Allied troops and camp administrators treated Jewish DPs with contempt, and even hostility. The Allies employed former German soldiers to work in many postwar jobs because they needed the labor. The Allies attempted to screen out former Nazi Party members, but this was not always successful, and sometimes a person's Nazi past was overlooked because they had a critically needed skill set. Some of these prejudiced people came in contact with Jewish DPs, which resulted in abuse. The DPs remained powerless to defend themselves.

With no other options, Basha and Samuel joined the masses of DPs and hoped for the best.

The escape from Poland to Germany freed Basha and Samuel from the potential grip of the bands of marauding, anti-Semitic Poles that had worried them, but it was far from a total solution to their monumental difficulties. They had merely crossed off one problem from a long list, but it was a start. Once they finally crossed the border into Germany without being sent back, they headed to Berlin. It was there that Basha received the news she had been praying for. Her father was still alive and living near Munich. She was overjoyed.

Isaac was anxious to reunite with his daughter and get her

started on the next phase of her life, so he sent a young man to Berlin to get her. However, the young man was intended to be more than an escort. In his enthusiasm to support his daughter, Isaac had taken the liberty of choosing him to be Basha's husband. He was a little late. Nevertheless, Basha and Samuel headed south to Munich to meet Isaac and celebrate their freedom as a family.

With no possessions to slow them down, Basha and Samuel set out quickly. As they traveled, the obvious economic disparity between the DPs and the Germans—who had started and then lost the war—was troubling to Basha.

"And, my God, I . . . we thought that after we were liberated, we would live in paradise, I mean, the world wouldn't know what to do with us. But what I saw, it really devastated me. German people at that time were already a little past the war. They were living in villas, living with beautiful curtains, sitting in their yards having picnics, and having a ball. And us, I couldn't even as a displaced person get a place to live." [278]

The situation was unquestionably unfair, but there was nothing Basha, Samuel, Dora, or Bernard could do about it. They kept going until the Allies found accommodations for them twenty miles southwest of Munich in a camp called Feldafing.

Feldafing Displaced Person's Camp

Feldafing, in Bavaria, was the first DP camp established specifically for former Jewish concentration camp prisoners. Opened on May 1, 1945, it was a quick response to a crisis. Advancing American troops had discovered cattle cars filled with Hungarian Jews parked on a railroad siding. They had been en route to a concentration camp in the Tyrolean mountains for execution by the *SS* when they were sidetracked. The troops could not leave them in the cattle cars, so they had to find immediate accommodations for them. They were aware of a former Hitler Youth summer camp in the American-controlled zone which had an adjacent railroad track, so the train of sick, malnourished prisoners was routed to the town of Feldafing.

The United States Army occupied the approximately two dozen stone and wood buildings of the former *Reichsschule Feldafing,* and requisitioned additional German homes and buildings sufficient to house the roughly three thousand Hungarian Jews that had unexpectedly fallen into their hands, and an additional one thousand Jews who would follow. [279] The Army set out to quickly create a facility where the former prisoners would have, at the very least, food, shelter, and medical care. Their hearts were in the right place but, initially, not much else. The lack of planning and resources was immediately apparent. Time would eventually resolve the problems, but it is fair to say the launch of Feldafing was not a superior example of American care. For Basha, the introduction to Feldafing became another unpleasant memory.

"They gave us . . . well, if you were single, you lived ten or twenty people together in one room, but I was married, so they didn't have no living quarters. They gave us a little room in the basement. And next to that little room was a slaughterhouse. When I woke up, half of the room was full of blood. When I got down from the bed, I was up to the knees in blood. And the first thing I remember after, I finally got a place, a little place on the first floor, was a little room and they separated us . . . one-half someone else lived. And they gave me the other half. [280]

"I used to have to go with a bowl to get some soup from the kitchen. It wasn't much better than the soup we got in the concentration camp. And we had to go there every day, that's what we brought. If we tried to go in [to] town and organize

something, like to buy, the MPs used to stop us and put us in jail. Would you believe? Would you believe something like this? While the Germans that lost the war . . . they lived like kings. They were dressed beautifully; they were dressed beautifully. Us they gave rags . . . old clothes." [281]

Many of the local citizens who lived well continued to maintain that they knew nothing of the concentration camps, or the murder and abuse of the Jews. The lies were infuriating to the people in the camps, especially those like Basha, who had seen the local citizens while imprisoned.

"We passed [them]. We went to work through their cities. They saw us walking to work. They saw the way we looked. They saw [the way] we carried our dead. They saw the Germans beating us. They were standing right there and looking, just looking on and not doing nothing. [282]

"The townspeople, they said they didn't know about it. They said they didn't know. I remember one incident [where] they attacked the camp [Feldafing]. They came in [from] the forest. The Germans [citizens] advanced, and they attacked the few survivors. That's how they felt about [us] after the war." [283]

News of the poor treatment of DPs in American-controlled camps reached the United States, and it was not well received. Most Americans considered it a core American value to care for the poor and oppressed. The stories that came back from Europe did not conform to that image at all. Congressman Earl G. Harrison, a former commissioner of immigration, was appointed to investigate the camps and the treatment of the DPs. On August 1, 1945, he presented his report, which noted "pathetic malnutrition," and stated, among other things: "We appear to be treating the Jews as the Nazis treated them, except that we do not exterminate them."

That was the last thing United States President Harry S. Truman wanted to hear. Deeply disturbed, he appointed an adviser to specifically work in the DP camps with the US military.[284] Truman also lobbied Congress for additional operating funds for the camps. Although he did not get everything he wanted, he got enough to make some quick improvements.

The war had broken up families and scattered members across the continent. Now that their basic needs for survival were accommodated, the DPs had time to focus on the search for their loved ones. The UNRRA created the Central Tracing Bureau, an organized system of gathering and dispensing survivor information. DP camp administrators posted lists of survivors and where they were currently located. Newspapers also printed survivor lists, and radio stations periodically read the survivor lists on air. DPs hopefully and prayerfully scanned the lists. Some rejoiced when they quickly found their families. For others, the search would go on for years.

Since the persecution and murder of the Jews had been a central component of Nazi philosophy, administrators within the United States Army, along with external Jewish relief org-anizations, worked to rebuild the Jewish religious traditions that had been stifled during the war. United States Army chaplain Abraham Klausner worked diligently on a plan to swap non-Jewish DPs in Feldafing for Jewish DPs being housed in the former Dachau concentration camp. Centralizing the Jewish population allowed camp personnel to restructure Feldafing in accordance with the recommendations in the Harrison report. [285]

DPs soon found the persecution they had endured for being Jewish replaced with long-missing support for their faith. For their part, the Jewish DPs moved aggressively to build a faith-based community within the camp. A Talmud Torah school, a yeshiva, synagogues, and seminaries were established along with a rabbinical council, secular schools including night vocational schools for adults, and a library with a large collection of Jewish religious books. Artistic and cultural endeavors received support, including theater troupes and an orchestra. It would have been preferable to be free to restart their lives outside the grounds of Feldafing, but until that day came, they made their small world as pleasant as possible.

Zionism was strongly supported in the camps, and many Jewish DPs, hoping for the eventual creation of a Jewish state, chose British-controlled Palestine as their intended future home. Zionist recruiters established training centers in the camps to teach Palestinian-bound DPs the basics of farming and other skills needed to prosper in the largely undeveloped land. After the Harrison report, President Truman encouraged the governments of the United States and Great Britain to give preferential treatment for DPs who wished to immigrate to the United States and Palestine. The British promptly reminded him that he had no authority to dictate what they did or did not do in Palestine. The United States Congress also pointed out they had a say in the matter. Progress would be made, but slowly.

The Zionist movement again caught the attention of Basha and Samuel, and after the new state of Israel was born on May 14, 1948, word came to them that they would be more than welcome there. They were both young—Basha was nineteen—the perfect couple for the proposed young country. The Israelis fought with their Arab neighbors and wanted young people to join the Israeli Defense Forces. It is unknown if this would have been a concern for Basha and Samuel, since another issue immediately surfaced. The Israeli recruiters felt Basha's father was too old to fit in with their plans. That was a deal-breaker. Basha refused to ever be separated from her father again. The move to Israel was off the table for good. [286]

Although religious and cultural opportunities increased at Feldafing, Basha did not take full advantage of them, something she later regretted. In particular, she would have liked to advance her education. It was not for lack of interest or motivation; it was a matter of her body not keeping pace with her ambition. She was still not in the best of health. When she was liberated by the Russians, she weighed sixty-seven pounds. The process of readjusting to food and regaining her health was slow, so she focused her limited strength and energy on improving her little room. She found and decorated a little box from which she made a stand for her radio, and sewed some good-looking window curtains from a piece of fabric she found. Then, with a burst of creative inspiration, she got some red shoe polish from Samuel, mixed it with floor wax, and buffed the floor of her room to a beautiful shine, adding color to her formerly drab quarters. Her room was spotless, and as attractive as possible. She was proud of it. To her surprise, one day she received two very important visitors.

The Harrison report had drawn the attention of some notable Americans who visited Feldafing personally to ensure the requested improvements had been initiated. One day, as Basha stood in her immaculate little room, Supreme Allied Commander, General Dwight D. Eisenhower, and General George S. Patton appeared in her doorway. Eisenhower was clearly impressed with what she had done to improve her Spartan accommodations and complimented her.

"See, if you want, what you could do with the room," Eisenhower remarked with a smile.

Basha had picked up enough English to have a conversation with him, and he lingered for a while to speak with her. Shortly thereafter, Eisenhower went to another barrack where, coincidentally, he inspected Samuel's room. Samuel had set up a shoemaking business there, which also impressed the officers. Fortunately, Eisenhower did not ask too many questions, since he may not have been happy with the answers. Samuel and Basha's daughter, Evelyn Kaplan, explains:

> *"In the displaced persons camp, my dad also started a little shoemaking business. He did work in there, in the camp. He got leather, from what he told me, from the black market. He got pieces of leather. He dealt with the group of people—other people who were trying to start up businesses—and they all tried to organize the supplies they needed for business. They shopped around on the black market."* [287]

Eisenhower left impressed with Samuel's ambition and craftsmanship, rather than his skill on the illicit trade market.

The quality of care in the American-managed DP camps was improving. The rudimentary, and frequently substandard, physical care provided when the camps first opened had been upgraded substantially. However, there was a complete absence of treatment for the DPs' psychological wounds. Finally out of harm's way, many had time—perhaps too much time—to reflect on the horrors of their past. Unsurprisingly, their emotional problems began to surface. In her testimony to Josey Fisher in 1981, Basha reflected on this aspect of her life in Feldafing and thereafter.

> *"It took quite a long, long time physically, and I think, mentally. I'm still not [over it] to this day. None of us is, because you can't be stable and live through what we lived through. You can't— for the most stable person. It had to leave scars, mentally and physically. In the DP camp there was something between us that we couldn't talk. I couldn't talk [to you] like this, the way I'm*

talking now; let's say ten years ago, I don't think I could have talked to you about it ... I can't even now, but I'm trying to. There was something between us [prisoners] *like we just couldn't talk ... I'm talking now of things that my sister-in-law* [has recently said]*, and all those years we lived together—I mean, we were so close and everything—and things that she tells me* [now] *that I didn't know, and I tell her things that she didn't know ... we just stopped talking. It wasn't just with me or with her; it was, I found out, with everybody ... It's just lately that I noticed people started—the survivors started to write books, they started to talk about it because they see that time is running short, that it has to be said for future generations to be on guard, and to watch that something like this should never happen again. To stay alert and see what's going on. That what happened to us should never happen to any Jewish person again.*

"*I remember in camp, there was a man there, and he always used to say, 'My God, I look at you girls and my heart swells up with joy. I see you* [in the concentration camps] *all without your hair and dragging in the mud, and now when I look at you and you look so much better. And you* [have] *started to lead a so-called half normal life.' Then he said, 'In my heart I'm just overjoyed.'*

"*He was also like a little bit older than us. That's what he used to say, and I didn't like to pass by him because he reminded me of this. I just tried not to touch it, that nobody should remind me about it or I would go berserk. I felt that I was going to explode once I talked about it, and I'll disappear. That once I start talking about it, it will be my end, and everybody felt—I'm speaking* [about] *my friends now—they all felt the same way that I did. And at that time, we didn't know. We just couldn't touch the subject.*"[288]

Jewish organizations worldwide stepped in to assist with the massive task of providing support for Jewish DPs. Although their intentions were certainly good, their skills and the scope of their programs were limited, a fact which troubled Basha.

> *"What I regret is . . . after the war they* [Jewish support groups] *didn't take a better interest in us to help us start to lead a normal life again, to get adjusted to a normal life to help us endure all of this fear and trauma and loss of family, the shock and all the torture, to ease our wounds, to help them heal. And there was nobody there, and this is what I think was a mistake from all the Jewish organizations. That's what I feel.*

> *"[To] help us talk and help us lead a normal life . . . [To] help us . . . because we constantly saw the Germans,* [momentary delusions caused by traumatic memories] *even if he wasn't there, behind my back. I always felt him there. I felt him for years there. I was afraid to walk from one place to another by myself. I wasn't used to it. I thought that I am not allowed. Even when I came to this country. They told me that I'll come to Philadelphia. I was afraid to go to another city. I thought I came here and that's where I must stay. It was always with me and I just couldn't shake it off. I could've been helped, but I wasn't. The years that I spent after the war would have been easier if anybody took an interest."* [289]

The United States Army was well aware of the psychological impact of war. During World War II, over half a million troops were withdrawn from combat due to "psychiatric collapse," also then known as "combat fatigue," and today as post-traumatic stress disorder (PTSD). There was little in the way of treatment at the time other than rest, a bit of counseling, and sometimes sedation.[290] The Army had its hands full dealing with combat veterans who returned psychologically scarred.

The DPs were on their own.

After what seemed like an eternity living in the camp, Harry Truman was reelected president and supported the Displaced Persons Act of 1948. The Act did not provide everything that Truman wanted, and he lobbied for additional legislation that would "reflect true American decency, goodwill, and freedom." However, flawed as it was, the Act increased the number of Jewish immigrants that the United States would accept. [291] Finally, Basha and many other DPs would realize their dream of moving to America.

Unfortunately, continuing the pattern in Basha's young life, there would be problems.

Notes

270. Bess Freilich interview by Marc Seligman, 35.

271. Dora Freilich, interview by Grossman, 4-2-54/55

272. "Kiclcc Pogrom," Wikimedia Foundation, last modified November 10, 2022, https://en.wikipedia.org/wiki/Kielce_pogrom.

273. Bess Freilich interview by Marc Seligman, 35.

274. Bess Freilich, interview by Fisher 4-1-45.

275. Dora Freilich, interview by Grossman, 4-2-56.

276. "Displaced Persons" *Holocaust Encyclopedia accessed June 28, 2022,* https://encyclopedia.ushmm.org/content/en/article/displaced-persons.

277. "World War II: Displaced Persons," Jewish Virtual Library, accessed May 8, 2022, https://www.jewishvirtuallibrary.org/displaced-persons.

278. Bess Freilich interview by Marc Seligman, 37.

279. "Feldafing Displaced Person's Camp," *Holocaust Encyclopedia,* United States Holocaust Memorial Museum, accessed June 28, 2022,

280. Bess Freilich interview by Marc Seligman, 37.

281. Ibid, 38.

282 Bess Freilich, interview by Fisher 4-1-49.

283. Ibid, 4-1-48.

284. "World War II: Displaced Persons," Jewish Virtual Library, accessed May 8, 2022, https://www.jewishvirtuallibrary.org/displaced-persons.

285. "Feldafing Displaced Person's Camp," *Holocaust Encyclopedia,* United States Holocaust Memorial Museum, accessed June 28, 2022.

286. Bess Freilich, interview by Fisher 4-1-46.

287. Evelyn Kaplan, email to author, June 6, 2022,

288. Bess Freilich, interview by Fisher 4-1-47/48.

289. Ibid, 4-1-49.

290. Duane Schultz, "Combat Fatigue: How Stress in Battle was Felt (and Treated) in WWII," Warfare History Network, accessed June 27, 2022, https://warfarehistorynetwork.com/combat-fatigue-how-stress-in-battle-was-felt-and-treated-in-wwii/.

291. Natalie Walker, "The Displaced Persons Act of 1948," *Tru Blog*, Truman Library Institute, April 29, 2019, https://www.trumanlibraryinstitute.org/the-displaced-persons-act-of-1948/.

CHAPTER 16

A New Country, a New Name, and a New Life

After roughly two and a half years in Feldafing, Basha, Samuel, Isaac, Dora, and Bernard were more than ready to get out of the facility and start new lives. They all registered to emigrate to the United States. The Displaced Persons Act of 1948 had increased opportunities to move there, but it had not made the process easy. One of the requirements was that the émigré must have a sponsor in the United States to ensure they would have a place to go and sufficient financial assistance to get them started in their new home; preferably, a waiting job. Fortunately, Basha and the group all had relatives living in the United States who agreed to be their sponsors. Basha's aunt Celia arranged for a group of relatives, whom Basha did not even know, to add their names to the paperwork required for her acceptance into the United States.

As the calendar turned to 1949, the families received permission to move to America. Dora and Bernard left first, with Basha, Samuel, and Isaac scheduled to follow shortly. They filled out the mountain of paperwork that would allow them to depart Germany, sail ten days on a passenger ship to New York, and then fill out the mountain of paperwork that would allow them entrance to the United States. One final step was a physical examination. That was Basha's first issue; a chest X-ray revealed spots on her lungs. They could be either active tuberculosis, which would be a serious problem, or scar tissue, which would not. The only way to tell would be to delay her departure by three months, have another chest X-ray, and see if there had been any change. It had not been easy to get tickets on the passenger liner, and Basha did not want to delay Isaac's departure. He had brothers in Philadelphia who were set to take him in, so she encouraged him to leave on schedule. She and Samuel would follow three months later after the second chest X-ray, assuming she was tuberculosis free. She was, but she also had a second issue: she was pregnant with their first child. In her condition, waiting three months to depart did not make the trip any more pleasant. Then there was a third issue. Getting passage on a regular passenger liner was not possible at that time, so she and Samuel would have to sail on a military transport, the USS *General W.C. Langfitt,* sharing the ship with soldiers and military equipment. Departing from Bremerhaven, Germany on April 16, 1949, it was still going to New York, and it would still only be ten days, but anything that could be considered luxurious on their originally planned ship was absent from the military transport. To make everything more challenging, Basha was having a difficult pregnancy. The trip would be memorable— for all the wrong reasons.

Basha and Samuel finally boarded ship in April 1949. Samuel was quite excited and viewed the trip as an adventure. A friendly, gregarious man, he made friends on the ship, including the captain, who took a liking to him and provided him with anything he thought he might like, including extra food. Basha, on the other hand, was not doing well at all. Years later she told her daughter, Evelyn, that she had been "a complete mess." [292]

While Samuel was getting an extra lunch, Basha was losing hers. She had a hard time even looking at food, but did her best to eat, knowing it was essential for the health of their baby. Some of it stayed down, but much of it did not. In addition to being sick from her pregnancy, she was also seasick. She never had any relief.

The constant nausea was pushing Basha to her limits, perhaps even affecting her judgment. One day it occurred to her that there might be a place on the ship that rocked less, which would give her some relief from the seasickness. She began exploring, hoping to find a place that was more stable. She eventually ended up in the cargo hold, completely lost. There were no passengers or crew down there to lead her out, so she wandered through the crates of military gear and vehicles alone, slightly panicked, looking for a way back to the deck. Adding to her misery, the smells of the cargo, motor oil, and general stench that accumulated at the bottom of the ship increased her nausea to a new level. The little she had eaten ended up on her dress.

It did not take long for Basha's absence to cause Samuel concern. He knew she was in no condition to walk too far or be gone too long, so something had to be wrong. He quickly searched the area near their quarters and did not find her, so he alerted the ship's crew to help him. Their immediate concern was that she might have fallen overboard. They searched the entire ship, finally finding her below deck among the cargo. Exhausted and vomit-stained, she was a pathetic sight. Samuel was enormously relieved to find her, but she looked like she needed immediate medical care, so he took her to the sick bay. Although she was five months pregnant, she did not look it. She informed the doctor, who checked for signs of problems with the baby, and they were all happy he had found none. They rehydrated her and told her they would keep an eye on her medical condition for the rest of the voyage. For Basha's part, she was satisfied that their quarters were as good a place as any on the ship, so she had best stay put.

Samuel's adventure, and Basha's ordeal, ended on April 26, 1949 when they set foot on American soil.

America, Land of the Free

For many years, freedom had been just a word. Now, standing on a wharf in New York City harbor, there were no walls or fences to contain them. There was no one to tell them what and when they could eat. There were no guards with rifles threatening to shoot them for little or no reason. Basha and Samuel could go wherever they pleased and do virtually anything they wanted. They had gone from having no choices to having a nearly infinite number of them. That can be overwhelming when you are not used to it. Fortunately, the requirement that immigrants have a sponsor was more than bureaucratic red tape; it had actual value. Basha's aunt Celia and her husband would be Basha's and Samuel's first guides in their new lives.

Celia was the sister of Basha's mother, Chava. The sisters had an incredibly close, loving relationship, and Celia's move to New York was painful for both of them. When Celia found out that Chava had been killed at Auschwitz she took it very badly, but she extended the love she had for her sister to Basha, Chava's only surviving child. Celia had always set aside a bit of her limited funds to send items to Chava and her family in Poland. When Celia found out Basha had survived the concentration camps and was living at Feldafing, she continued the practice. Basha was deeply moved when she was among the first of the camp inhabitants to receive a gift parcel. It was from Celia.

The welcome on the wharf was extremely emotional. When Celia looked at Basha, she saw all that was left of her beloved sister. As the years passed, Basha and Celia developed an incredibly close, loving relationship that lasted for the remainder of Celia's life.

Meeting on the dock that day, Celia likely had no idea how incredibly much she meant to Basha. It was not just the packages and financial support she had provided. Basha was well aware of the extraordinary love between Celia and her mother, but there was something else. Basha had developed the image of Celia as an extraordinarily kind and loving person. In a sense, that image of Celia had lived in Basha's heart for years. During the dark days in the concentration camps, the hope of someday joining Celia gave her a goal, hope, and perhaps even a reason to live.

> "*I* [wanted] *very much to live near my aunt because she was like . . . I must say, she had a lot to do with me surviving. Because sometimes I used to write addresses, my mother's letters to her, and I remember 1992 St. John's Place, Brooklyn. I remember. And so many times, you know, when things were so bad, I was thinking and pretending that I was coming to her on St. John's Place and I'll be able to live with her. She was very dear to me.*"[293]

Celia's plan was to meet Basha and Samuel at their ship and take them to her apartment in Brooklyn, where she could become acquainted with her niece and Samuel. After two or three weeks, Basha and Samuel would move on to live with another family member.

Celia correctly assumed that after all Basha had been through, she would need some love and care. The first step was obvious. It was over ninety degrees and humid in New York City, something Basha was entirely unused to. Being pregnant did not help the situation at all, nor did the hot silk dress she was wearing. Celia took her shopping at Macy's to get her started in a more comfortable wardrobe. Basha told the story to her daughter, Evelyn Kaplan.

> "*She bought my mom some outfits, some maternity dresses, and she bought my mother a topper coat* [a waist-length cotton coat]. *And my mother never stopped talking about the topper. It was a green topper coat. My mother at that time was a redhead. And so, the green of the coat . . . it looked so beautiful on.*"[294]

Celia's love and generosity were very moving to Basha. She had not experienced anything like this since their family was forced out of their home in 1942. Her emotions got the best of her, as she later stated in one of her testimonies.

"You know, all those years, I guess the tears left me. I couldn't cry, but when she bought me that topper, I just broke down. And I became so hysterical, and I cried for so long, she didn't know what was up with me. Because the idea that someone cared, that somebody cared for me. Because we were all alone between a wall of enemies. Everyone [in the concentration camps] *was out to destroy me. And here this woman, she wasn't wealthy, she was a little bit above poor, and she saved her pennies to buy for me this topper."* [295]

Basha's tears were completely understandable—except they did not stop. She cried so hard and uncontrollably that a concerned saleslady came to see what was wrong. Basha told Celia she would pay her back for all the items, but Celia unequivocally rejected the idea. They were gifts. Basha's tears not only did not stop in the store, but they continued off and on for days. She had lived a life of deprivation for seven years. Before that, even her loving family had not been able to provide her with extraordinary gifts such as these.

"I cried for days. The idea that I finally found such a good friend that cared. And I was very good to her after. She used to live with me. I used to send her money. I tried to give her back which she gave us—sending to Poland money and packages." [296]

Evelyn Kaplan stated she has never seen another relationship between an aunt and niece as the one between Celia and Basha. Basha continued to do all she could for Celia until Celia's death in the mid-1970s.

Since Samuel was a skilled craftsman, there was little concern about him finding a job. According to his daughter, Evelyn, he was not just a shoemaker; he was a shoe designer. All the shoes he made were custom, form-fitted for each individual customer. He would measure their feet and create a pair of shoes that would allow for any deformities, such as bunions or corns, to ensure that every customer experienced maximum comfort. In Europe he had his own sewing machines, and partnered in a business with his father and his brother, Bernard. He looked forward to doing the same thing in the United States. But it was different here; it did not work out that way.

Shoes in the United States were made in factories. No one's feet were measured, and all the shoes in a specific size were identical. They were either comfortable for the customer, or they were not. All the shoemaking machines were different from those he had used before, as was the method of manufacturing. There was not anything he could do about that except take the job that was offered. He started work on the basic machines, but eventually was moved up to designing. However, the shoes were still made in bulk, with no individual measurements taken. [297] He was not happy with his job, but realized it was highly unlikely that the American shoemaking business was going to change to conform with his higher standards. He went to work every day and, as always, he did his best.

From New York to Philadelphia

After three happy weeks with Celia, Basha and Samuel moved to Manayunk, Pennsylvania. That did not go nearly as well. They would be staying with the wife of one of Isaac's brothers, who appeared not to want them. In fact, she was not even nice to them.

"She put us in the attic, and I was pregnant, and it was hot. It was

a very hot May, and I wasn't used to the climate. It was terribly hot. And being pregnant, my legs were swollen. She made me stand [Recording unclear. It sounds like "day in and day out."] *washing her clothing by hand. It was another . . . oh God, it was torture.*

"And she, I remember, in the refrigerator she used to have food, so she always ate. And she said, 'Basha you can't eat because you vomit all the time from the pregnancy. You're not allowed to eat.'

"And my husband, the next day, he went to . . . work in the shoe factory. And he was sitting at lunchtime, not eating nothing, and all those people that worked with him they said, 'Sam,' they said, 'how come you don't eat nothing?'

"And he said, 'I don't have nothing to eat. My aunt hides everything, whatever she has.'

"They couldn't get over it. They took him out for lunch. And I remember, she never offered us a dinner. That's the way she was. And my husband took the last couple of pennies—we came with $13, I think, to this country—and he bought . . . the Tasty Cake [which] *was twelve cents. And we split the Tasty Cake between us. And that's what we ate for dinner. She never offered a dinner. Never nothing."* [298]

Basha was miserable, Samuel was miserable, and the aunt, who was probably always miserable, was more miserable. Obviously, this living arrangement was not going to work. The question was, how would Basha and Samuel resolve the situation?

Meanwhile in Philadelphia, Isaac was planning to move. His living arrangement was intended to be short-term as he adjusted to his new country, and it was time for him to strike out on his own. His brothers supported this but also wanted him to have family close by. They contacted Basha.

"So, my father lived with the brothers, but the brothers wanted very much for me to come to Philadelphia . . . so he should live with me. They insisted." [299]

Basha did not particularly want to move to Philadelphia. If anything, she wanted to move back to Brooklyn to be near Aunt Celia, but being with her father was also important to her, so she and Samuel packed up the little they owned and moved to an apartment in Philadelphia. It was the three of them until August 1949 when baby Evelyn was born and made it four. The family moved to an apartment on South Eighth Street in South Philadelphia, and Samuel continued his work at the shoe factory. Basha and Isaac were happier, particularly with the new baby. Samuel was a proud father, but it did not entirely outweigh the fact that each day he went to a job he did not like. He had to support his family, so he continued his routine at the factory until he had an accident, severely injuring his back. He was rushed to the hospital in excruciating pain. When he had recovered, he could no longer load and unload the machine he had been operating. The factory could find another job for him, but it was likely to be one he liked even less.

Basha and Samuel had discussed opening a shoe store, but Samuel had serious concerns. Although he was a fine craftsman, his business experience had been in Poland, not the United States. The endeavor was daunting to him, and he took his time considering the situation from all angles.

Basha took a different approach. One day while Samuel was at work, she went out and leased a storefront. When Samuel returned that evening, he was greeted by Basha, his baby Evelyn, and the news that he was in the retail shoe business. Surprise!

Samuel was a practical man, aware of his responsibilities to care for his family. This shoe store that Basha had suddenly created out of nothing appeared to be full of risks that made him uncomfortable. Evelyn remembered Basha telling her the story.

> *"And, of course he* [Samuel] *was in shock. He said, 'How are you going to get inventory? How are you going to pay the rent?' All that stuff. She said, 'We'll figure it out as we go along.' She was very business oriented. She was kind of aggressive in that way. She wouldn't let anything stop her. If she wanted to do something, she did it."* [300]

One positive thing about the shoe store was the location. It was in a very nice area of South Philadelphia. The neighborhood was prominently Jewish and Italian, and everyone got along. People socialized with their neighbors and cared about them. It was a great opportunity to develop customers who were also friends. The storefront was also very convenient. In fact, it could not have been more convenient; it was located directly below their apartment.

One more new thing: Now a business owner, Basha decided to Americanize her name. From then on, Basha would be known as Bess. She did not pick the name randomly. "Basha" is a Yiddish name—"Batia" in Hebrew."Bess" struck her as an American name that reflected on her origins and maintained a connection to her roots.

Samuel's cousin provided critical help launching the new shoe store. He personally introduced Samuel to the shoe jobbers, wholesalers who supplied merchandise to the retailers. Since Samuel and Bess had little money and had not developed credit, the cousin told the wholesalers he would financially back up Samuel and Bess if necessary. With the personal introduction and guarantee of payment from the cousin, Bess and Samuel were able to acquire enough inventory to get the business off the ground. Not far off the ground, but they were moving in the right direction. Or so they thought.

With a lot of hope and a little bit of inventory, they opened the door to the store. Unfortunately, they were the only ones opening it. They had no customers. Basha remembered:

"It wasn't easy. The street was full of competitors, people who had been in business for so many years. And we didn't have no stock, we didn't have no money. So, my husband had a cousin, he was in the shoe business. He went and took lots of empty boxes and filled up the shelves of our store, pretending we had a lot of stock. And the couple shoes that we had, I used to stay the whole night in the window switching them this way and that way . . . I remember the milkman—in those days they brought the milk to the door—and he was delivering milk already, and I was still in the window messing around with the shoes to put them in a place where they could catch the eye of the customer. It was very, very hard. It was very tough. A lot of times we thought it's not going to work. In fact, my husband had to go to work and I had to manage the store. I was managing the store with the baby and another baby on the way. It wasn't easy."[301]

It was not a happy time. Every day, Samuel went to the factory job that gave him no pleasure while Bess cared for the baby and worked in the store alone, trying to figure out what they were doing wrong. One day she discovered the answer while looking through the store window at all the potential customers who walked past their shop without slowing down. She looked at their feet, and then at their window display. The problem was obvious to her, according to Evelyn.

". . . They opened the store in South Philadelphia, which is the very high-stylish Jewish and Italian neighborhood. The people were . . . into fashion. The shoes my father ordered were basic family-style shoes. The door never opened in the store. No one came in. And she [Bess] was very observant. She was watching

the ladies who were shopping in the street, and she realized that the shoes they were wearing, and the shoes they were selling [in the store] *were not right for this clientele."* [302]

Certain that she had found the problem, Bess acted quickly to remedy it. So quickly that she, once again, did not tell Samuel what she was up to. She formulated a plan and acted on it very early one morning. Evelyn remembers the day everything changed.

"She [Bess] *went out one morning by herself, took two trolley cars, and she said* [to the children] *she was going out and she was going to pick the shoes. And she introduced herself . . .* [to the wholesalers.] *They never saw her before. She had an eye for high style. They* [the popular shoe style] *were called 'Springolators' at the time. They were like Cinderella slippers. They were made from glass and Lucite, really fancy. She got them to give her the samples. And one of the wholesalers, he did. He bundled them up for her. And she was coming back with two bundles of a dozen pair. She took the trolley . . . she went back with the two bundles of shoes on the trolley car and had to walk a city block to get to the store. And the bundle, while she was getting off* [the trolley], *the rope broke. So, they fell all over the trolley tracks. The driver had to stop the trolley and help her put the bundles back together. And she was so nervous and upset when she got into the house. She was sweating, and she was a wreck. We didn't know what happened. Then she got us dressed, fed, and took us to school.*

"When I came home for lunch, she was just finishing the window in the store. Displayed all these beautiful shoes with the glass heels and long stems. It looked like Cinderella slippers. And she put them on a turntable so they were spinning around. And she put a spotlight on them. As a kid coming back from lunch, I was in awe of the window. It was so beautiful; I couldn't leave it.

Watching shoes go around. So, I had lunch, went back to school, and when I got home, half the shoes were gone. Sold them. So, when my father came home from the factory, he didn't know how those shoes, the remaining ones, got into the window. And she said, 'We have to go to New York, and we have to get these shoes.'

"The next day, they took a trip to New York and the whole store changed, the whole business changed; they were so busy they eventually had to remodel the store." [303]

Bess and Samuel got along well with their Jewish and Italian neighbors. They came in to shop, but became friends as well as customers. Evelyn remembers her childhood in the multiethnic middle-class neighborhood, and the many nice people who came into the store.

"South Philadelphia was a very tight-knit community. Everyone seemed to know each other . . . Everyone got along pretty well. The Jewish people and the Italian people got along beautifully. Most of my father's customers in the store were Italian. Like when Christmas came, they would bring soup, they would bring cakes, they would bring cookies to the store. He developed a relationship with his customers where they were like family. This child was getting married, this one was going into the Army. Everything new, everything about everybody. There were a lot of them that were in show business that knew Joey Bishop, Mario Lanza, and Bobby Rydell. Pop culture. American Bandstand was big. The kids would go—dress up and go to dance on American Bandstand. It was that kind of community." [304]

However, it was not perfect. In any large group of people there are always a few with poisonous attitudes they enjoy inflicting on others. Among all the wonderful people who shopped at the store, there was a minority that would lash out at Bess and Samuel, sometimes in the cruelest of ways.

"We went through an awful lot. With ignorant people that didn't know where we came from, and what we went through in life, and didn't have any compassion whatsoever. The first little thing that touched them—a word that you said that they didn't like—they'd say, 'You greenhorn. I'm going to send you back to Germany where you came from. And Hitler should've killed you all.' I heard that constantly. Sometimes even now. And that really . . . it made my heart ache so much. And so many times I just cried through the whole night. Living this through." [305]

It is difficult to imagine why people do things like that. It was painful, but Bess and Samuel had certainly gone through much worse. They just did not need to be reminded of it.

With a good business—and mostly good customers and neighbors—Bess and Samuel had much to be grateful for, including their three children. Evelyn was born in 1949; Howard, in 1953; and Mark, in 1964. Mark's birth was the final fulfillment of the Gypsy's prediction.

Isaac had moved out of their apartment into his own place and engaged in various business activities, but he remained very much in their lives. When Dora and Bernard arrived in the states they lived in Brooklyn with their baby Elaine, born in 1949, and Harold, who arrived a few years later. Like Samuel, Bernard had gone to work in a shoe factory. Also like Samuel, he was very unhappy with the job. Samuel began searching Philadelphia for a location where Bernard could open a shoe store, and he found one in the northeast part of the city that Bernard liked. They would both be in the shoe retailing business, but not competitors. They were all pursuing what was known as the American Dream, and they were succeeding.

Back then, the postwar American Dream included leaving the crowded cities for suburbia. Basha, Samuel, and their children joined in, moving to the Philadelphia suburb of Havertown in 1960. There, they joined a synagogue where Howard and Mark attended Hebrew school. Evelyn was not all that thrilled with the idea and elected not to go. Aunt Celia warned her she would regret it someday. She does. Back then, she was not aware of how important the religious and cultural experience would be to her. Today it is a central component of her life.

———

Maintaining their growing shoe store was hard work, but their labor was rewarded with the resources to enjoy a social life. Bess and Samuel belonged to an organization in Philadelphia, called at the time the Association of Jewish Holocaust Survivors. The members all had the common experience of Nazi barbarism, but that was not something they dwelled on. They had a gala once a year, and dinner dances every two or three months held in a synagogue. The group included some family members as well as friends, and they got together for special outings such as bar mitzvahs, weddings, and summer trips to the Catskill Mountains resorts in southeastern New York. The shared experience bound them together. [306]

Family life was especially important. They had lost so many family members, and they especially cherished the ones who remained, as well as their growing families. Isaac, the entrepreneur, created a business that provided years of enjoyment for his family, as Evelyn recounts.

"Our best times were when we went to Atlantic City in the summer. My grandpop [Isaac] had these little side businesses. He was originally a butcher, a kosher butcher, but he couldn't get certification. He needed a storefront and a lot of other rules for kosher certification. So, what he used to do was rent the whole boardinghouse, and then he would rent out individual rooms in

*the summer. And that's how he made a living. We, as a group,
enjoyed being together—my cousins and my part of the family,
the Anushes."* [307]

Summers at Isaac's Atlantic City boardinghouse were like a big
party. Isaac's brother Philip came with his daughters, along with
an assortment of cousins, spouses, and their children. Friends of
the family, particularly friends of Bess and Samuel, would also
rent rooms with their families, and their friend, a rabbi, would
come with his family. The boardinghouse was really too small
to support the number of people staying there, but they were
all friends and family having a great time. They spent their days
on the beach, and nights, on the boardwalk. They also observed
the Sabbath, and Jewish religious holidays and traditions. The
summer experiences created a lifetime of memories for Evelyn
and the rest of the family. Bess and Samuel bought a one-bedroom
condo in Atlantic City, and the tradition continued. Not just
the tradition of gathering on the beach, but also the tradition of
cramming as many people as possible into one dwelling. Evelyn
continued:

*"I had my kids, and my husband, and I—we would all go down.
The whole thing would regenerate. My girls always talk about
the memories they have from Atlantic City. And there were times
when I was there with my girls, and my brother and his fiancée
at the time, and my younger brother. We tried to pack into this
one bedroom. We had mattresses under the bed that we pulled
out. We had sofa beds. My father and younger brother Mark
eventually couldn't deal with it—all the people in the tiny place.
They called another cousin, who had a big house, and she said,
'Come over and visit with me.' They couldn't take it, so they went
to my cousin's house. Then they would come back in the morning,
and the whole family would be together, and we would go to the*

beach. My kids said that was the greatest memories." [308]

The women shared cooking duties in the crowded little beach house, which was a special experience in itself. They had different styles of cooking and favorite dishes, so meals were always a feast. Bess loved to cook, whether at the beach or in their home. Jewish holidays, in particular, were always a special event at mealtime. Evelyn remembers that her mother had an amazing, innate talent for cooking.

> *"My mother didn't have cookbooks, didn't have measuring cups, but was an incredible cook. And the meals were unreal. Everything out of her head. She used her imagination and made the most delicious meals. And she could cook night and day for the Jewish holidays. For Shabbos, for Passover, you could smell the cooking when you were down the street . . . They used to stick their heads out the window and say, 'It smells like Bubbi's [Bess's] house.' There was never one main dish; there were three or four. And I think this was part of the concentration camp mentality. She told me when she came [to America]—when she told me her stories—she vowed that there would never be a hungry person in their house. And it was true."* [309]

Even with a wonderful family, beautiful home, and strong business, Bess could never shake the memories of the Holocaust. As with most survivors, the ghosts of the camps lingered in the shadows of her mind, sometimes presenting themselves strangely in her peaceful suburban American life. They even lurked in the simple task of cooking, which gave her such pleasure.

One evening after dinner when Evelyn was a child, she went to help her mother clean up the kitchen. Her father emphasized that Evelyn insist that Bess sit down.

"Tell her. She'll listen to you."

Bess had a problem with blood clots in her legs, so she did as

Evelyn requested and stepped out of the kitchen to rest. As Evelyn put the leftovers in the refrigerator, she saw a bowl containing very small balls of aluminum foil, each about the size of a marble, which she had never noticed before. She thought, what on earth could be in these little balls? She took the bowl to her father and asked if he knew what they were.

"Open them up," he said.

Evelyn opened one of the tiny balls and found it held crumbs left over from the bottom of a bag of bread. The concentration camp mentality and the ghost of starvation had manifested in an obsession with saving minute bits of food.

Puzzled, Evelyn asked, "Do we have to save these crumbs?"

"No, throw them out," Samuel told her. "But she'll be mad when she finds they're missing."

"That's what the concentration camp did to Mommy." [310]

Notes

292. Evelyn Kaplan, interview with the author, June 6, 2022.

293. Bess Freilich interview by Marc Seligman, 38.

294. Evelyn Kaplan, interview with the author, June 6, 2022.

295. Bess Freilich interview by Marc Seligman, 39.

296. Ibid.

297. Evelyn Kaplan, interview with the author, June 6, 2022.

298. Bess Freilich interview by Marc Seligman, 39.

299. Ibid, 38.

300. Ibid, 40.

301. Ibid.

302. Evelyn Kaplan, interview with the author, June 6, 2022.

303. Ibid.

304 Ibid.

305. Bess Freilich interview by Marc Seligman, 40.

306. Evelyn Kaplan, interview with the author, June 6, 2022.

307. Ibid.

308. Ibid.

309. Ibid.

310. Ibid.

CHAPTER 17

The Lessons

History teaches us lessons if we are willing to look and learn. The stories teach us of humankind's horrible potential for cruelty. They also teach us of humankind's remarkable ability to survive. Sometimes it teaches us both lessons in the same story. The Nazi regime targeted Europe's Jews for annihilation for no reason other than their faith and ethnicity. For millions, there was no escape; yet others, through a combination of inner strength and luck, survived. The dead cannot speak, so the living must speak for them.

At Auschwitz, Chava Anush immediately knew her fate. She knew she would not be the one to tell the story. She implored her daughter to survive because she loved her, but also so someone would live to tell the story. For this reason, the barbarism of the Holocaust should not be kicked aside as a historical sidebar. It had to be told, and it had to be told by someone who experienced it. Many times, Basha wanted to give up. The hunger and horror and pain had become nearly unendurable, but Chava's plea imbued her with a will to live stronger than the worst tortures and indignities the Nazis could inflict on her.

One would think that the Holocaust, one of the worst genocides in history, would be familiar to all. However, years later, in her shoe store in Philadelphia, customers continually reminded Bess of the ignorance of the masses. The tattoo on her arm, 33327, was clearly visible, especially in the summer when she wore short-sleeved blouses. People would ask: "Is that your lucky number?" "Is that your Social Security number?"

Their lack of understanding and compassion was like picking the scab off an old wound, once again starting the emotional bleeding. Surprisingly, it was sometimes the young, school-aged children who seemed to understand. They saw the tattoo and whispered to one another. Bess did not need to hear their words to understand their conversation. They knew this kind woman had suffered, and they knew it was not right. Later in life, Bess frequented the University of Pennsylvania for medical care. During one visit, a nurse noticed the Auschwitz tattoo.

"What's that?" Bess asked, shocked. "Where did you live?"

"She wasn't that young. If she was a very young girl, maybe I could forgive her, but she was in her late thirties. She said she didn't know anything about it [the Holocaust], *and I just couldn't believe it. This woman, a nurse, she must* [have had an education, yet] *didn't know nothing. 'What is this?' I felt like the sky fell on me. I mean, I would forgive it to someone ignorant, but a nurse . . . she killed my day that time."* [311]

Thoughts of the Holocaust were painful, as was speaking about the ordeal. Nevertheless, it was clear to Bess that, just as she had promised her mother, she must go out into the world and leave a record of the Nazi atrocities. She gave verbal testimonies to Gratz College and the USC Shoah Foundation so her experiences would be recorded forever for researchers, and those who wanted a first-person account of this dark period in history. She also spoke her nearly unspeakable story at schools and organizations, which moved audiences. Even those who thought they knew about the Holocaust learned things that had previously been beyond their imagination. She honored her mother's wishes. She lived and told the story.

Samuel Freilich, a fit seventy-two-year-old without a gray hair on his head, suddenly collapsed in their shoe store in February 1993. He died in a hospital several days later. Dora and Bernard had good lives, retiring to Florida, and then returning to live in a high-end assisted living facility near their daughter. Bernard passed away at the age of eighty-three, and Dora at the age of eighty-five.

Bess passed away peacefully on September 18, 2006, but her spirit lives on through her family, as expressed by her daughter, Evelyn Kaplan:

"My Mom, Bess (Basha) Anush Freilich, was a woman of valor. She is called a 'Holocaust survivor.' I prefer to call her a 'warrior.' Her teen years were spent in hell on earth, Auschwitz, the notorious Nazi concentration camp. Possessed with an indominable spirit and will to live, she survived. She witnessed the most horrific atrocities known to mankind and endured the most unimaginable acts of barbarism; yet, she emerged from this horror with a most beautiful, generous, and loving heart.

"I see her beauty and spirit everywhere; in the mountains every morning when I awaken, in the flowers and the trees, in the art that I create, and in the gorgeous faces of her grandchildren and great-grandchildren whom she never met. She is far away, but she is always nearby. Her beautiful spirit and sweet soul live on.

"Mom generously shared her wisdom. She taught us to tap into our capacity for forgiveness and fairness. She emphasized that whenever we feel anger or frustration, we must stop and listen to the voice within our hearts. It tells us to exercise goodness, express love, and to forgive. She lavished her family with so much love. She taught us to use our capacity to heal. To approach every situation with goodness in our hearts. To always stop and smell the roses, and to love one another and be a source

of joy to others. My mom was a woman of courage and wisdom. She was and always will be my heroine. Despite her most traumatic and horrific life story, she was the most loving, caring, compassionate, intelligent, and beautifully elegant woman. She was a joy to every life she touched.

"My mom and dad saw in their children the totality of their hopes and dreams. What was denied to them would be achieved and enjoyed by their children. There was no such thing as being hungry in our home. Upon Mom's liberation from Auschwitz, she vowed that no one in her family would ever be hungry again. Education was strongly emphasized. We had lovely clothes, a home that was always full of the scent of delicious food cooking on the stove, sweet memories of vacations at the beach, and so much love . . . we were totally lavished with love.

"My parents listened to our dreams for the future and encouraged us to reach for the stars. The whole universe was within our grasp. Every step we took, little or big, was always a grand achievement. My brother Marc, who is married to Lisa, helped in the family's shoe business for a while. He later followed his passion for cars and became involved in the automobile business. My brother, Howard, became a gastroenterologist. My parents were so proud of "their son, the doctor!" He and his wife, Sharon, have two daughters, Hayley and Carly. Hayley is a graphic designer and Carly is a physician assistant. Carly and her husband, Dan, have three small children; George, Henry, and Rosealie. Howard is currently practicing medicine in South Carolina. I taught preschool, and at the same time followed my heart and became a mosaic artist. My work has found its way to galleries and homes throughout the world. My husband, Jay, and I have two daughters. Our eldest, Lisa, is a partner in a prestigious Philadelphia law firm. She is married to Paul, and

together they blessed us with a beautiful granddaughter, Sky Bailey. Sky is named using the initials of my parents. My younger daughter, Renee, is a business lady. She owns the Old Bisbee Ghost Tour and the clothing company, Sweet Midnight. She is a fashion designer, a graphic designer, a toy designer, and an author. She is married to Jimmy. All of us followed our dreams with the lessons we were taught alive in our hearts. I know my parents are beaming with all the accomplishments of their children, grandchildren, and what their great-grandchildren are yet to be.

"I believe that Mom and Dad are a link in the eternal chain of Jewish destiny. The Jewish people have survived unspeakable horrors throughout their history. Yet, they have experienced many miracles as well. We are the legacy of this horrific time. We are the legacy in flesh and blood. We are the proof that hatred, indifference, and anti-Semitism may be our past, and sadly continues today, but we are the future. We are survivors, and we shall—and we will—continue to thrive. Our history lives within us. It flows through our veins and the veins of the Jewish people. It is in the DNA of my children and will be in the DNA of their children. History lives in who we are and how we live our lives.

"As an inmate in a Nazi concentration camp, it takes courage to fearlessly believe in the possibilities of another tomorrow. Under such horrific conditions, it would be considered a totally irrational or insane thought. All Mom's barbaric experiences and everything she witnessed in the camps, illustrated a most horrible outcome. But when she was pushed to the brink of despair, she never gave up hope. She held on to the seemingly impossible dream that tomorrow may be better . . . maybe even magnificent. That Basha would live seemed unrealistic,

unfeasible. It was a crazy thought that came to pass against all odds. Mom never gave up hope . . . her unrelenting spirit reigned supreme.

"I remember during a very down time in my life, Mom tried to offer encouragement. She told me that the Torah teaches us that we are a light upon the nations, and that anything is possible with the help of G-d. That G-d will help. The survival of my parents and my grandfather, Isaac, is a miracle that exemplifies that the light of the Torah shall never be extinguished. I believe this was the essence of her survival, and she and the Jewish people will always continue to flourish." [312]

Bess suffered in her young life, but she emerged a conqueror. She stood up to physical and emotional pain and abuse, and in the end, she became a symbol of love, persistence, and the indomitable power of the human spirit. Now, fulfilling her promise to her mother through her story and words in this book, her voice lives on, exposing her pain to other generations so the perpetuation of a tragedy like the Holocaust will never again be inflicted on the innocent.

Notes

311. Bess Freilich interview by Marc Seligman, 40.

312. Evelyn Kaplan email to author, October 19, 2022.

Bibliography

"Auschwitz-Birkenau: Crematoria and Gas Chambers," Jewish Virtual Library, accessed November 4, 2021, http://jewishvirtuallibrary. org/crematoria-and-gas-chambers-at-auschwitz-birkenau.

"Auschwitz-Birkenau: The Revolt at Auschwitz-Birkenau," Jewish Virtual Library, accessed November 4, 2021, https://www. jewishvirtuallibrary.org/the-revolt-at-auschwitz-birkenau.

"Block 11," Wikimedia Foundation, last modified July 2, 2022, https://en.wikipedia.org/wiki/Block_11.

Borkin, Joseph. *The Crime and Punishment of I.G. Farben* (London: Collier Macmillan, 1978).

"Budy," Subcamps of Auschwitz, accessed September 18, 2021, https://subcamps-auschwitz.org/auschwitz-subcamps/wirtschaftshof -budy-mannerlager/.

Butler, Rupert. *The Gestapo, History of Hitler's Secret Police 1933-45* (Havertown: Casemate, 2004).

"Combat Fatigue: How Stress in Battle was Felt (and Treated) in WWII," Warfare History Network, accessed June 27, 2022, https:// warfarehistorynetwork.com/combat-fatigue-how-stress-in-battle- was-felt-and-treated-in-wwii/.

"Displaced Persons," United States Holocaust Memorial Museum Holocaust Encyclopedia, accessed June 28, 2022, http://encyclopedia. ushmm.org/content/en/article/displaced-persons.

Dwork, Deborah and Robert Jay Van Pelt. *Auschwitz* (New York: W. W. Norton and Company, 2008).

Editors, *The SS* (Alexandria: Time-Life Books, 1988).

"Ethnic Origins and Numbers of Victims of Auschwitz," Państwowe Muzeum Auschwitz-Birkenau w Oświęcimiu, accessed September 27, 2021, http://70.auschwitz.org/index.php?loption=com_content&view=article&id=89itemid=173&lang=en.

Evelyn Kaplan, interview by author, April 7, 2022.

Evelyn Kaplan, interview by author, May 25, 2022.

Evelyn Kaplan, interview by author, June 6, 2022.

Evelyn Kaplan, interview by author, June 16, 2022.

Evelyn Kaplan, interview by author, July 21, 2021.

Evelyn Kaplan, email to author, October 19, 2022.

"Feldafing Displaced Persons Camp," United States Holocaust Memorial Museum, accessed June 28, 2022, https://encyclopedia.ushmm.org/content/en/article/feldafing-displaced-persons-camp.

"Feldafing Displaced Persons Camp," Wikimedia Foundation, last modified November 24, 2021,https://en.wikipedia.org/wiki/Feldafing_displaced_persons_camp.

Fisher, Josey G. Holocaust Testimony of Bess Freilich, Holocaust Oral History Archive, Gratz College, 1981.

"Flight and Expulsion of Germans 1944–1950," Wikimedia Foundation, last modified

December 1, 2022, https://en.wikipedia.org/wiki/Flight_and_expulsion_of_Germans_ (1944%E2%80%931950).

"Geneva Conventions," Wikimedia Foundation, last modified December 9, 2022, https://en.wikipedia.org/wiki/Geneva_Conventions.

Gerwarth, Robert. *Hitler's Hangman, The Life of Heydrich* (New Haven: Yale University Press, 2011).

Goldfarb, Kara. "How Dachau Guards Got Their Comeuppance," accessed April 17, 2022, http://allthatsinteresting.com/dachau-reprisals.

Grossman, Helen. *Holocaust Testimony of Dora Freilich*, Holocaust Oral History Archive, Gratz College, 1984.

Hart-Moxen, Kitty. *Return to Auschwitz* (New York: Atheneum, 1982.)

"Herva Kaddisha," (Chevra Kadisha) History of the Jews in Poland, Jewish Virtual Library, accessed September 4, 2021, https://www.jewishvirtuallibrary.org/glossary-c.

"History of the Jews in Poland," Wikimedia Foundation, last modified December 10, 2022, https://en.wikipedia.org/wiki/History_of_the_Jews_in_Poland.

Hoess, Rudolf. *Commandant of Auschwitz* (London: Weidenfeld & Nicolson, 1950).

Höhne, Heinz. *The Order of the Death's Head: The Story of Hitler's SS* (London: Penguin, 1960).

"Irma Grese," Jewish Virtual Library, accessed September 27, 2021, http://jewishvirtuallibrary.org/irma-grese.

"Janina Nowak," Faces of Auschwitz, accessed September 24, 2021, https://facesofauschwitz.com/gallery/2018-4-3-faces-of-auschwitz-janina-nowak/.

"Joachim Pieper," Wikimedia Foundation, last modified November 30, 2022, https://en.wikipedia.org/wiki/Joachim_Peiper.

"Josef Mengele," Wikimedia Foundation, last modified December 8, 2022, https://en.wikipedia.org/wiki/Josef_Mengele.

"Juana Bormann," Wikimedia Foundation, last modified November 3, 2022, https://en.wikipedia.org/wiki/Juana_Bormann.

"*Kanada* Warehouses-Auschwitz," Wikimedia Foundation, last modified March 11, 2022, https://en.wikipedia.org/wiki/Kanada_warehouses,_Auschwitz.

Karez, Jan. "Recollections," Auschwitz-Birkenau State Museum Archive, No. 196, 118.

"Kielce Pogrom," Wikimedia Foundation, last modified November 10, 2022, https://en.wikipedia.org/wiki/Kielce_pogrom.

Kogon, Eugen. *The Theory and Practice of Hell* (New York: Farrar, Straus and Giroux, 1950).

"Malchow Concentration Camp," Wikimedia Foundation, last modified May 26, 2021, https://en.wikipedia.org/wiki/Malchow_concentration_camp.

"Maria Mandl," Wikimedia Foundation, last modified November 21, 2022, https://en.wikipedia.org/wiki/Maria_Mandl.

Mattogno, Carlo, "The Morgues of the Crematoria at Birkenau in the Light of Documents," Committee for Open Debate on the Holocaust (CODOH), accessed November 2, 2021, https://codoh.com/library/document/the-morgues-of-the-crematoria-at-birkenau-in-the/en/?page=1.

"Nemmersdorf Massacre," Wikimedia Foundation, last modified November 15, 2022, https://en.wikipedia.org/wiki/Nemmersdorf_massacre.

"Operation Barbarosa," Wikimedia Foundation, last modified December 9, 2022, https://en.wikipedia.org/wiki/Operation_Barbarossa.

Peck, Michael. "The Battle for Moscow: How Russia Stopped Hitler's Military During World War II," The National Interest, accessed September 8, 2021, https://nationalinterest.org/blog/the-buzz/the-battle-moscow-how-russia-stopped-hitlers-Nazi-germany-17641.

"Pruzhany History," Our Family History, accessed September 4, 2021, http://www.flora-and-sam.com/pages/PruzhanyHistory.htm.

"Ravensbrück," United States Holocaust Memorial Museum, accessed March 26, 2022, https://encyclopedia.ushmm.org/content/en/article/ravensbrueck.

Reitlinger, Gerald. *The SS: Alibi of a Nation 1922-1945* (New York: Viking, 1957).

Roberts, Andrew. *The Storm of War* (New York: Harper, 2011).

Seligman, Marc. Testimony of Bess Freilich, University of Southern California

Shoah Foundation, 1996. (Video interview transcribed by the author.)

Shirer, William L. *The Rise and Fall of the Third Reich* (New York: Simon and Shuster, 1960).

"Sonderkommandos," United States Holocaust Memorial Museum, accessed November 4, 2021. http://encyclopedia.ushmm.org/content/en/article/sonderkommandos.

Steinbacher, Sybille. *Auschwitz: A History* (New York: HarperCollins, 2005).

"The Displaced Persons Act of 1948," Truman Library Institute, accessed June 27, 2022, http://trumanlibraryinstitute.org/the-displaced-persons-act-of-1948.

"The Extermination Procedure in the Gas Chambers," Memorial and Museum Auschwitz-Birkenau, accessed November 2, 2021, https://www.auschwitz.org/en/history/auschwitz-and-shoah/the-extermination-procedure-in-the-gas-chambers/.

"The Great Sonderkommando Revolt of 1944," Sky History, accessed November 2, 2021, https://www.history.co.uk/article/the-great-sonderkommando-revolt-of-1944.

"Trials of SS Men from the Auschwitz Concentration Camp Garrison," Memorial and Museum Auschwitz Birkenau, accessed March 26, 2022, https://www.auschwitz.org/en/history/the-ss-garrison/trials-of-ss-men-from-the-auschwitz-concentration-camp-garrison/.

Tusa, Ann and John Tusa. *The Nuremburg Trial* (New York: Atheneum, 1990).

Urievich, Zalman. *Pruzhany Jews in Ghettos and Camps* (Tel Aviv: Pruzhany Yzkor Book, 1958) accessed September 16, 2021, https://www.pruzh.org/yzkor_pruzhany/guettos_camp.htm.

Wachsmann, Nikolaus. *KL: A History of the Nazi Concentration Camps* (New York: Farrar, Straus and Giroux, 2015).

"White Busses," Wikimedia Foundation, accessed March 26, 2022, https://en.wikipedia.org/wiki/White_Buses.

"World War II: Displaced Persons," Jewish Virtual Library, accessed May 8, 2022, www.jewishvirtuallibrary.org/displaced-persons.

About the Author

Douglas Wellman is a former Hollywood television producer-director, and assistant dean of the School of Cinematic Arts at the University of Southern California. For over forty years he has been a historian and researcher of the twentieth century, particularly World Wars I and II. His primary interest is exploring and relating the lives of people caught in conflict. He also currently works a few days a week as a hospital chaplain.

Other Books by Douglas Wellman

On August 6, 1945, twenty-two-year-old Kaleria Palchikoff was doing pre-breakfast chores when a blinding flash lit the sky over Hiroshima, Japan. A moment later, everything went black as the house collapsed on her and her family. Their world, and everyone else's, changed as the first atomic bomb was detonated over a city.

From Russian nobility, the Palchikoffs barely escaped death at the hands of Bolshevik revolutionaries until her father, a White Russian officer, hijacked a ship to take them to safety in Hiroshima. Safety was short lived. Her father, a talented musician, established a new life for the family, but the outbreak of World War II created a cloud of suspicion that led to his imprisonment and years of deprivation for his family.

After the bombing, trapped in the center of previously unimagined devastation, Kaleria summoned her strength to come to the aid of bomb victims, treating the never-before-seen effects of radiation.

Fluent in English, Kaleria was soon recruited to work with General Douglas MacArthur's occupation forces in a number of secretarial positions until the family found a new life in the United States.

Heavily based on quotes from Kaleria's memoirs written immediately after World War II, and transcripts of United States Army Air Force interviews, her story is an emotional, and sometimes chilling, story of courage and survival in the face of one of history's greatest catastrophes.

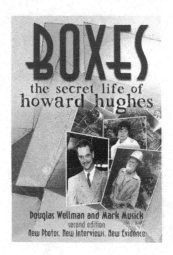

This second edition of *Boxes: The Secret Life of Howard Hughes* continues the history-changing story of Eva McLelland and her reclusive life married to a mystery man she discovered was Howard Hughes.

New witnesses have come forward with personal stories, additional evidence, and photographs. Hughes's links to the murder of mobster Bugsy Siegel and the killers of President John F. Kennedy are revealed as well as the real identity of the long-haired crazy man that Hughes placed in the Desert Inn Hotel to distract the world while he escaped.

Eva McLelland kept her secret for thirty-one stressful years as she lived a nomadic existence with a man who refused to unpack his belongings for fear he would be discovered and have to flee. Only her husband's death finally released her to tell the story that had been burning inside her for decades.

John Byner is a man of many voices and characters, from impersonating the slow, rolling gait and speech of John Wayne, to lending his voice to The Ant and the Aardvark cartoons. His dead-on impersonations, as well as his unique talents as a character actor, have put him on the small screen in peoples' homes, the big screen in theaters, and no screen on Broadway.

Growing up in a big family on Long Island, John discovered his uncanny ability to mimic voices as a child when he returned home from a Bing Crosby movie and repeated Bing's performance for his family in their living room. He discovered his talent made him the focus of everyone's attention, and allowed him to make friends wherever he went, from elementary school to the U.S. Navy.

John started his career in nightclubs in New York, but soon found himself getting national acclaim on The Ed Sullivan Show. With that he was on his way.

This memoir is the best and funniest moments of his life, career, and relationships with some of the biggest names in entertainment, both on and off the screen.

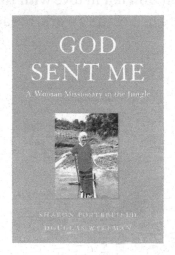

Raised in wealth and privilege in Southern California, the last thing Sharon Porterfield ever expected was to become a Christian missionary in the hostile, unforgiving jungles of Southeast Asia.

Her parents were atheists, but something inside her told her that there had to be a Creator. After years of searching and study, she became a committed Christian. In her mid-thirties she found a church she loved and ministered to at-risk women. She thought she had found her perfect place in Christian service. She was wrong.

One night a missionary spoke at her church. Disinterested and half listening, she suddenly felt God pull her to investigate. Seemingly against her will, she was strongly compelled to visit Burma and the Karen people who live there.

She gave in and went. The country was hot, humid, and alive with scorpions and malaria infected mosquitoes, and the Burmese Army was always a threat, periodically launching genocidal attacks against the Karen. The most basic of creature comforts, like indoor toilets and easy access to food, were absent.

Despite all this, Sharon fell in love with the Karen people and knew this was going to be her life's work, because God Sent her.